GENERAL WOLFE

By the same author

General Gordon
Famous Characters of the Wild West
Stories of Famous Ships
Anatomy of a Grand Prix Driver

GENERAL WOLFE

RICHARD GARRETT

Arthur Barker Limited
London
A subsidiary of Weidenfeld (Publishers) Limited

Published in Great Britain by Arthur Barker
Limited, 11 St John's Hill, London SW11

ISBN 0 213 16553 8

Printed in Great Britain by
Willmer Brothers Limited, Birkenhead

CONTENTS

ILLUSTRATIONS

BETWEEN PAGES 118 AND 119

The author and publisher would like to thank H.M. the Queen, the Mary Evans Picture Library, the McCord Museum, Montreal, the National Maritime Museum, the National Trust and The Public Archives of Canada for their kind permission to reproduce the above illustrations

AUTHOR'S NOTE

For readers who are not familiar with the organization of the Army as it was at the time of James Wolfe, these notes may be helpful. A regiment was, to all intents and purposes, the property of its colonel. That officer was responsible for its finances; and, in some ways, it could be compared to a commercial enterprise. If it made a profit, he was in pocket. Similarly, if it lost money, he had to make good the deficit from his own funds.

To remain solvent, a regiment depended on as many men as possible. To assist in recruitment, the Government provided a bounty; but, if the amount was not sufficient to attract people, the colonel added to it – again from his own pocket. To keep the numbers as large as possible, these officers were not particular about the type of men who enlisted. Poor physique and a criminal record were certainly not deterrents – and, to maintain the strength, deserters were hunted down remorselessly.

Among the main sources of revenue were uniforms, which were paid for partly by Government grants, and partly by deductions from the men's pay known as 'off-reckonings'. More often than not, the money obtained from these sources was greater than the expenditure. Indeed, in some instances, the clothing contractors added to the profit by actually paying the colonel for his custom. However, the wealthier officers were not dependent on these amounts: a number of them contributed to the funds and were able to parade especially elegant turnouts of men.

Although the colonel was in nominal command of the regiment, he was seldom concerned with the daily running of it. For this task, he had a deputy – a lieutenant, one might say. This officer was known as a lieutenant-colonel and was, effectively, the commanding officer. In battle, the colonel's place was on the right of his regiment – though, frequently, he was involved with other duties. At the Battle of Dettingen, for example, Colonel Scipio Duroure was Colonel of the 12th Foot. Nevertheless, he did not fight with the 12th since he was employed as Adjutant-General to the force. Similarly, James Wolfe's father, Edward Wolfe, was, at one time, Colonel of the 8th Foot *and* Inspector of Marines.

Within a regiment, a sergeant was in command of no fewer than twenty men and not more than thirty; a subaltern had charge of between thirty and fifty; and a captain of between fifty and one hundred. Thus, in a company of one hundred men, there would be one captain, three subalterns and five sergeants.

During James Wolfe's employment as a lieutenant-colonel, he was continually hard-up in spite of his relatively senior rank and a very modest style of living. The reason for this was that officers were extremely badly paid. Since they had to buy their commissions (which, in the view of the King and the Government, was one way of ensuring that the service was officered by gentlemen) it was assumed that they had sufficient private income to keep themselves. Consequently, they received little more than a token salary.

There have been many changes in the Army since the days of James Wolfe, but one thing remains the same. The instructions of this period made it clear that, when a regiment moved into camp, the captains and subalterns had to see that the men were settled in before pitching their own tents. In an age when discipline was harsh, and the troops were more or less paupers, there was at least some concern for their welfare. James Wolfe was particularly preoccupied with this aspect of soldiering. Doubtless because his own health was so bad, he realized that battles are won by men who are physically fit. He worked hard to ensure that his own men were in this condition.

RICHARD GARRETT

THE PATH OF GLORY

'The paths of glory lead but to the grave'

THOMAS GRAY *Elegy Written in a Country Churchyard*

The last few hours had been, in themselves, a lifetime. So much had happened: everything had gone faultlessly. One could conceive a plan, run through it over and over again, studying and revising the smallest detail; and yet, even then, something could go wrong – a small thing, a trifling mistake, which would turn the whole operation into chaos. But the execution was unblemished. It was almost too good to be true.

He had put on a brand new uniform before setting out. The material, a bright scarlet, was still stiff. It smelt of the tailor's shop: fresh, immaculate. Whatever the outcome, one should look one's best. Death which, next to birth, is the greatest of all events, deserved spruceness.

Time is relative. In boredom, it stretches itself; in action, it becomes compressed. There had been the short voyage to the landing place – the men sitting silent, reflective and disciplined, in the flat-bottomed boats. No effort was needed, no straining at oars. The St Lawrence River, that potent and unwitting ally, had carried them soundlessly into position.

It was as dark as the inside of a witch's hat. Round about dawn, it began to rain. It seemed to accentuate the scent of the pine trees.

The worst part had been the struggle up the cliffs leading to the Heights of Abraham. The distance had only been – how far? About two hundred and fifty feet, but the going had been steep and rough, and Wolfe was afraid. He did not fear the French and Canadian forces at the top. They were an enemy he could fight.

What he dreaded was his weak, elongated shell of a body, the disease which brought pain and fever, and sucked away the strength he so badly needed. It did not require a hostile musket ball to end his life. Before very long he would die in any case. His sickness was just as effective as the product of an alien armourer.

Somehow, grabbing at trees and bushes, clawing at the loose earth, occasionally helped by his soldiers, he reached the top. The small success seemed to revive him; the prospect of battle released him from his personal torture chamber. There would be victory; and, if it was bought for the price of his life, what did that matter? It would end the agony which could only achieve the same conclusion.

The first musket ball hit him in the wrist. It was a trifling injury, and he paid no attention to it. The second and third injuries threw him off his feet. He called to one of his men. 'Support me,' he said. 'Let not my brave soldiers see me drop. The day is ours. Keep it.' This, he now knew, was the end of his story; but it had been paid for with glory – the glory which, as he so often remarked to himself, leads 'but to the grave'. How right Thomas Gray had been!

The rain continued to fall. A light breeze ruffled the grass. Three men attended him: he refused to call a surgeon, for he knew it would be of no avail. For a few brief moments, his consciousness seemed to come and go. One of his aides, noticing that the French were in flight said: 'See how they run.' Wolfe stirred. Who was running? Had he been unconscious, or did nothing seem to matter any more? Then he stirred himself.

In a final moment of awareness, he grasped the situation. The enemy was in flight. They had to be stopped: their retreat must be cut off. He gave an order for one of his colonels to take up a position calculated to achieve this.

> The boast of heraldry, the pomp of pow'r,
> And all that beauty, all that wealth e're gave.
> Awaits alike th' inevitable hour.
> The paths of glory lead but to the grave.

He knew the lines so well: he had quoted them to himself again and again. The paths had now reached their destination. In those final moments, he seemed to be happy. He had fulfilled the task to which destiny had assigned him. James Wolfe, the youngest major-general in the British Army, could take his leave. He was thirty-two years old.

Part I
THE PATH

I

THE BIRTH OF A SOLDIER

The wedding of Lieutenant-Colonel Edward Wolfe of His Majesty's 3rd Foot Guards and Henrietta Thompson, the daughter of what still might be described as 'landed gentry', took place in the Yorkshire village of Long Marston on 12 February 1724. He was nearly forty; she was twenty-four. Edward was a professional, and very competent, soldier. Henrietta's family traced its origins back to King Edward III. The connection was remote. It might have been closer, if her ancestors had not shown a tiresome talent for producing daughters. The fourteen generations which lay between her and the long dead monarch witnessed the birth of only three sons. Two of them, admittedly, became Dukes of Northumberland, but they were in the very early days. Afterwards, the apparently never ending line of girls had to content themselves with marrying knights – and, latterly, country gentlemen.

Edward Wolfe came from an Irish family. Until the Civil War, they had spelt the name 'Woulfe'. Afterwards, a change seemed to be expedient, and these were simple fellows. They might have settled for Smith or Jones or Robinson, which would have guaranteed them anonymity. Instead, they merely dropped the letter 'u'. The fact that any Cromwellian investigator worth his salt would have spotted the deception did not occur to them. Fortunately for the future of the clan, their confidence was not misplaced.

Ireland had little but misfortune to offer the Wolfes – though, in all fairness, they seemed to court it. Edward Wolfe's grandfather had been a misguided soldier named Captain George Woulfe. His great-uncle was a stubborn Franciscan friar. Both men lived in Limerick. When, in 1650, the Duke of Ormond arrived with the intention of fortifying the town against the

Roundheads, the reckless friar refused him the keys. The people of Limerick were, he suggested, perfectly capable of looking after themselves. Ormond wearied of the argument and departed for France. Captain George and his devout brother were left to do the best they could – which wasn't very much.

One year later, the Roundheads under the command of General Ireton duly arrived. Ireton was made of sterner stuff than the Duke. He put the town to the siege. With a ring of iron outside and an epidemic of plague within (could anyone wish for a better ally?) the people capitulated. Ireton's terms were not ungenerous, though he had prepared a list of twenty men who, in his opinion, had tried to frustrate his mission. Among them were the friar and Captain George Woulfe. The former joined his ancestors by way of the axeman's block; the latter was more fortunate. He managed to escape to the North of England.

Dropping the 'u' from his name, he settled in Yorkshire, where people either did not know that he had been condemned to death, or else did not care. Presently he married and his wife gave birth to a son whom the couple named Edward.

Edward Wolfe was determined to be a soldier. Somewhat surprisingly, he set off to seek his military fortune in Ireland. Until the sad affair at Limerick, the Woulfes had been Roman Catholics. When he came to England, however, George, who took a less intransigent view of the faith than his brother, decided to become a Protestant. Were they not *all* children of God? It would be foolish to let a quibble of religious faith jeopardize his life, which was in peril enough.

But the Irish, Papists to a man despite anything Cromwell's men may have tried to teach them, turned down Edward's services. He was sent back to England, where he was compelled to contain his ambitions until William of Orange swept away the last traces of Catholic establishment. Then, and then only, was he permitted to become the first Wolfe to bear arms on behalf of a reigning English monarch.

Thereafter, it did not seem to occur to the Wolfes to adopt any other profession. His son, Edward, was a placid individual, careful in most things – even cautious. One looked in vain for the death-or-glory image, the eruption of battlefield bravado. Edward

Wolfe did not lead charges, but he helped to make them possible. He was, in short, the very model of a conscientious staff officer who was unlikely to trouble his superiors.

With such qualities, he was bound to succeed. He entered the service as a second-lieutenant in Viscount Shannon's Regiment of Marines, and, contrary to the custom of the times, he achieved promotion when he was still a young man. During the War of the Spanish Succession, he served with competence – if with little distinction – under the Duke of Marlborough. The Jacobite rebellion of 1715 found him soldiering in the Highlands under General Wade.

Before his marriage to Henrietta, he had been on half-pay for a good many years – a condition which, since he had little money of his own, prevented his settling down earlier. It was, perhaps, a pity, for Lieutenant-Colonel Wolfe seems to have been the settling type. His bride brought him a modest dowry, and, for the first two years of their married life, the use of her parents' town house in York. In 1726 the couple moved south to Westerham in Kent. Edward was now fully employed, for his regiment was engaged on that last barrier between eighteenth-century soldiers and unemployment – the building of military roads.

If Edward Wolfe was undemanding and of an equitable disposition, his wife seemed determined that life should provide what was only right and proper for a descendant of the blood royal. She was a tall and imposing lady, not, some people protested, without beauty. If her classical lines had a fault, it was that her chin appeared to have hesitated. The rest of her face had become all that an artist could ask of it; but this feature, far from bringing it to a seemly conclusion, had given up the struggle. What should have been a headland was scarcely a hummock.

Mrs Wolfe knew what her husband may have suspected during those long years on half-pay: everything depends on money. Without it, rank and position mean nothing. What, indeed, shall it serve to be well connected, if one cannot keep up with one's assiduously sought connections? If she had children, she was obviously going to see that they married well (which meant: married money). As for her husband, she would ensure that he was geographically in a position where he would be exposed to the danger of being noticed. How, otherwise, could he win promotion, and recognition – and, what must be the inevitable result of both, a higher salary?

Physically, she seems to have been adequately robust, though she had a tendency to catch colds. Like so many other sufferers from minor complaints, she had the makings of a first class hypochondriac. During her twelve years at Westerham, she compiled a book of recipes. Most were unremarkable, but one cries out for attention. It was entitled 'A good water for Consumption' and was compounded, among other things, of garden snails, beer and sliced earthworms. Heaven knows in what manual of the black arts it originated, but Mrs Wolfe's belief in it was absolute. She dosed her family with it repeatedly, and they, compliant creatures that they were, swallowed it without a murmur.

The Wolfes lived in an old house named Spiers on the edge of Westerham. It dated back to the fourteenth century, though much of it had been rebuilt. Although it was reasonably close to the centre of this slumbering Kentish town, it was not near enough for Edward's liking. Consequently, at the end of 1726 – when Henrietta was far gone in her first pregnancy – he caused her to be moved to the vicarage. She would, he felt sure, be in better hands if the baby was born when he was away on one of his military road building exercises.

On 2 January 1727, the child arrived. Nine days later, he was baptized James in the local church, and they all moved back to Spiers. Almost exactly one year later, a second son was born. He was christened Edward. A nursemaid named Betty Hooper was employed to look after the boys. By all accounts they were devoted to her. When, many years later, Mrs Hooper's own two sons grew up, James took them into his regiment. They were, he said, 'two of the finest soldiers in the camp'.

The Colonel was stationed at Maidstone to begin with. Later he was employed on the building of a military road which stretched south from Westerham to Edenbridge. It was a matter of small importance; but it kept him busy. When he was at home, his talk was mostly about the Army, and it never occurred to either boy that there was any other profession worth following.

Indeed, their anxiety to shed the fetters of childhood and join a regiment was almost precocious.

As warriors in the making, James and Edward might have seemed to be unlikely material. Both were delicate and Mrs Wolfe's recipe book was in frequent use. Furthermore, both boys easily became tired. Even their most ardent admirer must have wondered whether either was up to the rigours of campaigning. But, at this period, it did not seem to matter much; for Sir Robert Walpole (the first statesman to assume the title of Prime Minister) was in power, and Sir Robert believed in peace. Since the nation had seldom been more prosperous, and since he appeared to be irremovable (his record of twenty-one years as Premier is still unbeaten), it was unlikely that the call to arms would come in the foreseeable future.

James Wolfe took after his mother. As in her case, nature seemed to have lost interest when it came to building his chin. Indeed, with his pronouncedly pointed nose, his profile resembled an angle of forty-five degrees. His head was capped by a fuzz of red hair, which looked the redder by comparison with his pale complexion. His legs were unusually long, and his frame had an apprently endless preoccupation for growing upward but not outwards. When at last this process came to an end, he was six feet three inches tall.

The appearance of Edward is not recorded, though everything suggests that he was an even paler copy of his brother. Certainly the two boys got on well together; and, when James led, Edward meekly followed. If the former owned his undoubtedly thrustful nature to his mother, Edward may have taken after his more docile father.

Five years after the Wolfes had come to Westerham, a large house about a mile down the road came on to the market. Its name was Squerryes Court. For some years, it had been in the possession of the third Earl of Jersey; now it was bought by a family named Warde. Among the properties of the large estate was the house in which the Wolfes were living. Thus, the Wardes became their landlords – but, which is more important, they also became their friends.

Sir John Warde, the reigning member of the household, was

the son of one former Lord Mayor of London and the nephew of another. His wife had been the sister of two countesses (Buckinghamshire and Effingham). She had died at their house in London, leaving Sir John with two sons. The elder was ten years old: the younger, George, was about the same age as James Wolfe. No doubt feeling that a home in the country was better suited to the life of a widower entrusted with the upbringing of two boys, Sir John had decided to retire from the capital and devote himself to the existence of a country squire. Nevertheless, he kept on the house in London.

James Wolfe and George Warde became close friends. They were a strangely matched pair. Whilst James was pallid, delicate and lanky, George was handsome and robust. However, one of James's letters suggests that he had some sort of infirmity in his speech – a stammer, perhaps. Whatever it was, it was not sufficient to prevent his making what turned out to be a very distinguished career in the Army. But it was *there*. Were the two boys drawn to each other by a bond of weakness? Strength, after all, does not engender sympathy. The Warde family, certainly, was devoted to James, and Sir John did everything he could to assist the young man's future.

Life proceeded pleasantly enough. The Wolfe boys attended a school run by a Mr Laurence on the edge of the town. Betty Hooper looked after them in her capable way, and Mrs Wolfe ran to her recipe book whenever one or the other was taken ill. The book is still in existence at Squerryes Court, and a quick glance at it is enough to show that the majority of the remedies were far more horrible than the complaints they were designed to cure. Doubtless the threat of another dose of the 'good water for Consumption' was sufficient to put the hardiest bug to flight.

In their free time, the Wolfe boys played with the Warde boys. The garden at Spiers was small, but the grounds of Squerryes Court were huge. They lent themselves admirably to the one game they really enjoyed – soldiering. They talked soldiers and, so far as they were able, they tried to *live* soldiers. Nothing else mattered. Riding, shooting, and similar country pursuits were excellent as a means to an end, and that was the Army.

James, whatever his physical shortcomings, threw himself into these fantasies with considerable energy. He may have looked frail, but he did not act as if he were. It was, indeed, the first of many contradictions which comprised his character and turned him, in the final analysis, into one of history's great mysteries. Throughout his life, his letters home contained enough information to suggest that, now and again, he was feeling unwell – but seldom sufficient to cause his parents anxiety. It was as if a strong mind was determined to turn upon the weak body which encapsuled it: to offer it no quarter, and to make it behave as though it were robust. Most men knew where to stop. James went beyond the bounds of reason. Far from making allowances for his constitution, he rebelled against it – and drove himself, almost literally, to destruction.

But physique was not everything. James Wolfe was a very serious minded young man. Every portrait suggests a rather grey personality, with eyes which are, on the whole, cold. It is difficult to like him, though he seems to have been popular – even, at times, humorous. Perhaps the clue lies in his mouth, which appears strangely at variance with the rest of his face. One has the impression that it is striving to conform, and yet it badly wants to smile. No doubt, in life, it sometimes gave up the struggle. Historians, certainly, go out of their way to show that James Wolfe could reel off a merry quip with the best of them. Unfortunately the argument is rendered thin by lack of illustrations. Such Wolfe jokes as have survived were cumbersome and lacking in ornament – rather like heavy pieces of kitchen furniture.

Lieutenant-Colonel Edward Wolfe was busy with his regiment, building roads. As Mrs Wolfe was only too well aware, the occupation may have been designed to advance armies, but it was not advancing his career. If he were to make any further progress up the hazardous ladder of promotion, he needed to be somewhere where people would notice him. Westerham was delightful, but nothing very much happened there, and Sir John Warde was the only man of influence in the town. To get on, an officer needed to be nearer London – nearer, that is to say, to the court of King George II from whom all mercies and benefits stemmed. At present the nation was enjoying the affluence of Walpole's statesmanship, but there was no mistaking the public mood. Motivated by some strange yearning, which clearly did not have much to do with money, the people wanted war. Sooner or later something would crop up which not even Sir Robert Walpole would be able to overlook. Once the first shots had been exchanged, a soldier's opportunities, which had been stagnant for so long, would multiply. Mrs Wolfe wished to be sure that, when this occurred, her husband was in the right place.

Largely for this reason, the Wolfes packed up their possessions at the end of 1738, and moved to Greenwich. It was not, admittedly, in the centre of London; but, at least, it was nearer. The first signs that the circle in which they now moved might be advantageous occurred in the following year. Six regiments of marines were formed in preparation for what a strong body of public opinion, led by Pitt, hoped would be a war with Spain. The command of one of them was entrusted to Edward Wolfe.

Greenwich was the scene of a good deal of naval and military activity in those days, and a clergyman named Samuel F. Swinden had anticipated the needs of the officers' sons. Shortly before the Wolfes moved into the town, he had set up a small school specifically for these children. James, who was now twelve, was enrolled as a pupil, and so was young Edward. Swinden liked James, though Edward seemed to be the brighter of the two. Both got on well with their school fellows: if not given to pranks, they were at least friendly boys and the other youngsters, all from service families, applauded James's determination to become a soldier. Most of them had similar ambitions.

At home, the attitude towards his chosen career was less straightforward. The colonel was, clearly, delighted: it was, after all, his incessant chat about military matters, and his stories of long-ago campaigns, which had created the ambition. Mrs Wolfe, on the other hand, was far from pleased. Fussy about her offspring's health, she doubted whether he was strong enough for active service. As an ambitious woman, with a strong concern for economics, she had misgivings about the financial rewards. After all, she was well experienced in the soldier's peacetime lot. The alternatives were a dead-end occupation, half-pay when full pay was little enough, or unemployment. Would not James do better to apply himself to business, or, even, politics?

The Colonel encouraged, his wife discouraged, and the Wolfe household was the scene of heated arguments. So far as James was concerned, Mrs Wolfe might have saved her breath. He had no ears for her point of view. He intended to join the Army. Nothing could make him change his mind; and, as he frequently made clear, the sooner he could get on with it, the better.

As for Edward (or Ned, as the family called him), he was only too happy to follow his brother's lead.

In 1739, the nation was given the opportunity it had been waiting for. The source of the trouble was Spain's determination to ban English goods from its colonies – and the resulting actions of the Spanish navy in searching British ships. Everything boiled over, when a captain named Jenkins asserted that a Spanish sailor had cut off one of his ears. War was declared; the nation became wildly excited; and, when Admiral Vernon scored a not very well deserved victory at Porto Bello in the West Indies, its enthusiasm reached even higher peaks. As wars went, it was a poor thing, which dribbled over into the equally uninspiring War of the Austrian Succession. But, from a serviceman's point of view, it meant an end to road-building.

Colonel Wolfe must have made his mark quickly at Greenwich. Hardly had he been given command of the 1st Marine Regiment, than he was appointed adjutant-general to an expeditionary force, which was being assembled on the Isle of Wight. Its destination was to be a port in the Spanish West Indies named Cartagena. No sooner had James heard about his father's appointment, than he begged to be allowed to go with him.

The fact that he was only thirteen years old, and that expeditions to far-flung islands were no places for children, did not deter him. Could he not, he asked his father, go as a Gentleman Volunteer? He would wear no uniform (for there was no uniform for this branch of the Army); he would probably not become involved in the fighting; indeed, his duties would be confined to making himself useful about the place. This, he promised, he would do very well.

Mrs Wolfe dug herself in. The idea was ridiculous; James

should not go. But the Colonel was no less stubborn – and nor, when it came to a crunch, was James. The man and the boy prevailed. In July 1740, the adjutant-general and his eldest boy set off for Portsmouth. The former was to come back two years later, after a disastrous campaign. Fever killed off more troops than the enemy accounted for; the Army and the Navy bickered incessantly; and, on his return, Edward Wolfe advised his son never, under any circumstances, to have anything to do with joint expeditions.

James never reached the West Indies. He had left home under unhappy circumstances. His mother had begun by rebuking him, and had followed this up by letters which were full of self-pity. On 6 August, young James sat down in his lodgings at Newport, Isle of Wight, and wrote to her. He was compelled to protest: '[I] am very sorry, dear Mamma, that you doubt my love, which I'm sure is as sincere as ever any son's was to his mother. . . . I am sorry to hear your head is so bad, which I fear, is caused by your being so melancholy; but, pray, dear Mamma, if you love me, don't give yourself up to fears for us. I hope, if it please God, we shall soon see one another, which will be the happiest day that ever I shall see.'

It was, perhaps, a strange letter from a thirteen-year-old to his mother, and his obvious anxiety about things at home must have robbed this big adventure of some of its charm. In one paragraph, he observed: 'I believe we shall not sail this fortnight.' It was a considerable understatement. Although a fleet of transports had been assembled, and there was much to watch in the way of regiments embarking, the force did not get under way until November. By then, James had become ill, and his father had been compelled to send him home. Doubtless, the effect of this ailment on history was considerable. That delicate youngster, James Wolfe, would never have survived the rigours of those awful two years.

Sick in body, dejected in mind, he came home to Greenwich. Mrs Wolfe got busy with her manual of witchcraft and, aided by Betty Hooper, she nursed him back to health. She was obviously delighted by the turn of events. Fondly, she packed him off back to school at Samuel Swinden's small academy. The old routine of lessons, and occasional visits to the Wardes at Westerham, was resumed. Perhaps, now, James would see sense, and take up some other occupation.

2

THE VERY YOUNG OFFICER

If Mrs Wolfe imagined that her son's expedition to the Isle of Wight had put the idea of joining the Army out of his head, she was to be disappointed. The illness, which made the experience a misery, had not dimmed his ambitions in the slightest. He was still determined to become a soldier, and his father supported his ambition. Not much is known about the married life of Edward and Henrietta Wolfe, but the placid colonel must sometimes have been roused to argument. He and his wife took entirely different views of their eldest son. She saw his weakness; he noticed only the boy's strength. Obviously, his confidence was sometimes misplaced. How, otherwise could he have conceived the notion that this frail lad, who was seasick even when the vessels were at anchor in Spithead, could have endured a voyage of some 5,000 miles – and survived on an island where fever was known to be commonplace?

But the fact that James had fallen ill, and had been sent home in the coach from Portsmouth, did not disturb his plans for the boy's future. He was determined to use whatever influence he had to obtain a commission for him. It would have to be in his own regiment, the 1st Marines.

Ever since private armies had fought in Europe, during the fourteenth century, the method of becoming an officer had been comparatively simple. An aspiring leader bought his way into the service. As originally conceived, a military unit was rather like a commercial enterprise. The officers were partners. If a man commanded, say, a regiment, his investment was greater than that of a company commander. When one of them decided to retire, he sold his stake. By this method, a more junior officer could, as it were, purchase his shares and consequently achieve promotion.

Similarly, if the owners of a regiment found one of their colleagues unsatisfactory, they could buy him out.

Anyone could purchase a commission; and there were, indeed, women and children who had been enrolled as ensigns. But more conventional warriors were not necessarily more effective. Some wanted to get into the Army believing it would open up a world of social opportunities. Others wished to serve briefly in a campaign – entirely for the prestige which such an experience conferred upon them. Few were motivated by professionalism. From time to time, there had been attempts to get rid of this iniquitous system. Cromwell had succeeded in his New Model Army. William of Orange had failed. In 1694, he had introduced an Act by which an officer had to swear he had not paid for his commission. It was largely disregarded, and in 1702 it was abandoned entirely. Eighteen years later, a tariff was laid down stating the maximum sums payable for commissions and preferment.

The attraction of the purchase system to the government was, perhaps, understandable. When a man felt he could soldier no more, he sold his rank. The payment, in theory at any rate, took care of him in his declining years – and absolved the authorities of any need to give him a pension.

Purchase, or else exceptional influence, was the only way of getting into the regiments of foot and the cavalry. There were, however, units known as non-purchase corps, into which admission was entirely by merit. They included the Royal Artillery, the Royal Engineers, and the Marines. Since the Wolfes were never well off, the attraction to Edward of his own regiment must have been considerable – financially no less than the fact that here, more than anywhere else, he was able to pull strings.

It was December 1741, Mr Swinden's school had broken up for the Christmas holidays, and James had ridden over to Westerham to stay with the Wardes. One afternoon, he and George Warde were playing at the top of a small hill not many yards from the house. It was a favourite spot of theirs: they used to fence and practise firing pistols. They heard a carriage crunching over the drive below, but neither paid any attention to it. Shortly afterwards, Sir John Warde came hurrying up from the house. He was carrying an envelope in his hand, addressed to 'James Wolfe Esq.'. Signed by King George II and by one of his ministers, it was James's commission as a second-lieutenant in his father's regiment. The document was dated 3 November. For some reason it had been delayed.

James and George, who was expecting his own commission to arrive before long, were in transports of delight. In a mood of more sober reflection that night, however, James may have had misgivings. The regiment was on active service 5,000 miles away. He was unlikely to be able to join it; and, in any case, his unfortunate experiences of the sea at Spithead, may have caused him to doubt his suitability for a regiment which had to do with ships. Nor were the Marines a corps which offered much in the way of a future.

The 1st Marine Regiment was seventy-five years old. It had originated as 'The Maritime Regiment of the Lord High Admiral of England'. William III had disbanded it; Queen Anne had revived the concept of soldiers fighting beside sailors, by turning three regiments of foot into marines. One of these was Edward Wolfe's.

Had James realized it, the future of the Marines was about to undergo another change – and one which was unlikely to benefit the prospects of officers serving in the corps. Having come under the Army, the authority was to be transferred to the Navy in 1761. This meant that all the colonelcies would be given to senior naval officers. Furthermore, any young officer who felt that his ambitions were being frustrated, would be unable to arrange a transfer back into the Army. The likelihood of rapid promotion in the other non-purchase corps was bad enough. In the Marines, it would simply not exist.

But it was a beginning. There was a war to be fought, and James Wolfe was now eligible to take part. That, for the moment, was all that mattered. On his return home, he found his mother a great deal less than enthusiastic. Nor were the poor woman's troubles over. In a year, young Ned was to follow his brother. For the time being, however, she had other things to think about. Her husband was on his way back from the West

Indies. Only ninety-six officers and men of his regiment had survived the expedition.

There is nothing to show precisely what happened during the next few months. Sir John Warde may have had a hand in it. James, though he was even now only fifteen, certainly did. Somehow he managed to exchange into the 12th Foot (until recently, the Suffolk Regiment). In the light of future events, it may have been that the regiment was severely under strength. Any officer, even a boy second-lieutenant, was welcome.

What had begun as the War of Jenkins Ear transformed itself into the War of Austrian Succession. The claimant to the throne was Maria Theresa; the opposition came from Prussia. France sided with Prussia, Britain with Austria. As with so many other conflicts in the eighteenth century, it became a struggle between Britain and France. The English forces were assisted by Hanoverians and Austrians. Spain, predictably, was allied to the French. The Netherlands, which were part of the Austrian Empire, took little interest in the proceedings.

Napier, in his *History of the Peninsular War*, observed: 'In the beginning of each new war, England has to seek in blood the knowledge necessary to ensure success; and like the fiend's progress towards Eden, her conquering course is through chaos followed by death.' He might have been writing about the War of Austrian Succession. A septuagenarian field-marshal named the Earl of Stair, who was dithering on the brink of senility, was wrenched from retirement to command the expeditionary forces in Europe. His army consisted of fifteen cavalry regiments plus the Horse Guards, fifty infantry regiments and the Foot Guards, and four companies of Royal Artillery. Few of the officers had been employed on active service, and the inexperienced majority had received no training. A man had to find out how to fight as best he could. Many never discovered the art.

On 27 April 1742, a fleet of transports was moored in the Thames off Deptford and Woolwich. On Blackheath common, Lord Stair's departing soldiers were paraded for inspection by King George II and his son, the twenty-one-year-old Duke of Cumberland. It was a fine sight, with the scarlet tunics standing bravely out against the pale green of the common. James was wearing a powdered wig for the occasion, and George Warde, who was now in the Dragoons, was resplendent in the uniform of a cornet. Among the huge crowd of spectators, were Mrs Wolfe and Ned.

Once the inspection was over, the troops marched down to the river and embarked. Like the campaign in front of them, the departure got off to a slow start. At the mouth of the Thames, the wind dropped and the ships were becalmed for several days. It was not until 10 May that the armada of troopships, escorted by the fifty-gun warship *Argyle*, reached Ostend. When the men disembarked, they found that their wives and camp-followers had reached the port before them. Someone made a joke about its being the only expeditionary force in which the advance guard was composed of women. From Ostend, the soldiers marched to Bruges and thence to Ghent.

This must have been an unusually lonely period in the life of James Wolfe. Later he was to become a solitary figure by choice; now, in the confusion of so many new experiences, he could have done with some companionship. George Warde's regiment had not yet arrived, and he found himself a boy in a man's world – unsure of himself and unready to enjoy the pleasures that appealed to his fellow officers.

James's was a guarded personality. In his early letters home, he told his parents precisely what he wanted them to know. He confined news of his health to the barest details – erring, frequently, on the optimistic side. Of his feelings he gave very little clue at all. They portrayed a rather dry, unemotional, youngster – an impression which must be misleading. For though James had sufficient confidence in himself, and he certainly did not want for physical courage, he was nevertheless shy. He betrayed this condition by blushing suddenly, and by plucking at his buttons and cuffs with his unusually long fingers.

The language of an officer of the period was larded with obscenities and covered a small field of topics. He was liable to drink heavily and he enjoyed the company of ladies at a fairly low level. By contrast, young James seldom swore; he drank moderately and sometimes not at all; and he felt uneasy in the company of women. He once wrote to his mother: 'I am often surprised at the little sensibility I feel in myself at the sight of the fairest and finest females.' He had, indeed, only one love in his life: his profession. He pursued it with a single-mindedness which must have dismayed his less dedicated colleagues.

Nevertheless, the other officers of the 12th treated their stripling subaltern kindly, and did their best to show him how to perform his duties. He was comfortably quartered in the town, though the local people did little for their visitors. All they wanted was to go about their lives in peace – and without hindrance from the military rabble that had descended on them. As one captain wrote home: 'They hate the English and we hate them.' There was an episode in which some infantrymen became involved in a fracas with a local butcher and his friends. There were casualties on both sides. Afterwards, the soldiers were locked up in barracks, and the town's magistrates decreed that 'whoever should offer the least affront to the subjects of the King of Great Britain should be whipped, burnt in the back, and turned out of town.'*

Mrs Wolfe's letters to her son were, as might be expected, full of motherly concern. James acknowledged them politely. 'I am vastly obliged to you for your good advice,' he replied on one occasion, 'and will follow it as much as lies in my power, I assure you.' To provide himself with an interest in his spare time, he bought a flute and took lessons from a local teacher. He may not have been very good at it; at all events the instrument was seldom mentioned. But now things were looking up. George Warde had arrived with his Dragoons, and the two friends were able to spend the odd hour or two together. The local theatre re-opened, which gave them somewhere to go in the evenings. Writing to his mother on 12 September, he said:

You desire to know how I live. I assure you, as to eating, rather too well, considering what we may come to. For drink I don't care much; but there is very good rum and brandy in this place, and cheap, if we have a mind to take a little sneaker now and then at night just to warm us. The weather begins now to grow coldish: we have had rain for the last two weeks, and people say 'tis likely to continue till the frost comes

* *Gentleman's Magazine.*

in. I have not begun with fire yet, neither do I intend till I know where we shall encamp.

This place is full of officers, and we never want company. I go to the play once or twice a week, and talk a little with the ladies, who are very civil, and speak French.

War, as most other field sports, had its seasons. No general would have dreamed of committing his troops to a campaign in winter, and the Earl of Stair was no exception. The army rested and shivered in Ghent. The canals and rivers froze over; traffic in Flanders came to a standstill; and it was not until February of the following year that Stair bestirred himself. On the thirteenth of that month, young Ned arrived to join the 12th as an ensign. James was now an accomplished officer. The flute had been put to one side, and he was studying the duties of adjutant. During December, there had been a rumour that the army would return to England in the spring, but it seemed unlikely. The reason for the British presence in Flanders was the threat of a French attack on Hanover. With the coming of warmer weather, it might thaw into reality.

In early February, Lord Stair ordered his men to march into Germany. The object was to link up with Austrian troops near Frankfurt. Those officers who could afford it travelled on horseback. Those who couldn't struggled along on foot beside the common soldiery. The Wolfe brothers took a middle course. Their assets were not sufficient to purchase one of these beasts apiece, and so they shared one. On one day James would ride and Ned would walk. On the next, Ned was in the saddle and James was on foot.

The going was horribly rough. Mrs Wolfe had instructed James that he was to write home once a fortnight, and he obeyed. Somehow he managed to keep it up throughout most of this ordeal. His letters recorded fatigue, cold and, later on, hunger.

'This is our fifth day's march,' he told her in mid-February; 'we have had very bad weather all the way. I have found out by experience that my strength is not so great as I had imagined; but, however, I have held out pretty well as yet. . . . I never come into quarters without aching hips and knees.'

It took them the better part of two months to reach the Rhine. Occasionally, the men were able to obtain eggs and bacon from the local people. For most of the time, they existed on Army bread. And the winter was slow in departing. On 7 April James was informing his mother that, less than a week previously, he had been 'obliged to walk up to my knees in snow'. As for sleeping at nights, he often had to lie 'upon straw'. By 7 May they were at Frankfurt and within a day's march of the French, who had come up from the south. There was now a feeling of impending action in the British lines. Ned wrote home: 'I don't expect to hear from you till we have beaten the French, and return to Flanders, which time is very uncertain.'

Rumours continued to abound. One was that the French might take it into their heads to make for Bavaria, and that the British would follow. This would have involved the army in another two months on the march. As Ned shrewdly pointed out in one of his letters home, 'there is no credit to be given to half is said here.'

But Marshal Noailles, who commanded the French, had no intention of taking his men to Bavaria. He was a superb tactician: he had his plan, and Lord Stair was behaving as he hoped he would. Indeed, the British commander-in-chief did not seem to realize just how close the enemy were. Unlike his opponents, His Lordship had a poor intelligence set-up.

Manœuvring in a comparatively small area, the two armies nonetheless managed to avoid each other. Stair evacuated some high ground near Frankfurt; Noailles occupied it. By early summer, the English, supported by 16,000 Hanoverians and an Austrian force, were encamped in the village of Aschaffenburg by the banks of the River Main. Ned was now beginning to show symptoms of fatigue, but this may have been because, like almost everybody else in the army, he was hungry. If Noailles's strategy worked, there would be no need for a clash of arms. The Allies would be starved into submission. Already, Stair's 37,000 men were on half-rations. It only remained to cut the line between the Allied army and its reserves a few miles away at Hanau, and the French operation would be complete.

George II seems to have been more aware of what was taking place than his man on the spot. On 21 June, accompanied by his son, the Duke of Cumberland, he arrived to assume command personally. It was just as well. Stair, while out on reconnaisance, had nearly been captured by a Fench patrol. His men were now living by marauding the countryside, and it would not be long before this frugal source of supply dried up. Something had to be done at once, and the monarch's first act was to promote Cumberland, who was only twenty-two, to the rank of major-general. He then prepared to march his beleaguered troops to safety.

James Wolfe had done well to study the duties of an adjutant, for he was now required to carry out this function. Indeed, the 12th was so short of effective officers, that he was virtually second-in-command of it. At first, having discovered the harsh reality of his constitution, he was afraid the work might be too tiring. As he became used to it, however, he was glad to note: 'I think it will agree very well with me.' Writing home on 21 June, he told his father: 'We are now nearly forty miles from Frankfurt, which we marched in two days and two nights, without nine or ten hours' halt, in order to gain a pass that is here, and now in our possession. The men were almost starved on that march. They nor the officers had little more than bread and water to live on, and that very scarce, because they had not the ammunition bread the day it was due. But I believe it could not be helped.'

Unless a miracle occurred, there would be no ammunition bread for many a day to come. Fires on the far side of the river showed that the French were closing in and burning villages. As if to make matters easier for them, Stair had forgotten to destroy the bridge over the river at Aschaffenburg. There was nothing, now, to prevent Noailles from attacking in the rear. It was almost as if the ancient English field-marshal had become mentally paralysed.

The French commander-in-chief was ready to bring off the *coup* which he had prepared with such superb skill. His nephew, the Duc de Grammont, had taken up a position with 30,000 men athwart a ravine which covered Stair's only possible line of escape. Now, with a further 12,000, Noailles was about to cross the river into Aschaffenburg, and push the Allies forward towards Grammont's guns.

Goaded into action by his sovereign, and only too aware of the impatient and scornful comments of Cumberland, Stair at last shook off his lethargy and did something. On 26 June, he issued the following order:

> After Tattoo this night the tents of the whole army to be struck without any noise and all the baggage and artillery to hold themselves in readiness to march; the army to remain under arms in front of their encampments.
>
> Tomorrow at break of day every regiment to march into their new ground; and as soon as the army are arrived in their new camp, they are to remain under arms in front of the new ground in the same manner as they did the night preceding till further orders, keeping a profound silence, no fires being suffered in the camp.

It was not very explicit. The 'new camp' was at Hanau, but the Field Marshal seemed unaware of Grammont's powerful force which lay between him and it. It was certainly a withdrawal; indeed, it was little short of flight. With the French pouring across the river, it seems inconceivable that even the elderly Earl imagined it could be carried off without a battle.

What was more, Stair could have saved himself the trouble of insisting on such security precautions as 'a profound silence'. Noailles heard about the order almost at once. He instructed Grammont to take up his final position, and began his own move into Aschaffenburg. The British were doing precisely what he had hoped they would do – even to the extent of believing that the main French attack would come from the direction of the village. They appeared to be unaware of the much more substantial trap which lay ahead of them.

The day began fine. On the left, the River Main made its languid way towards the Rhine. To the right, the hills, coated with pine trees, looked like a giant wall in the thin light of dawn. Down in the valley, the Allied troops went about their business quietly. At 4.0 am the army got ready to move. In his headquarters to the rear of the lines, George II finished his toilet and ate a hurried breakfast. Like a scarlet giant, the army began to move. The first shots were fired at seven o'clock when a French battery opened up on the British cavalry at the approaches to the village of Dettingen. The effect was to cause the drivers of the baggage-train to panic. Leaving their vehicles unattended, they ran off into the woods. Then it began to rain.

If Grammont had done what was expected of him, and remained in his position, he would have annihilated the British army in Europe. It would have been too easy. Nothing could have prised his men out of their natural fortress. With good marksmanship, they would have committed a fearful slaughter, until Marshal Noailles's force came up from the rear and delivered the *coup de grâce*. But Grammont was young and impatient. He could not wait. To the astonishment of his uncle, he ordered his men forward to meet the oncoming British. Robbed of their natural defences, the French were now compelled to fight the British on equal terms.

The prelude was an exchange of artillery fire lasting about two and three-quarter hours. At noon the two forces marched towards each other, and at about one o'clock the battle proper began. A French regiment attacked the Scots Fusiliers and broke through the first line. 'But', Wolfe told his father some days later, 'before they got to the second line, out of two hundred, there were not forty living.... These unhappy men were of the first families in France. Nothing, I believe, could be more rash than their undertaking.'

Although he was in the centre of the line, where the fighting was thickest, young James Wolfe had time to watch other sections of the battle with a critical eye. He noted that the British cavalry did badly: fighting with pistols, when sabres would have been a more effective weapon. 'Their excuse for retreating', he observed, '[was that] they could not make their horses stand the fire!' However, since they had not been in action before, they might be excused. He hoped they would do better next time. (They did.)

The colonel of the 12th, a man named Duroure, was acting as adjutant-general. Since the regiment had no lieutenant-colonel, the command was entrusted to a major, with Wolfe as his second-in-command. Before the battle, Colonel Duroure had loaned James a horse. During the fighting, the animal received a ball in one of its rear legs. 'So', James wrote, 'I was obliged to do the duty of an adjutant all that and the next day on foot, in a pair of heavy boots. I lost with the horse, furniture and pistols which cost me ten ducats; but three days after the battle got the horse again, with the ball in him – and he is now almost well again – but without furniture and pistols.' The loss of these personal effects seemed to distress him very much.

The English musket (or firelock) of the time was a weapon known as Brown Bess. Its range was limited to three hundred yards; with a reasonably able shot, it could discharge three rounds a minute. Indeed, it was really more effective as a mounting for a bayonet. The French were, perhaps, better marksmen, but when it came to fighting at close quarters there was no one to beat the British infantryman.

James and his commanding officer were well aware of the folly that came from opening fire too soon. It wasted ammunition, and distracted the men, when they would be better occupied in marching towards the enemy. James wrote: 'The Major and I . . . before they came near, were employed in begging the men not to fire at too great a distance, but to keep it till the enemy should come near us.' Their instructions seem to have gone unheeded at first. At all events, as he sadly admitted, they did 'very little execution' with their first fusillade.

Stocially, with tired eyes and pinched faces, the soldiers trudged forward through the pouring rain. They halted, fired, reloaded, and moved on once more. With each pace their ranks seemed to thin. So long as he kept going in the right direction, a man assumed that all was well. The only witnesses were the trees which thronged the hillside, and they could not applaud.

Encouraged by their sovereign, the men behaved well. James was pleased to note: 'The King was in the midst of the fight; and the Duke [of Cumberland] behaved as bravely as a man could do.' While at the head of the second line, His Royal Highness received a minor wound in the leg, but it did not deter him. The Wolfe brothers were unharmed, though it was a close thing. Wrote James: 'I sometimes thought I had lost [Ned], when I saw arms, legs and heads beat off close by him. He is called "The Old Soldier", and very deservedly.'

When it was all over, the French were put to flight leaving behind four thousand killed and wounded. The British lost about half that number. It had been a far from glorious victory: if Grammont had not made his disastrous mistake, it would have been a crushing defeat. But at the time nobody thought about that. Stair seemed to have become rejuvenated by the success. He was all for following up the fleeing French. But the King, who had just achieved the distinction of being the last British sovereign to command his troops in battle, thought otherwise. There were plenty of toadies only too eager to keep him busy during the next few days, as they overwhelmed him with their congratulations. It was an experience His Majesty thoroughly enjoyed. Having linked up with their reserves at Hanau, the Allies went into camp at Worms. The enemy lived to fight another day.

As for James Wolfe, when the fury of battle had ended, the smoke of gunpowder had blown away, and the dead had been buried, a reaction set in, He told his father: 'The fatigue I had the day we fought and the day after made me very much out of order, and I was obliged to keep to my tent for two days.' The malady whatever it was, succumbed to the time-honoured cure of bleeding. Writing home on 4 July, he reported that the removal of a few pints of blood had been 'of great service to me, and I am now as well as ever.'

During the long march into action, as the French cannon balls crashed into the ranks and he saw the British cavalry beaten back, did he experience fear? If he did, he made no mention of the fact; but to admit to such a sensation would have been unmanly. James Wolfe had been compelled to grow up quickly. Throughout most of his life, he kept his emotions under perfect control. Certainly, in the heat of battle – as his lanky figure stumbled through the mud imploring his men to fire with accuracy and economy – his mind had no time to reflect on danger. Then, as in all his career, James Wolfe was preoccupied with only one thing: his duty.

3
THE LONG ROAD TO SCOTLAND

When their sons were receiving their baptism of fire at Dettingen, Colonel and Mrs Wolfe were busy settling down in a new home. They had moved into the West End of London and acquired a house in Old Burlington Street. Significantly, the Wardes had a residence in the same road. The object was similar to that which had caused the departure from Westerham to Greenwich: ambition. They would now be even closer to the influential circles Mrs Wolfe so assiduously tried to cultivate. In February of the following year, her quest for preferment with the help of a removal van was successful. Her husband was promoted to the rank of brigadier-general.

Meanwhile, under more modest circumstances, her son James was adding to the sum of family achievement. His exertions on the field at Dettingen had been noticed by the Duke of Cumberland. On 13 July, he was given the rank of lieutenant and made substantive adjutant of the 12th. He was very busy. After the battle, when he was still feeling unwell, the Earl of Stair had demanded detailed reports on the condition of the troops; a return of men and horses still fit for service; an account of the state of the regiment's arms; and a list of things which were needed to bring the unit back to fighting strength. All this had to be done within twenty-four hours.

During this period, James seems to have been more or less running the regiment. The colonel was seriously ill with dysentery, and the major appears to have been similarly afflicted. Indeed, there was a lot of illness in the British lines, and James was lucky to escape with a minor complaint which yielded to bleeding.

Some officers might succeed in drawing full pay despite the fact that they spent only half the time working. The adjutant, on the other hand, earned every penny he received. His duties were listed in a contemporary document, and they were nothing if not demanding. He was not only responsible for maintaining a link between the regiment and brigade via the brigade major: he had also, for example, to inspect all detachments before they went out on duty, and to ensure that a sergeant was in charge of them. He should, the document instructed, 'always choose three or four good sergeants that can write well'. Every Friday morning, he had to give the brigade major a list of the men who were out on detachment, on leave, sick, in hospital, discharged from the service, dead, or who had deserted. He was in charge of the training of new recruits; he had to see that all offenders were brought to justice, and that the punishments were carried out; and he had 'to keep constantly to all the rules and forms of discipline and exercise now used in the British Foot, and on no pretence whatever to change or let fall any of the said customs till further orders.'*

It was an enormous burden to place upon the shoulders of an officer who was still only sixteen and a half years old, but James coped admirably. Indeed, later on, when leave was granted, he never received any. Somehow, this boy adjutant seems to have made himself indispensable. His father had always been a good staff officer, and this ability had rubbed off on to him. It sometimes seemed that he was held captive by his own sense of duty. No part of the outside world was allowed to intrude. In one sense, he was wretchedly old for his age: in another, almost childishly ignorant. He lived in a narrow corridor, his existence governed entirely by the requirements of the service. There was no place for art or literature, for entertainment, or even for conversation which went beyond the banalities of regimental gossip.

The camp at Worms was well fortified; and there were constant rumours that the French, having recovered from their mauling at Dettingen, were about to attack. James thought that the health of the troops might benefit from such an encounter. He wrote to his father: 'We have a great deal of sickness amongst us, so I believe the sooner we engage (if it is to be) the better.'

* *Orders for a Battalion and an Army*, first published in 1768.

The thought that battle might serve as a cure for illness was certainly original. But the French did not go into the offensive. Lord Stair, despairing of ever seeing eye to eye with his sovereign, resigned – and the King went home to London, where Handel was busy composing a *Te Deum* in honour of the recent victory. Presently, as autumn approached and the war seemed likely to die of sheer inertia, the British army moved back to Flanders. They were quartered, briefly, in Brussels. When James celebrated his seventeenth birthday, on 2 January 1744, he was stationed in Ostend.

Ned Wolfe had endured the rigours of campaigning less well than his brother. Towards the end of 1743 he fell ill and was sent home on leave. James had nothing to say about it. Perhaps he remembered his own return from the Isle of Wight. Or, possibly, he tried to ignore Ned's frailty. Since his own life was an almost constant struggle against physical weakness, he seemed to take the view that ill health simply did not exist. 'Don't talk to me of constitution', he once remarked of a fellow officer; 'he has good spirits, and good spirits will carry a man through anything.' It was a convenient philosophy in an age when medical science was more a matter of luck than judgement.

At any rate, when he wrote to Ned that winter, his letter was mostly concerned with regimental matters. The two of them were 'to be tented together next campaign. The marquee is making and will cost us about £4.' There had been only one promotion: an officer known as 'Thickhead' had taken over his father's company. The rest was devoted to some rather heavy-handed badinage about girls. 'I am . . . in some pain about Miss Warde. Admire anywhere else and welcome – except the widow Bright. Miss Paterson is yours, if you like her, and so is the little staring girl in the chapel [at Greenwich hospital] with twenty thousand pounds'; and so on. Mrs Wolfe, apparently, was suffering from one of her innumerable colds, but she had sent James a plum cake, which 'was very good and of singular service to me.' Possibly in playful deference to Ned's nickname as 'The Old Soldier' in the regiment, the letter was addressed to 'Capt Wolfe'. There was no reference to the young man's health.

The remark about the cost of the tent illustrates the economics of the army of that period. Even the other ranks had to pay for their uniforms. Money for this purpose was stopped from their pay, and the sums were known as 'off-reckonings'. The amounts collected were usually more than enough to pay the tailors' bills. Consequently, some of the profit went into regimental funds; the rest became the property of the colonel. Between the years 1739–44, a Colonel Handaside is reported to have netted £384 from this source, and the commanding officer of a Guards regiment made £578. As any commercial activity, an investment in the Army was required to yield a dividend.

By the end of February 1744, Ned Wolfe had recovered sufficiently to return to duty with the 12th. He was promoted to lieutenant, and settled down to a period of discomfort and inaction on the banks of the River Scheldt. Four months later, James was given the rank of captain. He was transferred to the 4th Foot (now part of the Royal Border Regiment), which was stationed at Ghent. As spring stretched out into summer, and the Flanders fields became a richer green, the outlook for the army was ominous.

Previously, the French sovereign had been constrained to limit expenditure on his forces. Suddenly, all economic considerations were swept to one side. Louis XV demanded glory at no matter what price. As a result, an army of 120,000 men took to the field in May under the command of Marshal Saxe. Its target was Flanders, where the Allied units were severely under strength. In early June, Ypres fell; and, as Ned Wolfe wrote to his father, 'we have some expectations of their visiting us next.' The clash of arms was averted by the arrival of a strong Austrian force – no doubt to the relief of Mrs Wolfe back in England. Ned had told his father: 'I don't doubt but she is in some apprehensions of our being in danger; but I hope she'll not fright herself while we continue in health, as we both are now.'

'Continue in health'? This must have been another example of the Wolfe brothers' careful editing. By the end of the year, Lieutenant Edward Wolfe, not yet seventeen, had died of consumption. James was in Ghent when he heard that his brother was ill. A letter from the young man's physician had failed to reach him, and he did not realize how serious the complaint was.

Consequently he went about his duties and thought little of the matter. And then, on a dismal day in October, he received the news. Ned, the Old Soldier, had passed away. For weeks afterwards, the thought that he had not been present during his brother's last hours tortured him. 'It often', he wrote to his mother, 'makes me angry that any hour of my life should pass without thinking of him.'

Eventually he consoled himself with the reflection that 'Nature is ever too good in blotting out the violence of affliction', and went on to give an unexpected assessment of himself. 'For all tempers (as mine is) too much given to mirth, it is often necessary to revive grief in one's memory.' Those who served under this strict and ambitious young officer might not have agreed with him; but James was in an unusual mood. It was almost as if, having exposed more of himself than he cared to, he was anxious to erect a façade. Indeed the death of Ned had affected him very deeply. It was customary in the Army to auction the effects of a dead man, and to spend the proceeds on the regiment. But James had not the heart to undertake such a thing. Declaring that 'we none of us want', he decided to give Ned's belongings away to those who had helped the young officer during his lifetime. His servant received his clothes; a friend named Parry was given one of his horses and his furniture. As for James himself, he was not unmindful of his deserts. 'His other horse', he wrote, 'I keep myself. I have his watch, sash, gorget, books and maps.' These, he assured his mother, 'I shall preserve to his memory.' There were other, smaller, bequests to people whose names he did not mention.

The year dragged on. The army in Flanders endured another winter. In April of the following year, the two sides clashed at Fontenoy. The 12th received heavy losses; James and the 4th however, were still at Ghent without any hopes of glory. Although they expected to be ordered into the field at any moment, he was not optimistic about the outcome. 'The army would', he wrote, 'make but an indifferent defensive figure for the rest of the campaign.'

But the French had another weapon. Skilfully used, it would reduce the British forces in Flanders to little more than a phantom army, and bring the conflict into the heartland of Britain itself. It (or, rather, he) was known as the Young Pretender. On 25 July 1745, backed with French money and the promise of military support, Prince Charles Edward Stuart landed at Moidart in the Western Highlands. The 'Forty-five had begun.

While James had been fretting at inaction and the state of the British forces in Flanders, fortune had been relatively kind to his father. In April 1745, this now aging officer was appointed Inspector of Marines and Colonel of the 8th Foot. In the following month, he received the rank of major-general. As for James, he had spent an otherwise very dull period studying industriously. The reward came on 12 June, when he was appointed brigade major. It was a remarkable achievement for a young man of his age, but he had deserved it. In spite of Ned's death, he had not been allowed home on leave, and he seemed to be unaware of the few distractions that a town such as Ghent had to offer. He went about his duties with a conscientiousness that almost exceeded their demands. In the evenings, while his colleagues were either drinking or womanizing or both, he pored over military manuals. The narrowness of his world was closing in still more. Unless he did something about it, he was in danger of becoming a first-class bore.

One of the King's early reactions to the landing of Prince Charles was to withdraw seven battalions from Flanders. Among them was the 4th of Foot. By November, the Jacobite forces had penetrated into England, and James Wolfe had reached Newcastle, where a force of ten thousand men had been assembled. They were commanded by an ancient warrior named General Wade, whose senility was almost a match for that of Lord Stair. Major-General Edward Wolfe (now at the head of a division) was also in the town. Unfortunately, he was suffering from an attack of gout. Since he was unable to ride a horse, he was compelled to go campaigning in a post-chaise. His wife was worried about his fitness for the field, but James was quick to reassure her. 'I really believe you need not concern yourself about my father's safety', he wrote, 'for 'tis the opinion of most men that these rebels won't stand the King's troops; and as to marching north and south with the army in his post-chaise, it does him so much service that I never saw him look better.'

For the time being, Prince Charles was 'standing the King's troops' very well indeed. By 4 December, his force had penetrated as far south as Derby – with Wade, still up in the north-east, putting on a performance of what can only be described as impatient indecision. But the kilted tide was turning at last. Prince Charles had overstretched himself; by the end of the year, he and his men were back in Scotland. Unfortunately for Wade, this elderly officer's contribution had not been considered sufficient. On 30 December, he was relieved of his command. His replacement was a brutish bachelor named General Henry ('Hangman' to his enemies: he had no friends) Hawley. He was an evil-tempered cavalryman, who seemed to enjoy cruelty for its own sake. Whether for practical purposes or from a grim sense of humour, his camp furniture always included a pair of gibbets. As the son of the Lord President of the Scottish Court of Sessions wrote: 'No mortal disputes Mr Hawley's genius for the management of a squadron, or prosecuting with rigour any mortal to the gallows; although at the same time, they wish that he had the lenity to make converts, or the absolute force to make them fly before him.'

Throughout the early days of his career as a brigade major in the North of England and Scotland, James Wolfe had been compelled to take a good deal of exercise without actually seeing any action. By 5 January 1746, Prince Charles's men were laying siege to Stirling. Three days later, the town fell; but the castle continued to hold out. Hawley, who now commanded eight thousand foot soldiers and thirteen hundred cavalrymen, was anxious to bring matters to a swift conclusion. But, before he could do anything else, he had to relieve the garrison at Stirling. The road from his headquarters (now in Edinburgh) lay by way of Falkirk. As if to avoid putting his enemy to too much trouble, Prince Charles decided to meet him half-way.

If Hawley imagined that this encounter (the word is James's: he would not use the term 'battle' as 'neither side would fight') would enhance his reputation, he was in for a rude shock.

Neither he nor his soldiers imagined that Prince Charles's Highlanders were a foe to be considered seriously. When, on a moor near Falkirk, a young soldier shinned up a tree, and noticed the enemy through his telescope, the General was busy elsewhere. Lord Kilmarnock was fighting with the Jacobites; his wife, no doubt eager to slow down the English advance, was entertaining the 'Hangman' to breakfast. Consequently, when he should have been out in front making a reconnaissance, the General was dallying with a charming lady over an excellent meal. It was certainly more pleasant than conditions outside, where a strong south-westerly wind was blowing and icy rain was sheeting down.

The result was that Prince Charles was able to place his men in a commanding position on high ground without any interference. When the news of this reached Hawley, he rode hurriedly from his hostess's house – leaving his hat behind. His troops were having a meal, and wondering what all the fuss was about. The Jacobites would never fight: the whole thing, in their opinion, was just another exhausting march – with nothing but sore feet and a wet uniform to show at the end of it. Like their leader, they were sadly mistaken.

As if to make matters worse, the force's artillery was out of action. At some point, the guns had become bogged down in a swamp. The Falkirk carters, who were employed to drive the horses, saw this as an excellent opportunity to escape the bad weather and the perils of combat. Cutting their charges loose, they hurried off home.

Hawley had not studied the land, yet he dispatched his cavalry to attack the Highlanders. The route lay across exceedingly rough ground, and they quickly came to grief. Furthermore, Prince Charles misled the General by carrying out a number of feints. He had used the same techniques at Prestonpans, and Hawley should have expected it. Instead, he fell for it. The one redeeming feature was that the Prince, by a surprise oversight, had left his own cannons behind.

When the two forces finally clashed, the time was four pm. It was becoming dark, and the encounter lasted for only about ten minutes. During this period, the Highlanders inflicted severe punishment on the English troops, with comparatively small losses to themselves. At the end of it, Hawley was dark with rage – though whether with himself, the enemy, or his own troops, is uncertain. Little is known about James Wolfe's part in the action. He was somewhere in the second line, prowling like an elongated shadow in the twilight. Afterwards, practical soldier that he was, he noted that 'the ammunition – on which we can only depend – was all wet and spoiled.' However, he refused to concede that this had been a defeat. 'Though we can't be said to have totally routed the enemy', he wrote to an uncle, 'we yet remained for a long time masters of the field of battle.' It was a considerable overstatement. He also observed that 'our retreat was in no way molested by the enemy.' This, too, was something for which the English could take no credit. The reason for Prince Charles's hurried departure was that he wanted to get back to Stirling and resume the siege.

Indeed, James's critical faculties, which were usually very sharp during an engagement, were curiously blunted on this occasion. Perhaps the poor light obscured his observations. Whatever the reason, it was no doubt a good thing; for, shortly after the battle of Falkirk, he was appointed as Hawley's aide-de-camp. Other generals might indulge in post mortems: 'Hangman' Hawley was unlikely to ask his ADC 'Where did I go wrong?'

Down in London, the Duke of Cumberland took a less euphemistic view of the Falkirk fiasco. He considered that Hawley had made a thorough mess of things. When the King heard his remarks, he told the Duke to make haste to Scotland and take charge. The royal general's arrival in Edinburgh on 30 January was greeted with delight by all the troops. Hawley was less enthusiastic.

Dissension within his own ranks caused Prince Charles to abandon the siege of Stirling and to retreat into the Highlands. Wherever he went, the Duke of Cumberland would not be long in following. Leaving behind garrisons of Hessian troops at Stirling and Perth, the Duke and his army entered Aberdeen on 28 February 1746.

Although the Duke of Cumberland was now supreme commander in Scotland, Hawley remained commander-in-chief of HM Forces in north Britain. The fact that he was in a subordinate position made little change to his life style. He continued to drink heavily; to use language which would embarrass a fishwife; and to assume an almost divine right to the property and hospitality of other people. Within the ranks, however, a considerable change was noticeable. Many of the soldiers remembered the Duke from the Flanders campaign, when he had won their approval by his conduct at Dettingen. Then, as now, he had been called in to supervise a general who was thought to be incompetent. There was no reason why he should not repeat his success. Morale perked up everywhere. Now, at last, the troops would be able to avenge their humiliations at Falkirk and Prestonpans.

The Highlanders were, at best, regarded with suspicion – at the worst, hated. James Wolfe was no exception. He was staunchly loyal to his monarch, and he deplored the Jacobite habit of referring to George II as 'The Elector'.* This had been Prince Charles's idea, for the Pretender regarded himself as the rightful king of Great Britain. If George wanted a title, he must content himself with that of minor European royalty. As for Scotland itself, James disliked intensely this rain-drenched corner of the realm, with its large hills and its perfidious population. He would far rather have been soldiering in Europe.

His introduction to the duties of ADC was at once petty and difficult. While they remained in Aberdeen, the Duke and Hawley were to be neighbours. The former helped himself to the house of a lawyer named Alexander Thomson – a man of proven loyalty to the Crown. Nevertheless, Thomson's trust in his King did not extend to the Duke of Cumberland. Before departing for lodgings in another part of the town, he took the precaution of locking up all his possessions. It was no doubt wise; but, once his unwelcome guests had departed, he found that his bed linen had been ruined, and his stock of sugar had been removed.

Hawley was quartered next door in a house belonging to a Mrs George Gordon. Although she was an Englishwoman, Mrs Gordon was suspect. Her husband owned large estates in the area of Aberdeen, and he stood fairly and squarely on the side of the

* Like his father, King George I, George II had retained the title of Elector of Hanover.

Young Pretender. Like Alexander Thomson, she, too, had locked up everything before departing. Unlike the Duke, however – whose depredations might be regarded as moderate – Hawley wanted everything. Early one Friday morning, as he lay comfortably in Mrs Gordon's bed, the General summoned James. He was to get hold of the keys at once. The young ADC dispatched an orderly to Mrs Gordon's rooms with a suitably worded message. She replied that, for the moment, it was impossible. They were with her maid, who was out shopping. A second request, couched in less diplomatic terms, produced them without any more argument.

That evening, James himself visited Mrs Gordon's lodgings. In the face of the enemy, his courage was beyond dispute. But here, in this small room, confronted with this pious (her nephew was Dr Bowdler, who removed the bawdy bits from Shakespeare) and stubborn woman, he was ill at ease. His normally pale face was flushed, and his long fingers were in a frenzy as they plucked at his buttons and cuffs. Mrs Gordon had a friend with her at the time, and he was politely asked to leave. Then James got down to business. Hawley, he explained, had been very angry at her delay in handing over the keys. On his instructions (as Mrs Gordon wrote to her sister in England), 'I was deprived of everything I had, except the clothes on my back.' But this, it appeared, was not quite so bad as it sounded – an opening shot, perhaps, designed to quell the fury of her outrage. 'After delivering this message', she continued, 'he [James Wolfe] said that General Hawley, having enquired into my character of several persons who had all spoke very well of me, and had told him that I had no hand in the Rebellion, and that I was a stranger there without any relatives in the country, he, the General, therefore would make interest with the Duke that I could have any particular thing that I had a mind to, and could say was my own.'

At this point, one begins to wonder who was fooling whom. Such a message sounds totally out of character so far as Hawley was concerned. Was James doing his uncomfortable best to mitigate the severity of his master's demands? As for Mrs Gordon, she had plenty of friends and in-laws in Aberdeen, and the words 'could say was my own' were well used. An inventory of the house's contents revealed that she was in possession of many things which, quite obviously, were not her own. It seems likely that her friends had believed that, since she was an Englishwoman, her property would not be confiscated. Consequently, they had persuaded her to hide their own belongings.

What, then, was Mrs Gordon going to seek James Wolfe's permission to keep? She began, very moderately, with her supply of tea. The young officer sadly shook his head. That, he was afraid, would be impossible. The army was short of tea. Chocolate, then, said Mrs Gordon. No, James replied, not chocolate. The army had nothing like enough of it. From consumables, she switched to more durable items. How about her china? James admitted that, since there were no women with the forces, their requirements in this respect were small. Nevertheless, Hawley happened to like nice chinaware. Perhaps Mrs Gordon would just retain *some* of it? Encouraged by this small victory, his unwilling hostess then laid claim to her pictures. But, Wolfe pointed out, there really were rather a lot of them. Surely she didn't want them *all*? Which ones, in particular, did she wish to retain? Mrs Gordon said that she couldn't remember every one of them, but that she would, indeed, like to keep a portrait of her son.

At this James became suspicious. Son? How old was he and where was he? She explained that he was fourteen (which was probably untrue – everything suggests he was older) and that he was staying with the MP for the county of Aberdeen. After telling her that, fourteen or not fourteen, she would still have to produce the lad, Wolfe returned to Hawley. There is no record of their conversation, but it cannot have been an easy one. The General was doubtless drunk; James, anxious to do the right thing by this unfortunate woman, was trying to wring concessions out of him. At some point, the Duke himself was called in.

On the following morning, Mrs Gordon told her sister: 'Major Wolfe came to me again and told me that the Duke of Cumberland had sent him to let me know that my petition had been read to him, and that he would take care that everything should be restored to me.' There was, however, a considerable gap between the thought and the execution. When Mrs Gordon immediately applied 'for a pair of breeches for my son, for a little tea for myself, for a bottle of ale, for some flour to make bread, because there was none to be bought in the town, all was refused me.' She was, on the other hand, allowed to keep the portrait of her son, though characteristically Hawley had ripped it from its expensive gilt frame. As for the china tea-service, Hawley took it with him. Some while later, when the campaign was over, he presented it to the Duke of Cumberland. The Duke was not interested in it, and passed it on to a prostitute friend. Since there were far more pieces than she needed, she sold the lot to a dealer; and it was in this man's shop that, some while later, a friend of Mrs Gordon discovered it.

But James had more to do than wrangle with a cantankerous ex-patriate Englishwoman over her possessions. The Young Pretender had established his headquarters at a house four miles east of Inverness, and there was news of a French sloop on its way with supplies of arms, money, and men, for the rebels. In fact, the vessel was driven ashore, and £12,000 plus a small host of cold and discontented Frenchmen and Spaniards were captured. On 8 April, the English army marched out of Aberdeen. They forded the River Spey (one Dragoon was drowned); and, on the fourteenth, they reached Nairn, where the columns halted. The following day was the Duke of Cumberland's birthday. There were extra rations of brandy for the men, and, for the moment, thoughts of the campaign were overtaken by loyal – and, in some instances, drunken – rejoicing. But the pieces were relentlessly falling into place for the final showdown. On a bleak brown expanse of moorland near the village of Culloden, the two armies were to meet very shortly, and a new Dark Age in Scotland was to be wrought with fire and death. But James Wolfe was unconcerned with such matters. For the moment, he had quite enough to do ministering to the irascible Hawley.

4
THE WIDENING HORIZON

While Cumberland's troops were celebrating the royal birthday, Prince Charles's forces moved cautiously towards them. The idea was to catch the redcoats unawares. Had they succeeded, the result would have been a fearful bloodbath, and a victory which would have thrown Falkirk and Prestonpans into insignificance. But Prince Charles miscalculated the distance. By the time his soldiers were within striking distance of the King's men, a watery dawn was splashing across the sky. The royal troops, though doubtless hung-over, were at least on the alert. The Highlanders withdrew.

The preludes to the battle of Culloden were a deception and a miscalculation, both of which were deadly to the Jacobites. The former began as a rumour, which later seemed to be substantiated by a forged document found on a captured officer. The gist of it was that the Young Pretender intended to show his enemy no mercy. James Wolfe wrote to a friend afterwards: 'The Rebels, besides their natural inclinations, had orders not to give quarter to our men. We had an opportunity of avenging ourselves for that and many other things, and indeed we did not neglect it, as few Highlanders were made prisoners as possible.' There is no evidence to suggest that any such orders were given. It was a cruel deceit, conceived by somebody either with thoughts of revenge – or else to convince the royal soldiers that they were, as they suspected, fighting a savage enemy. And it worked. If James was taken in by it, so must everyone else have been.

Prince Charles should, on the other hand, be blamed for that miscalculation. The battlefield was of his own choosing. In selecting Drummossie Moor, he had assumed that the soft ground of this soggy wilderness would make it impossible for Cumberland to bring up his artillery. In fact, it was possible, and the effect of the guns on the Highlanders was devastating.

At six o'clock on the morning of 16 April, the two forces came within sight of each other. As always, it was raining. There were about six thousand men in Prince Charles's ranks, about eight thousand in Cumberland's. The battle took place in the afternoon, with the royal troops firing with unusual accuracy. Wrote James: 'They [the Highlanders] waited till we came near enough to fire cannon on them, and were greatly surpris'd and disorder'd at it, and finding their mistake, they charged upon our front line in thick solid bodies, throwing down their arms without exploding them, and advancing furiously with their drawn swords. . . . The front line on the Rebels' near approach began a most violent fire, which continued 8 or 9 minutes, and kill'd so many of their best men that they could only penetrate into our Battalion.'

General Hawley was busy commanding five squadrons of Dragoons on the left – carrying out an attack which, according to James, 'was done with wonderful spirit and completed the victory with great slaughter.' Since he was not a cavalryman, James, presumably, was fighting with his own regiment. If this was the case, he had a rough time of it. He wrote: 'They were attacked by the Camerons (the bravest clan amongst them), and 'twas for some time a dispute between swords and bayonets; but the latter was found by far the most destructive weapon. The Regiment behaved with uncommon resolution, killing some say almost their own number, whereas 40 of them were only wounded, and those not mortally, and not above ten kill'd.' In fact, he must have been uncertain about the actual figures, for these do not agree with other reports. Furthermore, in another letter written shortly after the battle, he put the regiment's losses as 'out of three hundred and fifty . . . one hundred and twenty officers and men killed and wounded.'

Of his own performance that day, he had nothing to say. Like so many of Wolfe's accounts of actions in which he took part, his letters read like stories filed by war correspondents. They carry authority and, on the whole, appear to be accurate. But they are entirely objective. He might have been a dispassionate eye-witness, observing the fray through a telescope but totally uninvolved. It is only at the end of one of them that he gives the smallest clue to his feelings. 'And may', he piously writes, 'they ever be punished in the same manner who attempt the like!' That is all.

However, a legend exists that, despite his apparent relish at the slaughter and the fact that few prisoners were taken, he was not entirely heartless. According to this story, he was riding over the battlefield afterwards with the Duke of Cumberland, when they noticed a body moving. The Duke reined in his horse, and asked the wounded man to whom he belonged. 'To the Prince,' he said. Cumberland is then supposed to have turned to James and said: 'Wolfe, shoot me that insolent Highland scoundrel who dares look on us with such contempt.' James refused. 'My commission is at Your Royal Highness's disposal', he is reputed to have said, 'but I can never consent to become an executioner.' The other officers in the party followed his example, and it was left for a private soldier to dispatch the unfortunate man.

Since the victim has been identified as a young man named Charles Fraser, Lieutenant-Colonel of the Master of Lovat's Regiment of Frasers, there seems little doubt that something of the kind occurred. But was the officer who ordered the execution really Cumberland? It seems more likely that Wolfe would have been with Hawley at the time, and such a command would have been typical of the 'Hangman'. Nor do suggestions that Wolfe's refusal permanently damaged his relationship with Cumberland cut very much ice. When one remembers that Wolfe became a major-general at the incredibly young age of thirty-two, it appears out of the question that this evil genius was hindering his career – though by this time Cumberland himself had been disgraced.

After Culloden, the Duke of Cumberland returned to London. His father, the King, presented him with £1,000 on the spot, and Parliament voted him the sum of £25,000 a year for the rest of his life. Hawley was less fortunate. He retired into lecherous obscurity, leaving James free to return to his regiment. As for the troops, they were invited to help themselves to the belongings of the now subdued Highlanders. Since they prosecuted the task of acquiring livestock with greater energy than the officers, an order had to be issued, stating that the loot should be shared out in proportion to pay.

For a while, James was stationed at Inverness. After the 1715 rebellion, a chain of forts had been established across the entrance to the Highlands. By the time of Culloden, they had fallen into disuse. Now it was decided to rebuild them. One of the lessons of the 'Forty-five, surely, was that the wild men of the hills should be *contained*. One clan in particular had always been troublesome: the MacGregors. With an amiable anarchy, they looted, burned, and laid waste their neighbours' lands. When anybody tried to stop them, they smiled and cut his throat.

The key to keeping this unruly tribe in check was the fort at Inversnaid, a tiny pin-prick of a place at the top of the eastern shore of Loch Lomond. The MacGregors had amused themselves by destroying it on countless occasions. True to form, it was now a mere charred ruin. James Wolfe was given the task of restoring it – if not to martial glory, then at least to a functioning outpost. He moved into the ruined fort; established six sections, each commanded by a sergeant, in the neighbouring hills; and got on with the job of rebuilding. The NCOs reported to him at weekly intervals; he reported to army headquarters fortnightly; and the MacGregors, chastened no doubt by the defeat of Prince Charles Edward (who was still at large somewhere away to the north), behaved with unaccustomed meekness. James remained there until the latter part of November 1746, when he received six weeks' notice to join his regiment on the Continent.

For the first time in over four years, he was allowed leave. Packing up his belongings, he made his way to London and the house in Old Burlington Street. It was not a particularly happy interlude. His father was still suffering from gout; and this, added to what he considered to be financial worries, made the old gentleman peevish. From time to time, he vented his rage on his son. James was to tell his mother: 'If ever my opinion of myself differs from my father's, 'tis certain to be in my own favour. I don't believe he ever thought better of me than I do of myself.' Since he held himself in far from low esteem, this hardly suggests an attitude of disapproval on the part of the General. However, the situation was certainly not eased by the money question.

Major-General Edward Wolfe's salary as Inspector of Marines was three years in arrears. This, in itself, gave him ample cause for complaint, and he was doubtless intolerant when James, who was also hard up, wished to borrow some cash to kit himself out for Europe. In the end, as sons so frequently do, he obtained the necessary sum from his mother.

In early January of the following year, James arrived at Breda in Holland to take up his new duties. Breda was dull; the routine of service life was dull; and he was becoming restive. He wrote to his father on 15 February:

> There is such a dearth at present of everything new and entertaining, it seems no easy task to fill a letter; at least to give it such a turn as may please. We military men don't accustom ourselves to moral topics, or seldom entertain one another with subjects which are out of the common role. . . . Nine-tenths of the letters from hence, I am persuaded, are filled with observations from what occurs in the army in general, or in the particular battalion to which the writer belongs. I know or at least guess by myself, how much every man's attention is taken up with the things about him; and the use of thinking constantly on the same matter weighs greatly with the mind, and in time becomes its first principles, so that setting aside a man's modesty and his diffidence, he had little else to talk about.

By May, things were brightening up a little bit. The regiment had been moved to the outskirts of Brussels, and he had made the acquaintance of a Miss Lacey, the daughter of an Irishman serving as a general with the Austrian army. Two of James's letters to her have survived. When one cuts away the playful badinage, they seem to be mostly concerned with the collection of a new scarlet tunic and waistcoat from a local tailor. There were evidently problems of communication. 'This letter you will be so good to direct, and let it be sent to the embroiderer. If you think my manner of correcting too harsh, it is left for you to soften; sure they must be dense if my French is useless, unless it could be in the least thought otherwise by you.' Miss Lacey sorted everything out, and James received his garments. Her reward, it seems, was a reflection on love as related to the role of a soldier. 'Sure it must never happen', James tells her, 'that a soldier can be unhappy in his love; if so, what reward for great and glorious undertakings, or what relief from despair. . . ? I write this in a moment of reflection; you'll pardon the style, 'tis unusual and has not in it the turn of gaiety that would perhaps be more pleasing to you.' Since Miss Lacey's reply has long been destroyed, there is no knowing how she reacted. In any case, so far as James was concerned, the relationship appears to have been no more than a well-mannered flirtation.

From the Jacobite point of view, the Young Pretender's adventures in Britain had been a squelching failure. From that of his French sponsors, however, the operation was by no means disastrous. By drawing away English troops from Flanders, it enabled Marshal Saxe to strengthen his position and build up reserves. The winter of 1746–7 was an unusually cold one in Europe. While the luckless British forces shivered in camp, poorly nourished and inadequately accommodated, the French troops existed in comparative comfort.

The Duke of Cumberland was now regarded as the King's super-general. After his victory at Culloden, there seemed to be nothing he could not accomplish. The Duke himself had much the same idea. But, as even he was compelled to admit, he could do nothing until his complement of guns and transport was at least equal to that of the enemy. His patience, ever on a slender thread, finally snapped in early June 1747. As he interpreted the situation, Saxe was about to lay siege to Maastricht on the frontier between Holland and Germany. This had to be stopped. His Royal Highness gave the order to march. The two sides met on 21 June at the village of Lauffeld, three miles to the west of Maastricht.

Battles are a series of clashes which, gathered together, win or lose a war. Few of them are decisive – as, for example, Culloden was. Most of them are colossal wastes of lives and materials. Lauffeld was an almost definitive example of this type of engagement. The French were in good position, both from the point of view of defending and counter-attacking. Cumberland was obstinate. This very insignificant village was going to be his, and never mind what it cost. The English troops made five attacks, and on each they were driven back. Austrian reinforcements failed to arrive in time; a body of Dutch cavalrymen, whom Cumberland had brought up to reinforce his tired and bloodied infantry, took fright and rode off in the wrong direction. Eventually, after a fearful carnage, the English survivors were compelled to retire. Cumberland had reckoned without the considerable numerical superiority of the French.

Wolfe was injured during the battle when a bullet pierced his body. Characteristically, mentioning the affair afterwards, he said little about himself. On the other hand, he had some fine things to say about his servant. 'He came to me', he wrote, 'at the hazard of his life . . . took off my cloak and brought a fresh horse; and would have continued close by me had I not ordered him to retire. I believe he was slightly wounded just at that time, and the horse he held was shot likewise. . . . Many a time has he pitched my tent and made the bed ready to receive me, half-dead with fatigue; and I owe this to his diligence.'

If James Wolfe was grateful to his servant, the Duke of Cumberland was no less delighted with James Wolfe. Afterwards, he was heard to speak admiringly of the young brigade major, who had been at once so fearless and so capable. It was certainly a good sign for the future. In the meanwhile, however, James spent a short spell in hospital (the wound does not seem to have been very serious). Then he went home. He arrived in London on the same day as the Duke: 13 November.

Mrs Wolfe was never slow to make new friends who would benefit her husband's career. Since they had taken a town house in Old Burlington Street, she had winkled her way into influential circles, pulling Edward fondly along behind her. James was now able to enjoy the social life to which this provided the entrance. His previous leave had been disappointing: this one more than made up for it. He was as vain as the next man – perhaps a little bit more so. At any rate, he had returned as a hero, and the young ladies treated him as such. It was very enjoyable. Miss Lacey was in the capital and so was Miss Warde (she about whom he had written to Ned). But he was particularly attracted by a girl named Elizabeth Lawson. Elizabeth was well connected. Her mother was the niece of the Earl of Peterborough, and she herself was a maid of honour to the Princess of Wales. But this was of little concern to James. He liked her as he had never liked a girl before, and that was all that mattered.

By the following spring, he was back in Holland – this time as brigade major to a combined force of Austrians and British. He did not relish the assignment; but, taking the longer view, things seemed to be good. He had been talking with the adjutant-general. During the course of their conversation, the latter had remarked that the Duke of Cumberland intended to give James the 'major's commission of Bragg's regiment for nothing, and (as he was pleased to say) in order to my being Lieutenant-Colonel to it, for Jocelyn [the present incumbent] is dying'. Alas, it came to nothing. Just over three months later, he was telling his mother 'if I rise at all, it will most probably be by means of my father's pocket.'

But for the first time in his life he was thinking beyond the Army. He had left school when he was thirteen. Now he was twenty-one. During this period, he had been on leave only twice. He had endured long spells in camp; fought in four engagements; earned promotion at an unheard of rate; and where was he? A man with little education whose only experience of life was that of the parade ground, the battlefield, and the orderly room. He could write a lucid and accurate account of a military operation, and he could turn quite a pleasant phrase when corresponding with a girl-friend. But what did he know of the world beyond Flanders and Scotland? What social accomplishments had he beyond the not very rigorous ones needed to pass muster in an officers' mess or a London drawing-room? He was, as he was becoming uncomfortably aware, inadequate. If he were to become the type of man his ambitions dictated, he needed to travel; and he proposed to apply for extended leave.

When they first heard his plans, his parents seem to have opposed the idea. His father, in particular, was afraid that it would hinder his promotion. But then, Wolfe Senior was a military man who had never looked for ideas outside the service. In a letter dated August 1748, James poured out his heart to his mother:

There will be difficulties in everything that contradicts a principle or settled opinion, entertained amongst us, that an officer neither can, nor ought, ever to be otherwise employed than his particular military functions. If they could beat men's capacities down, or confine their genius to that rule (to be observed with the expected nicety, so as to exclude all other attachments), no man would ever be fitted for a higher employment than he is in. 'Tis unaccountable that he who wishes to see a good army can oppose men's enlarging their notions, or acquiring that knowledge with a little absence which they can't possibly meet with at home, especially when they are supposed masters of their present employment and really acquainted with it.

Replying to his father's objections, he pointed out that 'attendance, or the frequent offer of one's person to their observation, has had hitherto little effect.' For a young man who had reached the rank of brevet major before his twenty-first birthday, this verdict might appear to be ungenerous. But, no doubt, his disappointment over the job promised by the Duke of Cumberland still rankled. In any case, he might have saved himself the trouble of writing. His application for long leave was turned down.

The War of Austrian Succession was grinding fitfully to a halt. The action had passed into the hands of the statesmen; the army waited, encamped and eager to go home. As for James, he continued to brood. In his last letter from Flanders, he told his mother: 'For my particular, I wish nothing so much as the means of escaping from noise and idleness. I never till now knew our army otherwise than as I could have desired it . . . but then I never knew what it was to wait, in smoke and subjection, the signing of articles of peace, and till now have always had, or imagined I had, a prospect of better times.'

He had sold his 'poor little grey mare', and he missed her. There was nothing surprising about this: James had always been fond of his horses. The strange thing, and one which must have worried his career-minded parents, was this new outlook. It was almost as if their son were becoming a rebel. In many of his letters, James has a tiresome habit of telling us everything except the root cause. Had the conditions of active service and the danger of battle become a kind of drug, something he needed to keep his enthusiasm up to the necessary pitch? Or, remembering his father's experiences, did he dread the prospect of peace? After all, an impoverished life on half-pay, or the unexciting business of building roads, were scarcely attractive prospects. Either argument will do; but a third needs to be considered. One somehow gets the impression that, for a few brief moments, a door in James's mind had opened. Through it, he had glimpsed an enchanting view; and then, equally suddenly, it had closed. He was left feeling restless and discontented. Somehow, he must get it open again – and, this time, it must remain so. Up to his twenty-second year, James Wolfe was not sufficiently complicated. Afterwards, he was in a desperate hurry to make amends.

5

THE OLD YOUNG MAN

At last, after eight years of war, there was peace. The troops came home: the statesmen rose from their chairs and left the conference room. Their deliberations were contained in a swatch of papers known as the Treaty of Aix la Chapelle. One of its clauses set down France's acknowledgement of the Protestant succession to the throne of Britain. There would no longer be any nonsense about Pretenders – Young or Old. Otherwise, the world was much as it had been before hostilities. A prodigious sum – measured either in lives or money, it didn't matter – had been wasted. The French celebrated the occasion by a display of fireworks in Paris. Fifteen people were trampled to death when the crowd became out of control. It was, in its grim way, a most fitting conclusion.

James Wolfe saw little to celebrate. His prospects in the Army seemed uncertain. Although he had served for some time as a major, his rank was only temporary. It appeared probable that he would be sent back to Scotland as a captain. As he saw it, the experience would be 'mortifying', and he had no taste for more soldiering amid the dark mists of the Highlands. The only things that promised any enjoyment were a spell of leave in London – and the opportunity to see more of Elizabeth Lawson.

Miss Lawson was tall and slender and about the same age as James. Since her beauty was generally admired, she had no lack of suitors. When James met her, she had just turned down a proposal from a young clergyman earning £1,300 a year. Currently, she was being hotly pursued by a knight, who was reputed to be very rich. He was also, in James's opinion, 'mad' and not to be treated as a serious rival. For the man who was fortunate enough to win her heart, Miss Lawson had a dowry of £12,000 to offer. In all conscience, it seemed to be enough, and James was the last person to regard matrimony as a financial investment. He was hopelessly in love with the girl he called 'my Maid of Honour' and that was what really mattered. Delving delicately into what he hoped might be the future, he was already putting out feelers to see how her mother and her uncle (General Sir John Mordaunt – an old friend of his father) would react to a proposal of marriage. Unfortunately, his own mother was also carrying out an investigation.

When seen in profile, James was not particularly attractive. His receding chin and pointed nose were neither of them examples of manly beauty, and his long thin legs and body were not suggestive of strength. But when you saw him full-face, the prospect was much more pleasing. His eyes were animated, and his quick smile was real and likeable. As a soldier, his exploits were sufficient to arouse romantic interest: and, as for his prospects, he had already accomplished a good deal. Miss Lawson might do well to consider him seriously.

Mrs Wolfe, on the other hand, was disinclined to consider Miss Lawson seriously. Ever conscious of money, that lady had other plans for her son. Twelve thousand pounds on the nail might seem to be a handsome sum. In Croydon, however, there was a Miss Hoskins, who would be able to enrich her spouse to the tune of £30,000. This, Mrs Wolfe told herself and her husband, was a much better proposition. When James wrote to a friend describing his passion for Elizabeth, he noted: 'The General and Mrs Wolfe are rather against it.' This was a fearful understatement. Mrs Wolfe was going to use every weapon in her formidable armoury to fight the match – and she had no doubt that, when it came to the crunch, the General would be by her side.

But would she need to fight? James, clearly, was going to be posted somewhere, and his next theatre of employment would not be London. Possibly absence, which is wrongly supposed to make the heart grow fonder, would do what it normally does. Indeed, Mrs Wolfe's hopes were echoed in James's fears. He astutely observed: 'Young flames must be constantly fed, or they'll evaporate.' He had been in London for little more than three weeks, when the orders arrived. As he had expected, he was to return to Scotland. On the other hand, his forebodings about being demoted to captain turned out to be groundless. He was invited to fill a vacancy for a major in Lord George Sackville's regiment, the 20th Foot (the Lancashire Fusiliers). This, in itself, was good news. Even better was the fact that the present commanding officer, Lieutenant-Colonel the Honourable Edward Cornwallis, was due to take up a job as Governor of Nova Scotia. With any luck, James would assume his responsibilities. It seemed as if the Duke of Cumberland's promise had not been entirely without substance.

When he joined it, the 20th was stationed in Stirling. It was a dreary town in which the inhabitants practised thrift and drunkenness in almost equal measure. There were, for example, seventy pubs serving a population of five thousand; and yet, among all the far from impoverished families, there were only four male servants. James detested the place, and referred bitterly to 'the very bloom of life [being] nipped in this Northern climate.' However, he did not have to endure it for long. He had joined the 20th in early April 1749. Less than one month later, the unit was ordered to Glasgow. Cornwallis departed for Canada, and James became a temporary lieutenant-colonel.

He was only twenty-two. Many of his officers were considerably older. His position isolated him from them; but, in any case, he would probably have chosen to keep his distance. As a young man who aspired to culture, he found their conversation boring. And, as something of a puritan, he disapproved of the way in which they spent their time off duty. For him, the move to Glasgow had one great attraction: the city possessed a university. The Army might refuse him the opportunity to travel abroad: now, albeit in not such an attractive way, fate had given him the opportunity to catch up with his lost education. Normally, any officer under the rank of brigadier had to live in camp or barracks with his regiment. Glasgow had no such facilities. The men were billeted in lodgings – and he was quartered at a house in the suburbs. One of his first actions was to arrange for two of the teachers from the college to come there each day. In the mornings, he put in a couple of hours studying mathematics. In the afternoons, he turned his attention to Latin. For the rest of the time, he was preoccupied in running the regiment – and worrying about money, his health, and his parents' attitude to Elizabeth Lawson.

As a commanding officer, he was conscientious and just. Early on in his service with the 20th, he compiled what later became known as *General Wolfe's Instructions to Young Officers*.* There were few better guides for a newcomer to the service – in Wolfe's or any other time. To anybody who imagined that serving with a regiment meant attending the occasional parade and enjoying a lavish social life, the opening sentence was enough to dispel the illusion. 'When a young gentleman betakes himself to the profession of arms', he wrote, 'he should seriously reflect upon the nature and duties of the way of life he has entered into, and consider that it is not, as the generality of people vainly imagine, learning a little of the exercise, saluting gracefully, firing his platoon in his turn, mounting a few guards (carelessly enough) and, finally, exposing his person bravely in the day of battle; which will deservedly, and in the opinion of judges, acquire him the character of a good officer: no, he must learn chearfully [Wolfe's spelling] to obey his superiors, and that their orders and his own be punctually executed.'

If they wished to succeed, young officers should make themselves 'perfect masters of the exercise of the firelock', so that they would be able to play a useful part in weapon training, and be present at roll call – not just to put in an appearance, but to learn the names of the men in their companies. This, however, was only a beginning. 'So soon as possible' they had to find out about their characters, 'that they may know the proper subjects to encourage, and point out an example; as well as those also whom it will be necessary to keep a strict hand over.'

They had to see that a proportion of the soldier's pay (in this case 2*s* 4*d* a week) was spent on 'good and wholesome provisions'; visit the men's quarters at least three times a week, ensuring that the rooms were clean and the beds well aired and well made; satisfy themselves that the food was properly cooked,

* It was published with other documents in 1768, nine years after his death – hence 'General'. He was, in fact, a lieutenant-colonel when he wrote them.

and intercede in all disputes between the men and their landlords.

A tiresome circumstance of life in Glasgow was that some of these landlords were prepared to trade liquor for their lodgers' rations. It was, Wolfe noted, more likely to occur in the case of 'those men who are billeted upon homes of the lowest class, as they are the most likely to be prevailed upon by the disobedient soldier.' It must stop. And so must the habit of 'always trusting to the reports of serjeants'. A young officer must see for himself.

Finally, Wolfe wrote: 'A young officer should never think he does too much; they are to attend to the looks of their men, and if any are thinner or paler than usual, the reason of their falling off may be enquired into, and proper means used to restore them to their former vigour.'

When the 20th was stationed in the city, Glasgow had no police force. Consequently, in addition to their normal duties, the soldiers had to help out in emergencies. Two occurred during this period. The first was a fire which laid waste to the southern bank of the Clyde. One hundred and fifty families from the Gorbals were made homeless by it. The military's function was to cordon off the streets and prevent looting. According to the local newspaper's report, 'Many of the soldiers exerted themselves in preventing the flames and saving people's lives.'

The second occasion was a riot. It was sparked off by a party of body-snatchers, who had been digging up graves and carrying the mortal remains to the college, where they proposed to sell them to the apprentice surgeons for dissection. When the mob heard about it, they attacked the university buildings. The ringleaders were arrested. Two of them were found guilty, and sentenced to be whipped through the town and banished for life. Not unreasonably, people considered that this was much too severe. Another disturbance appeared to be in the making; but, fortunately perhaps, the men escaped one Sunday morning when the rest of Glasgow was at church. The three men responsible for stealing the corpses do not seem to have been prosecuted.

Most of the time, however, was occupied with routine duties. The regiment was required to work with the excise officers in helping to prevent contraband goods being smuggled into the

Highlands; and to thwart the attempts of French recruiting officers, who were on the prowl for the services of dissatisfied Scotsmen. A detachment of two captains, six subalterns, six sergeants, six corporals and three hundred men, had to be sent off to work on a road running from the Pass of Lancey to the head of Loch Earn. For this assignment, the men received extra pay (2*s* 6*d* a day in the case of lieutenants, 1*s* 0*d* for sergeants and 6*d* for privates). They were allowed to wear rough working-clothes – though any pattern with a check in it was forbidden. It was too much like tartan, which had been banned since Christmas Day of the previous year.

The men under his command did not, in James's opinion, amount to a great deal. Problems of discipline were constantly at the top of his mind. The prescribed penalties were harsh; but, whenever possible, he tried to temper them with humanity. Nevertheless, this could not always be done. For some misdeeds, soldiers were sentenced to shortish spells in an institution known as 'the Black Hole'. During these periods, their diets were restricted to bread and water. The sergeant of the guard was allowed 2*d* per man per day to spend on these frugal supplies. There had been one or two cases of NCOs and sentries smuggling in rather more succulent items for the captives. Anyone who did so in future, Lieutenant-Colonel Wolfe decreed, would be punished.

For many offences, flogging was the penalty. If, for example, a man failed to turn up at 'exercises or a review' for any reason other than sickness, he should, Wolfe ordered, 'immediately be tried and whipt at the head of the company he belongs to'. It was an NCO's responsibility to make sure the men knew about these parades. If he failed to warn them to be present, 'he shall be broke' (i.e., deprived of his rank). Later on, the penalty for failing to come on parade was made more severe, and the culprit was sent to the Black Hole.

An outbreak of theft had occurred. When the accused men appeared before the commanding officer, they invariably alleged that they had *found* the supposedly stolen items. In future, Wolfe ordered, 'a soldier who finds goods, money, or anything else of even the most inconsiderable value, do immediately shew the same to one of the sergeants of the company, whose duty it is to acquaint the officer, in order to its being restored to the owner; any man who disobeys this order shall be punished as a thief.'

When a sentry was knocked down and injured, Wolfe pointed out what he expected from men on guard duties. 'The Colonel takes this opportunity to tell the soldiers', he wrote, 'that he looks upon sleeping or any want of vigilance in the sentry, to be the highest breach of military discipline, and of the most fatal and dangerous consequences; he therefore warns them all, that he is determined to make a dreadful example of the first offender.'

A grenadier named Rigby had accepted a bribe from a Highlander. His crime was regarded as so serious that he was condemned to six hundred lashes. However, it is doubtful whether he received them. Wolfe noted that his 'youth and former good behaviour' were the only considerations that 'could induce the Lieutenant-Colonel to pardon him'.

Deserters (and there were a number of them in 1749) who were recaptured were to be 'tried by a general court-martial, and may expect no mercy'. There had also been complaints from the local landed gentry about troops poaching their game. As a result, Wolfe wrote the following: 'The soldiers are not to fish in the gentlemen's ponds or lakes without permission; nor are they to go above two miles into the country without leave in writing from the officer commanding the company. Any soldier who shall take his firelock out to shoot, or who shall be known to use nets or snares for catching game, will be punished very severely.'

But poaching was not the only sport which was liable to land a man in trouble. There was another, hidden, peril within the regiment itself. The first indications of it appeared in an item sandwiched between a piece about road building duties, and another announcing that 'all the rigour of the strictest justice' was to be meted out to those found guilty of dishonesty. 'If', Wolfe wrote, 'any woman in the regiment has a venereal disease, and does not immediately make it known to the surgeon, she shall upon the first discovery be drummed out of the regiment, and be imprisoned in the Tolbooth* if ever she returns to the corps.' Fair enough; but the order may have come too late. A few days

* The local prison.

later he was observing that 'the worst and idlest soldiers are those that are most frequently in venereal disorders by which they are incapable of serving and their duty is done by better men; he therefore thinks they should suffer for their intemperance; and orders that six shillings be paid for the cure of the pox [syphilis], and four shillings for the clap [gonorrhoea]; which sums of money be employed in providing necessities and conveniences for the hospital.'

Later on, the officers appear to have been the victim of a plague of anonymous letters. 'As this is a mean and underhand practice', Wolfe said, 'it is positively forbid.' Anyone discovered would be severely punished. But, as he pointed out, it was quite unnecessary. Soldiers who wished to make complaints should 'address themselves in person to their officers'.

Happily, all was not bad in the ranks of the 20th. On one occasion, Wolfe was able to write: 'The Colonel is extremely well pleased with the behaviour of the five companies . . . and hopes they will continue the same regularity and sobriety, which they must be sure is of advantage to themselves, creditable to the regiment, and so useful to His Majesty's service.' He was a disciplinarian, but always just. And, when something was well done, he did not hesitate to give praise. Nobody could have asked more of a commanding officer.

If regimental life had its ups and downs during this period, Wolfe's personal affairs were no easier. Although he was by no means extravagant, he was perpetually short of money. At one time, according to his reckoning, he was left with one shilling a week pocket money – once he had covered his other expenses. It was hardly surprising. Parliament took the view that if an officer could afford to buy a commission, he did not need much salary. During these frequent financial crises, he was compelled to write to his parents for loans. As he usually pointed out, he would vastly prefer to live off his own resources, but they were not sufficient. Largely due to his mother's prodding, the necessary cash nearly always came promptly. On one occasion, however, the old General seems to have been obstinate. He would, he said, far rather leave his son a substantial sum when he died, than send him occasional hand-outs during his lifetime. Writing to Mrs

Wolfe, James immediately took issue with this philosophy. He pointed out that, 'undoubtedly he must observe that, as I am as likely to make a good use of it now as I can possibly be at any other time, and much more certain, for who can tell which of the two [of us] shall survive? But suppose I should stay a few years behind, would it not be highly pleasing to him that the person he intends for his successor should in his presence and under his eye, flourish while he lives and give him some convincing reason to hope that what he has been at pains to collect would not be idly or basely employed? Would he not receive some additional satisfaction when the very principles he has taken care to instil are generously exercised for his credit more than mine?'

Doubtless the message was passed on by Mrs Wolfe – who probably used it as further evidence in her case against Miss Lawson. How, she must have wondered, would her son live on that young lady's paltry £12,000? With Miss Hoskins's £30,000, he could, if he wished, buy himself into the Guards – *and* afford to live in the regiment.

Nevertheless, James's argument was successful, and General Wolfe obliged with a generous amount. His son was suitably grateful. 'I promise you these sums are not employed but in a manner that you yourself might approve', he assured his father, 'and I should be ashamed ever to ask, but to such purposes as become your son . . . for though I had rather be indebted to you for any kind of aid than to any man alive, yet the name of a debt is more than enough to make it disagreeable in the affair of money alone.'

Money was not the only thing he required from London. Possibly the shops of Glasgow were inadequate; at any rate, he was, at one moment, wanting a dozen black stocks ('*not* Bank Stocks nor South Sea', he quipped). The next he was asking his mother to order him a new wig, costing thirty shillings. One of his sergeants, who was going to the capital, would collect it.

Socially, his life was bleak. As commanding officer of the 20th, he made it his duty to attend church every Sunday morning. Although he was not lacking in religious zeal, he found the sermons tedious, and observed that 'the generality of Scottish preachers are excessive blockheads.' However, as he told his mother, 'I got the reputation of a very good Presbyterian' by his regular attendance. Later, a chaplain was posted to the regiment. 'I'm now back to the old faith,' he wrote, 'and stick close to our communion. The example is so necessary, that I think it is a duty to comply were that the only reason, as, in truth, it were not.' The need for this 'example' stemmed from what he judged to be the character of his fellow officers. 'Few of my companions surpass me in common knowledge, but most of them in vice,' he wrote. 'This is a truth that I should blush to relate to one that had not all my confidence, lest it be thought to proceed either from insolence or vanity. . . . I dread their habits and behaviour, and am forced to keep an eternal watch upon myself, that I may avoid the very manner which I most condemn in them. Young men should have some object constantly in their aim, some shining character to direct them.'

Outside the regiment, he found himself 'surrounded either with flatterers or spies and in a country not at all to my taste'. The men of Glasgow were 'civil, designing and treacherous with their immediate interests always in view; they pursue trade with warmth and necessary mercantile spirit, arising from the baseness of their other qualifications.' As for the women, they were 'coarse, cold and cunning, for ever enquiring after men's circumstances. They make that the standard of their good breeding.' The observation was made in a letter to a friend. He might have been hesitant to address such a remark to his mother. As the affair of Miss Lawson versus Miss Hoskins was making uncomfortably clear, Mrs Wolfe was using precisely the same yardstick in her assessment of eligible young ladies.

Indeed, that matter seemed to be reaching a head. James had been doing his best to persuade his parents of Elizabeth's virtues, but they remained unconvinced. For a longish period, Mrs Wolfe gave up writing to her son – observing, one might say, a huffy silence. At others, she complained about her own health. In fact, she was only suffering from sciatica, but she was a hard working hypochondriac. At one time, she was attending three doctors – and taking that number of cures for an equally varied selection of complaints. Did she hope that, by exaggerated accounts of her ill health, she might sway her son by winning his sympathy? In one letter home, he felt obliged to tell her that 'any disorder that we have been accustomed to for any length of time, tho' not to be perfectly cured, often admits of some alleviation from our acquaintance with it.'

His love for Elizabeth was undiminished. 'Your opinion of Miss Lawson', he told her, 'has inflamed me anew, and you have exactly hit upon the part of her perfection (her behaviour) that worked the strongest upon me; for I have seen a hundred handsome women before, and never was in love with one.... I don't think you believe she ever touched me, or you could never speak with so much indifference....' As Mrs Wolfe obviously hoped, the conflict between James's duty to her and his love for Elizabeth was beginning to wear him down. At one point he almost capitulated, but it was no good. Miss Hoskins could keep her £30,000: James wanted only his 'Maid of Honour'.

While Mrs Wolfe, was going to one physician after another, her son became more seriously ill. It was a wretched summer that year in Scotland, and he spent much of his leisure huddled over a fire in his quarters. Throughout the years of campaigning, often existing off inadequate rations, his health had stood the test. Now, when he should have been living off a reasonably balanced diet, he went down with scurvy. It was, he said, 'the most lazy and indolent disorder I have ever been oppressed with; 'tis pain to undertake the slightest business; and what used to give me pleasure in the work, is now tedious and disagreeable.... I must drive off this heaviness by some means or other, and not be thus uneasy to myself, when everything about me looks gay and pleasant.' Eventually, he recovered; but the effect of the sickness had been all too apparent. In a letter to Mrs Wolfe dated 19 July, he wrote: 'It is not easy to describe me in my present state. If I say I'm thinner, you'll imagine me a shadow or a skeleton in motion. In short, I'm everything but what the surgeons call a subject for anatomy; as far as muscles, bones, and the larger vessels can serve their purpose, they have a clear view of them in me, distinct from fat or fleshy impediment.'

Poor James: nothing seemed to be going right. Lord George Sackville was about to give up his colonelcy of the regiment. The two men had got on splendidly. Sackville was undemanding, and it was this which gave James the time to pursue his studies of mathematics and Latin. He was also sympathetic. On one occasion, he suggested that a change of air might do his young lieutentant-colonel good. James was only too eager to accept the idea. But the authorities thought otherwise. When he applied for four months leave to escape the Scottish winter and to improve his health in London, he was turned down. In November 1749, Lord George departed, and Lord Bury replaced him. The new colonel, who had been a former aide-de-camp to Cumberland, showed little inclination to visit his latest acquisition. He remained in London; James had to give up his studies, and spend the time writing long reports on regimental affairs. However, as his health improved in the autumn, he was able to find time to shoot and hunt (the regiment owned a pack of hounds). He did this, he insisted, strictly for exercise. For entertainment, he preferred reading.

The term of duty for a regiment in Scotland was six years. The prospect filled James with concern. He told his friend, William Rickson: 'My stay must be everlasting; and thou know'st how I hate compulsion. I'd rather be a Major upon half-pay, by my soul...! Besides, I am by no means ambitious of command, when the command obliges me to reside far from my own.... Would to God you had a company in this regiment [Rickson was serving in Ireland], that I might at least find some comfort in your conversation.'

For perhaps the first time in his life, James was thoroughly lonely. No doubt this was one of the reasons for his outpourings of letters to his parents – in which he revealed more of himself than he had ever done before. What with the cares of command, ill health, and the wretched conflict of being torn between Elizabeth and his mother, this was a singularly unhappy period. The only solution seemed to be to get away from Scotland, to carry out his earlier plan of seeing something of the world. But the Army remained obdurate. James Wolfe must stay at his post.

In November 1749, the 20th received instructions to march to Perth. The journey, which covered one hundred and fifty miles, was not a bad one. After the ghastly summer, the weather mended its ways. There was little rain; the morale and conduct of the troops was improving under his leadership; and there might be happier times ahead. A report from two of his friends who had been stationed in Gibraltar ('they complain of being too strictly confined, and too much duty') put him in a better frame of mind to suffer Scotland. What was more, his health seemed to be getting better from a new regimen he had set himself. 'I am', he told his mother, 'entirely at leisure to prosecute such entertainments as I find of use to my health and agreeable to my taste. As the latter is generally subservient to the first, I have improved and strengthened my constitution beyond what I have hitherto known.' Since this was written in mid-winter, he must indeed have been feeling more robust.

He was still only a temporary lieutenant-colonel. In March 1750, however, he was given the substantive rank. It was an occasion for family rejoicing. James detected the Duke of Cumberland's hand in the matter, and he was grateful. 'The Duke', he wrote to his father, 'has employed his power and influence upon this occasion where, at least, it is sure to be remembered. There are not many opportunities in life, and the prospect, as things stand at present, very distant; but if ever he commands the army of this nation in its defence, I shall wish to be with him.'

Only the matter of Elizabeth Lawson continued to trouble him. And this would not be resolved until the spring of the following year. It might have been easier for James and his family, if, as he had predicted, the 'young flames' had evaporated in the rigours of separation. Unfortunately, they did nothing of the kind.

6
THE TRIAL BY FRUSTRATION

On the march to Perth, riding at the head of his men, and savouring the clear air of the southern Highlands, Wolfe felt better. Glasgow had produced so many difficulties that things, surely, could only improve. He was unusually optimistic, and even prepared to enjoy life. Unfortunately, the euphoria lasted no longer than the journey. When he inspected his cramped and uncomfortable quarters in the town, the old weariness returned. It would be easy to blame it on circumstances. Part of the truth, however, was that he was hopelessly under-nourished. The only green vegetables available in Scotland were cabbage and kale, and then only in season. There was a sparse crop of potatoes. The one fish obtainable was salmon, and there was little fresh meat. For much of the year, the army – officers and other ranks alike – had to exist off salt beef. It was hardly surprising that he had contracted scurvy; nor that, before the year was done, he should succumb to another attack.

His mind and his body were clamouring for release, to get away from this narrow life which had to be endured in such uncongenial surroundings. For want of anything better, he decided to take two weeks' holiday in the country. He stayed at a farm, bathed often and drank large quantities of goats' milk. Afterwards, he professed to feel better, but the brief interlude was brought to a brusque conclusion. For the first time since he had acquired the regiment, Lord Bury proposed to visit it. Wolfe's presence was required back at headquarters.

Bury had been kept well informed by his lieutenant-colonel's long and dutiful dispatches. For three hectic weeks, His Lordship watched the men parading. He visited the detachments in the surrounding countryside, and then he hurried back to London. During this hubbub of activity, James had tried to sound him out on the prospect of extended leave. His Lordship pushed the matter aside. It was out of the question: the 20th was shortly to be moved to Dundee. Some of the men were still inadequately provided with uniforms – there was too much to be done. Wolfe must remain where he was. There could be no argument.

Wolfe remained. Conditions in the Highlands were calm; the natives were still subdued by the carnage and privations which had followed Culloden. Nevertheless, as he was only too well aware, this state of affairs depended on a strong military presence. 'Such a body,' he wrote, 'is now so disposed throughout the whole Highlands that any attempt [at another revolution] must be crushed in the beginning.' The military supervision was, indeed, so thorough that the clansmen were even deprived of their favourite pastime of stealing one another's cattle. They were James observed, 'either reduced to live honestly and industriously, or starve through excess of idleness'.

For want of any other recreation, he went off into the hills for some shooting. Afterwards, he was very tired – which was hardly surprising. Over a period of three days, he had been on the go from five in the morning until nightfall. The results had been satisfactory: there was a large bag of game – despite the fact that he was a self-confessed 'very bad shot'.

When he was out hunting, or was occupied with running the regiment, his mind was on other things. James Wolfe was a very ambitious young man. Regimental life was beginning to bore him; but, if he were to advance himself beyond that, a wider knowledge of military affairs would be necessary. One place he particularly wished to visit was a school of engineering and gunnery at Metz in northern France. What was needed, he decided, was ten month's leave. He would spend four weeks in Metz, wander down the Rhine as far as Switzerland, and then return home through France and Holland. As the time went by, he polished the plan lovingly. It would take him away from the abhorred Scotland during the coming winter and beyond. He would return as a military savant worthy of senior rank – and with the culture and social graces that such a position required.

The months struggled by. In August, as might have been expected, he succumbed to a second attack of scurvy, but the ordeal was made tolerable by a four-day visit from George Warde. As it happened, this young man was destined to have a brilliantly successful career in the cavalry. After this particular encounter, however, James was unsure about his friend's future. Although he was grateful for the understanding George had shown, James considered him extremely indifferent 'as to preferment and high employment in the army . . . principally from an easiness, or rather indolence, of temper that make him unfit to bear a heavy part in life.' Possibly he was comparing his guest with his own view of himself – or perhaps his malaise made him see everything and everybody as inadequate.

By September he had recovered, and was composing a letter to Lord Bury, applying for ten months' leave to go abroad. His Lordship was less sympathetic than Lord George Sackville: the 20th was being run to his liking, and he was not eager to put the regiment in anyone else's hands. When he was asked to approach the Duke of Cumberland about it, he did not press the case very hard. The reply, when it came, was negative. The Duke, it seemed, had no objection to James Wolfe having a spell of leave – providing he did not go outside the UK. James made two attempts to have the verdict changed, but on each the Duke was adamant. 'He accompanied his denial', Wolfe wrote, 'with a speech that leaves no hope – that a lieutenant-colonel was an officer of too high a rank to be allowed to leave his regiment for any considerable time.' Cumberland may have feared that, if he were let loose on the Continent in his present frame of mind, this uncommonly promising young officer might be persuaded to accept a commission in the Prussian army.

James was bitterly disappointed. The assembly of ideas, which he had erected with such care, had come crashing to the ground. It was unfair to himself; but, which was even worse, it seemed a poor look-out for the Army. 'How does the Duke mistake my sentiments', he asked his father, 'or how greatly does he oppose the only method that can be fallen upon to preserve any knowledge of military affairs in the Army. I shan't say to introduce it, for infinite pains have been taken to make us acquainted with some particular branches, which yet, do not amount to all that may be required from an officer.'

However, for better or for worse, he was granted four months leave in England. He set out from Dundee on 4 November 1740, and – after a journey which was unusually fast – reached York two days later. He dutifully called on Thompson relations in Yorkshire, and then took the stage to London. He arrived in Old Burlington Street on the fourteenth. If he hoped for respite from the worries of regimental life, he was to be quickly disillusioned. His mother was determined that the time had come to deliver a death blow to what she called his 'senseless passion' for Elizabeth Lawson, and to drive him into the arms of the affluent Miss Hoskins. She had no doubt worked out her offensive tactics with considerable care, but one vital ingredient was missing. She manifested an almost unbelievable lack of insight into her son. Far from smothering James's love for Elizabeth, she was more likely to increase it

To begin with, she avoided a head-on confrontation. She asked whether James had heard the rumours? When he said that he had not, she hinted that Miss Lawson had agreed to marry another man. It was nonsense, and James saw through the ploy at once. He allowed the matter to pass without much comment. As if to change the subject, he began to plan his comparatively long period of leisure.

London was a paradise for anybody who enjoyed gambling, heavy drinking, or whoring. None of these things was to James's taste. To pass the time, and to escape from the thundery atmosphere of 10 Old Burlington Street, he visited Parliament. The debate was about North America, and he found it adequately absorbing – especially since his old friend William Rickson had recently been appointed to Cornwallis's staff in Nova Scotia. He deplored the government's reluctance to send more troops to the colonies, which he 'took to be a bad prognostic'. 'A minister cool in so great an affair', he wrote to Rickson some while later, 'it is enough to freeze up the whole! but perhaps there might be a concealed manœuvre under these appearances, as in case of accidents, "I am not to blame", "I was forced to carry it on", and so forth.' The ideal solution, he decided, would be to recruit 'two or three independent Highland companies' for service in North America. Their members would be 'hardy, intrepid, accustomed to a rough country, and no great mischief if they fall. How can you better employ a secret enemy than by making his end conducive to the common good?'

He spent a fortnight listening to the debate, and then he lost interest. Admittedly, he had learned a good deal from the experience – a mass of facts about the northern part of America, all of which he passed on to Rickson. But he was still brooding about the Duke of Cumberland's refusal to grant him a chance to go abroad; and this led to bitter reflections about Army officers. 'We fall every day lower and lower from our real characters', he observed, 'and are so totally engaged in everything that is minute and trifling, that one would almost imagine the idea of war was extinguished amongst us.'

For some people, the hardest part of any war is the peace which follows it: the difficulty of adapting to new circumstances, in which honour and self-sacrifice seem to be replaced by the utterly trivial. Wolfe was in such a condition now, and circumstances at home did little to help. Having found her son unmoved by her false reports that Miss Lawson was courting somebody else, Mrs Wolfe now turned her guns on to the girl's mother. It was common gossip in court circles that, before her marriage to Sir Wilfrid Lawson, Lady Lawson had committed one or two indiscretions. There may or may not have been any substance to the story: this hotbed of tittle-tattle seldom concerned itself with the truth. But, for Mrs Wolfe, they provided valuable ammunition. Was James aware, she wanted to know, of the kind of family into which he proposed to marry? If the mother had such a background, what could one expect of the daughter? She then unleashed a torrent of propaganda in favour of Miss Hoskins, with her impeccable, dull, and rich, relations. This was too much. James could stand it no more; he walked out of the house, and took lodgings in a neighbouring street.

James Wolfe's private life was normally beyond reproach. He drank little, never swore – and, when his fellow officers were at the gaming houses, he was at home in his lodgings reading or studying. But Mrs Wolfe had pushed him too far. It was as if, having heard his loved one humiliated, he wished to subject himself to the same treatment. Others might abandon themselves to the vices of London for pleasure: he was doing it from despair. In his letter to Rickson, he gave only the barest outline. 'In that short time', he wrote, 'I committed more imprudent acts than in all my life before. I lived in the idlest, dissolute, and abandoned manner that would be conceived, and that not out of vice, which is the most extraordinary part of it.'

One evening, or so the story goes, he made a public declaration of his love for Miss Lawson at a ball. He then threatened to whip a man whom he supposed to be his rival. At other times, he sank without trace into a swirl of alcohol, keeping company with women who, no doubt, made good other deficiencies in his education. But the wretched young man's constitution was not up to this sort of thing. After a week or so of debauchery, he became ill. From the babble of the salons and the pothouses, he passed into the dark quietness of his rooms. The curtains were drawn as he lay in bed, fighting a sick body and trying to escape from the fog of dejection which seemed to stifle his mind. Presently, he recovered; and it must have been with a good deal of relief that, in early April, he set off to join the 20th, which was now stationed at Banff.

So far as Miss Lawson was concerned, this disastrous leave marked the end of the affair. Since Wolfe's letters to his mother have been preserved, a good deal is known about their side of the question. Unfortunately, nothing is known of Elizabeth Lawson's attitude. She must have sensed that this young officer, who wooed her so industriously, had, in fact, an element of weakness. He was torn between herself and Mrs Wolfe, and he was not strong enough to cut free from the maternal entanglement. But was it quite so simple as she suspected? Did he realize that, in spite of his comparative seniority in the service, he was still financially dependent on his parents? If he wedded Elizabeth against their wishes, this source of income would immediately dry up. He would have only his pay and her £12,000. Was this sufficient on which to base a marriage? Wolfe aimed high in everything, and he may have doubted it.

We know that he loved her as he had never loved anyone before. But what were her feelings for him? A mutual friend suggested that she was 'amiable' but 'cold'. When James heard the remark, he wanted to know whether she was 'as much a mistress of her own as of the hearts of all her acquaintances'. Was she, he wondered, 'the extraordinary woman that has no weaknesses? Or happily constructed without passions?' It certainly suggested that their affair was somewhat less than torrid – a meeting of minds, perhaps; certainly not a junction of bodies.

A miniature painted of Elizabeth at about this period shows a gentle, beautifully modelled mouth; but the eyes seem to contradict it. There is, to be honest, a trace of coldness, even calculation, about them. It is possible to guess that she might be demanding – unwilling, perhaps, to share. The attitude was not likely to find great happiness out of a marriage to James. Whoever took him for a husband would have to realize that the greater part of him belonged to the Army. However much he might grumble about it, his duty in any conflict of responsibilities would be to the service. It is questionable whether Elizabeth would have accepted him on these terms. How, for example, would she have endured the uncomfortable alternative of months of separation or long periods in lodgings at uncongenial places? Neither her family background nor her experience at Court had equipped her for such things. Was, perhaps, Mrs Wolfe thinking beyond money, when she discouraged the match? But this may be doing less than justice to Elizabeth. Whilst Wolfe's heart lived to love another day, she never married. She died in the early part of 1759 – just one month after James had departed on his final mission to Canada. As for Miss Hoskins, while Mrs Wolfe was scheming to drive her son into her arms, she had been otherwise engaged. In February 1751, when James was lying ill in his London lodgings, she confounded everybody by marrying John Warde, George's brother and the heir to Squerrye's Court. Out of the whole unsavoury drama, she was the only player to escape with happiness. But then, she had £30,000.

Back with the regiment, James became filled with remorse. He passed much of his spare time covering reams of paper with protests of apology to his parents. With an abandon that may suggest a hidden uncertainty about his feelings for Elizabeth, he threw his heart at both the General and Mrs Wolfe. To the former, he wrote: 'I am very glad . . . to be able to make you some sort of apology for every particular instance of vice or folly that has very luckily fallen under your notice while I had the honour to be near you. I say very luckily, for if you or some other perfect friend had not discovered them, so as to make them known to me, I might have continued in the conceit of there being no such thing in my composition, and consequently they must in time have taken root, and increased beyond the power of any remedy.'

His mother, as one might expect, was harder to appease. By mid-July, James had still not received any letters from her, and he had 'begun to think myself exiled to all intents and purposes without the consolation of being so much as thought of in this state of bondage and confinement'. Then he received a note which was unusually short, but nevertheless gave him hopes of forgiveness. Indeed, Mrs Wolfe's silence was not entirely due to her ill temper. The General and herself were on the move once more – this time to a house in Blackheath.

The trouble with James at this period was that he was reading too much. His letters home reflected the fact. The styles swung from that of one writer who had influenced him to another. Frequently, he delivered brief homilies to his parents – such as (to Mrs Wolfe): 'It is fit that some share of evil should fall upon us in this life, to teach us to enjoy the best that we are formed to taste.' At others, he became downright incomprehensible. In one attempt to describe his philosophy, he remarked, half-way: 'I have had a mind to burn this letter.' It might have been as well if he had – it would certainly have saved his mother a good deal of trouble (assuming that she had the patience to trace her way through the confusion of thought). But one thing was clear: his unfortunate experience with Miss Lawson had not entirely put him off the idea of one day becoming married. 'I have', he wrote, 'a certain turn of mind that favours matrimony prodigiously, though every way else extremely averse to it at present, and you shall know it. I love children, and think them necessary to us in our latter days; they are fit objects for the mind to rest upon, and give it great entertainment when the amusements of other kinds have lost their value.' The author of this was only twenty-four; but, in his mind, James may already have seen himself as middle-aged. His very reasonable concern with his health, coupled with the experience of poor Ned, had already convinced him that he was not likely to enjoy a very long life.

At Banff, the routine was much as it had been at Dundee. Detachments were scattered in outposts over the surrounding countryside. Every Monday morning, the headquarter company paraded on the green. Drunkenness was a problem, as well it might be. What other source of recreation was there in these outlandish parts? In an effort to cut it down, the wives of soldiers were forbidden to sell liquor; but there were no doubt other sources available – even in a neighbourhood where the natives were suspicious and resentful of what was, all too evidently, an army of occupation.

In the summer of 1751, James became ill again. This time, his complaint was gravel – a urinary infection which manifests itself in the formation of crystals. The regimental surgeon had prescribed soap, to be mixed with water and taken internally. It was a commonly used treatment for the complaint. From the patient's point of view, however, it was unpleasant and utterly useless. Having sampled it with a predictable lack of success, James decided to take the cure at Peterhead, a small spa about thirty-six miles away. For over a hundred years Peterhead's supposedly healing spring had been comforting the sick. The water had acquired a modest reputation as a specific for his ailment, and James considered it well deserved. He had, he said afterwards, 'found great relief from it'. Although the month was July, he considered the weather of this north-easterly corner of Scotland to be as cold as England in November. 'I could not imagine', he wrote, 'that the climate in any part of this island could be so severe.'

However, there were consolations. The population of Peterhead included a number of women – 'some of great vivacity, and others very handsome' – and he enjoyed their company. 'A man', he observed, 'could not fail to be pleased with such variety.'

The spate of letters home continued. He had received a report that his father, who was now in his sixty-seventh year, was in low spirits. Had his conduct in London been to blame? Still nursing a heavy sense of guilt, he poured forth a further stream of apologies. 'I had much rather be quite out of your thoughts', he told the old gentleman, 'than take a place in them to torment you.' To his mother, he mentioned his health. Honey had been recommended: could she send him six or eight pounds? In addition, he said, he proposed 'to nourish [himself] with chocolate and milk'. In moderately better health, he returned to the regiment.

Winter in Scotland, he had remarked, extended from the beginning of August until mid-May. The 20th had been ordered to leave Banff at the end of September and move to Inverness. It was not a prospect which filled him with any pleasure. The town was the very breeding ground of Jacobite sympathies, and the troops could expect no better treatment from the local people than they had received at Banff. Furthermore, when the thick snow crept over the surrounding countryside, there was little to do but eat and sleep. It promised to be a period of gloom and, so far as he was concerned, further attacks of bitter introspection. However, before he went into enforced hibernation, he proposed to pass the time with sightseeing.

Five years had passed since the battle of Culloden. Now, he took the opportunity to revisit the battlefield, and to run over the events with critical retrospection. The affair had not been as well managed as he had, at the time, believed. He was a little vague in his assessment of the mistakes; but he pointed out: 'The actors shine in the world too high and bright to be eclipsed; but it is plain they don't borrow much of their glory from their performance on that occasion, however they may have distinguished themselves in later events.' He also paid a visit to Fort George, where £160,000 were being sent in an attempt to make it the most considerable fortress and the best situated in Great Britain. But he was not impressed with the progress. Although he found that 'a vast quantity of earth (had been) thrown up for ramparts', he considered that 'there's work for six or seven years to do'.

And then there was Inverness, with the long Highland nights; cut off from the civilized world by snow, and a population which, all too evidently, was hostile. When the regiment marched into town, the morale of the men was low, and its commanding officer wrapped in a mood of melancholy. It was as he had suspected. 'A little while serves to discover the villainous nature of the inhabitants and the brutality of the people in its neighbourhood. Those, too, who pretend the greatest attachment to the Government, and who every day feed upon the public purse, seem to distinguish themselves for greater rudeness and incivility than the open and professed Jacobites.'

When the weather allowed it, he went riding for exercise. For the rest, he fretted at the delay of a ship which was bringing reinforcements and supplies of uniforms from the south. 'I shall be broke for not completing the regiment,' he wrote to his father; 'they sent me a reprimand for not doing it last year, though I was all the winter in London.' His senior officers' views of justice were, it seems, less correct than his own.

During the evenings, he settled down before a blazing fire in his lodgings to read, to write letters, or just to brood. His career was no longer making the progress his insatiable ambition demanded. He talked about having to be 'content to be a little lower than Caesar in the list'. He worried some more about the old General's well-being, and was pleased to hear that he was taking a reasonable amount of claret. 'He is never better than when he uses it freely but without excess,' he told his mother. In this letter, a flash of optimism intruded. He talked about being 'young and in health [and] all the world is my garden and my dwelling.'

Life was not entirely lacking in diversions. There were fortnightly dances, when officers of the 20th spun round the floor with ladies named Macdonald, Fraser, and McIntosh. In their hearts, these young women were known to be still lamenting the Young Pretender. But they behaved themselves very well: abandoning their principles, as James observed, 'for the sake of sound and movement'. He himself had taken the floor with the Laird of Kippoch's daughter. Her father had been killed at Culloden, but this did not seem to spoil the experience.

A more significant meeting took place between James and Simon Fraser, a relative of the young officer he had refused to shoot after Culloden. They met in a mood of reconciliation. James was anxious, as the fortnightly dances suggested, to appease the Jacobite gentry. They were part of the United Kingdom. What purpose could this atmosphere of silent hostility serve to either side? Fraser, who had been pardoned for his Jacobite sympathies in 1750 after a spell of imprisonment, seems to have adopted a similar view. At any rate he listened with interest when Wolfe described his idea of independent companies of Highlanders being recruited to serve overseas. The conversation bore fruit five years later, when Fraser raised the 78th Regiment of Foot (known as 'Fraser's Highlanders'). More than eight hundred of the men were enlisted from his father's estate.

But James was still attending to his own education. Just as at Glasgow, so at Inverness did he employ a tutor. The man was a local schoolmaster named Barber. The subjects chosen were algebra and geometry. 'I have read mathematics', James wrote to his father, 'till I am grown perfectly stupid, and have algebraically worked away the little portion of understanding that was allowed me. They have not even left me the qualities of a cox comb; for I can neither laugh nor sing, nor talk an hour about anything.'

The long night continued. At Christmas they made a larger fire than usual, and ate bad mince pies prepared by the sutler's wife. The mail to London was delayed by snow; and then – suddenly, it seemed – it was spring. James closed his books and climbed into the saddle for some fresh air. As he saw himself, he was undergoing a gradual change. One of his uncles had stopped corresponding with him. That gentleman, apparently, disapproved of what he considered to be his nephew's radical views. They were all becoming (or seemed to be) coarsened by this life in the northern extremity of the UK. In his own opinion, James was no exception. He chided himself for an attitude which was 'rustic, hard-tempered and severe'. 'We use', he reported, 'a very dangerous freedom and looseness of speech among ourselves; this, by degrees, makes wickedness and debauchery less odious than it should be, if not familiar, and sets truth, religion and virtue at a great distance.' As he told his mother, 'I hear things every day said that would shock your ears, and often say things myself that are not fit to be repeated.... The best that can be offered in our defence is, that some of us see the evil and wish to avoid it.'

The snow cleared, and the sun forced its way through the thick overcast. In Inverness there was a lightening of spirits – almost an atmosphere of gaiety. But even spring had its snags. Among those who were stretching themselves to dispel the winter lethargy was Lord Bury. His Lordship had decided, after an absence of nearly two years, to visit his regiment again. The 20th would have to be spruced up. Its commanding officer applied himself to rehearsing the old argument for leave to go abroad. And the citizens of Inverness, although they did not realize it, were about to receive an unpleasant surprise.

7
THE UNBECOMING CONDUCT

James had done a great deal for the 20th Regiment of Foot. Inevitably, stationed in such a remote corner of the UK with so few diversions, the men grumbled. But, on the whole, morale was high. Even the officers – either impressed by their lieutenant-colonel's example, or else because there were no alternatives – were mending their licentious ways. As he proudly told his father, 'we are allowed to be the most religious Foot officers that have ever served in the North for many a day.' Their conduct appealed to the pious leaders of Inverness society, and relations between the occupying power and the townspeople took a considerable turn for the better. As a self-appointed diplomat, James could consider himself successful.

Unfortunately this new understanding, which had been wrought with such care, was not proof against the regiment's colonel. The work of months was destroyed by one foolish remark from Lord Bury. Sensitivity had never been among that gentleman's virtues. On this occasion, he used his boorishness to wicked effect.

George Keppel, Viscount Bury, was three years older than James. His father, the second Earl of Albemarle, had taken over as commander-in-chief in Scotland after Cumberland's departure. During the campaign which had culminated in Culloden, the two young men had struck up an acquaintance. Since James was acting as aide-de-camp to Hawley, and Bury was carrying out similar duties on behalf of the Duke of Cumberland, it was natural. Their daily responsibilities ensured that they saw a good deal of each other.

It was Bury's boast that he had been the target of the first round fired in the battle. It had occurred when the two armies were still five hundred yards apart, sniffing each other like a pair of suspicious animals, and each forming into line. At some point, a young Highlander broke out from the Young Pretender's ranks. When he was in full view of the royal troops, he threw down his weapons. He ran forward over the heather, crying out that he was the Duke of Cumberland's prisoner, and begging for quarter. Since the troops had other matters on their minds, nobody knew what to do with him. He was passed back to the rear, until he came across a distinguished figure of a man, mounted on an unusually good horse and rigged out in a superb uniform.

The Highlander suddenly came to a halt. Groping inside his rags, he pulled out a musket. Without taking adequate aim, he discharged it at the officer. Predictably, he missed. Seconds later, he was shot down by an English private. Even if his marksmanship had been better, this suicidal mission would have had no effect upon the day's outcome. In his zeal, the young man had hoped to assassinate the Duke of Cumberland. Instead, misled by His Lordship's finery, he had fired at Lord Bury.

After the battle, Lord Bury was assigned by the Duke to carry the news of the victory to London. The ship which was supposed to take him south ran into head winds. After five days of heavy weather in the North Sea, her captain gave up the unequal struggle. Bury was put ashore at North Berwick. He made the rest of the trip by post chaise. When he reached the capital, he was rewarded by the King, who gave him £1,000. It was more than adequate payment for a difficult journey.

When Lord George Sackville ceased to be colonel of the 20th, James might have hoped to be given the regiment. He had, after all, the necessary experience: his father was an officer of high rank and, by this time, the Wolfes were well-connected. Unfortunately, Lord Bury could depend on even more influence. Not only was his father an earl; he had spent his time with the Duke of Cumberland to good purpose. He had been lavish with his flattery, and had even copied some of his master's more braggart mannerisms. The performance was entirely to the Duke's liking. Young Viscount Bury was obviously destined for big things. In 1746, he became Member of Parliament for Chichester; and, when the colonelcy of the 20th fell vacant, he was instantly awarded it. In the shadow of such powerful opposition, James's claims were not even considered.

Down in London, Bury continued to cultivate Cumberland. From time to time, the Duke even asked his opinion on military matters. Bury could be relied upon to produce answers which would please His Highness. So far as James was concerned, the new colonel of the 20th was yet another source of frustration; for the Duke's refusal to grant him a long period of leave to go overseas may have been partly on Bury's advice. After all, the latter's regiment was in excellent hands. He was able to divide his time between the Court and Parliament. Why should he run the risk of putting the 20th in the hands of a, possibly, less adequate lieutenant-colonel? It was entirely in his interest to ensure that James's applications were turned down.

In the early spring of 1752, Bury decided to expose his constitution to the rigours of northern life. He would visit the 20th and enjoy a little sport into the bargain. James wrote to his mother: 'Lord Bury comes down in April; he'll stay six weeks, and then swear there's no enduring it any longer, and beg leave to return. "Wolfe, you'll stay in the Highlands; you can't, with any face, ask to quit the regiment so dispersed; and when you have clothed and sent them to their different quarters, towards the end of November you shall come to London, my dear friend, for three months." This will be his discourse, and I must say, "My Lord, you are very kind"!'

His Lordship arrived. The detachments were brought into Inverness from their stations in the hills, and the regiment was paraded for review. Shortly afterwards, a delegation from the local Council called. As Lord Bury was no doubt aware, the fifteenth of the month was approaching, and this was the Duke of Cumberland's birthday. As a gesture of goodwill, the town would like to celebrate the occasion by providing a suitable entertainment. Had he, they wanted to know, any objections?

This was a tremendous step forward. Cumberland had been loathed throughout the Highlands for the butchery which had followed Culloden. Even in 1751, five years afterwards, the hatred had continued. When news reached Inverness that the Duke had been seriously injured by a fall in the hunting field, a few people were glad that he had not been killed. The majority, on the other hand, took a less kindly view. And now, here were these selfsame people proposing to honour the anniversary of a man they had detested. It was a more than ample tribute to Wolfe's diplomacy and the conduct of the 20th.

But Bury either did not understand, or else he was determined to be unpleasant. Unlike his lieutenant-colonel, he had not spent months getting to know these people – probing into their troubles and trying to find points of contact. He had been down in London, cocooned in the silk of privilege, the spoilt darling of society and the friend of a royal duke. He had not taken part in fortnightly hops with the local ladies – his experience was limited to court balls. What did he know of these people? What, indeed, did he care about them?

When the civic dignitaries put their proposal to him, he muttered something about its being a kind thought. But, as he took care to point out, he was a friend of Cumberland. He knew him well; and, whilst His Royal Highness would doubtless appreciate the thought of birthday celebrations, he would much prefer the following day to be honoured. The date would be 16 April – the sixth anniversary of the Battle of Culloden. The meeting became silent, either from disbelief or else from anger on the part of the delegation. Presently the leader announced that this was too big a decision for him and his colleagues to make on their own. They would have to consult the rest of the Council. In a good deal of confusion, they withdrew.

The very idea was preposterous, and nobody can have been more aware of this than James Wolfe. As for the Council, they did not require long to debate the matter. They could not possibly celebrate an event in which a high proportion of their fellow citizens had been killed, and they sent a message to this effect. Bury promptly put on his Duke of Cumberland face. The proposed festivities were not to be cancelled. If they were not held on the sixteenth, he could not, he said, be responsible for his soldiers' conduct. It was a threat, and the councillors capitulated. There had been enough violence in Inverness.

Doubtless out of loyalty to his colonel, James recorded no comments on this affront to the town's civic pride. In any case, he was more preoccupied with the much exercised topic of permission to spend a long leave abroad. He never gave up. Other officers might have pigeonholed the application in a box labelled 'Lost Causes', but not James. He clearly had a poor opinion of his colonel, but this did not deter him.

As he had written during the previous winter: 'Lord Bury professes fairly, and means nothing; in that he resembles his father and a million other showy men that are seen in palaces and the courts of kings. He desires never to see his regiment, and wishes that no officer would ever leave it. This is selfish and unjust.' Nevertheless, his hopes remained despite odds which, as he must have admitted, appeared to be impossible. Shortly after Bury's arrival, he was writing: 'His Lordship pays my attendance upon him with fair words and promises; and he thinks it highly reasonable that my long confinement should have an end, though he is far from sure of the Duke's consent. I tell him the matter of fact, that when I feel any extraordinary restraint, and am kept longer with the regiment than is equitable, I hate the sight of a soldier.'

The debate continued – with Bury using Cumberland as a convenient shield. As his own experience now confirmed, the 20th was being excellently run: it would be difficult to find a better commanding officer.

But the regiment was not to be in Inverness for much longer. After the 'Fifteen Rebellion, a chain of three forts had been constructed along the line of the Caledonian Canal. There was Fort George at the mouth of the Moray Firth near Inverness; Fort Augustus in the middle between Loch Ness and Loch Lochy; and Fort William down at the south-westerly end. During their stay at Inverness, the 20th had been employed in restoring Fort George from the Jacobite depredations. Now they were ordered to Fort Augustus. As before, detachments were spread out over the surrounding countryside. If James had any regrets when he said good-bye to the people of Inverness, the greater part of them were for Mrs Grant, his landlady. During his residence in the town, she had treated him with kindness and fussed about his health. As for the rest of the population, after Lord

Bury's behaviour, it was a relief to get away from their accusing eyes.

Like James, Bury enjoyed shooting. There was some good sport to be had at Fort Augustus, and His Lordship spent most of his time out in the hills with a gun in his hands. His lieutenant-colonel trailed along beside him – acting, it seems, as a servant. James wrote to his mother: 'He'll keep me to carry his powder-horn and flints; we shall ramble from post to post till he's tired and goes off.' It was not, indeed, long before Bury found Fort Augustus rather dull for his liking. He made his excuses, and departed for Fort William – which, presumably, he found equally lacking in entertainment. Before very long, he was on his way south to the joys of London.

His departure was a relief for James. Not only was he glad to see the back of his colonel: before going, Bury had promised to make another plea on his behalf to the Duke of Cumberland. The matter was now more urgent than it had ever been. James's teeth were giving trouble, and he had learned that the best dentists were to be found in Paris. 'They put in artificial teeth', he told his mother, 'that are every way as serviceable as the natural ones. . . . I see no harm in repairing any loss of this kind, as we really can't eat nor speak properly without them.'

During its stay at Fort Augustus, the regiment was involved in a manhunt. The estate of Charles Stewart of Ardshiel had been confiscated after Culloden. The property was taken over by the Court of the Exchequer, which appointed Colin Campbell of Glenure as factor. One of his first actions was to expel all the tenants. While walking through a wood one day, Campbell was shot dead by an assassin concealed behind a tree. As James heard it, the killing had been carried out by two Highlanders – at the instigation of the wife of a banished rebel. James was not optimistic about the outcome of the investigation. It would, he felt sure, 'be very difficult to discover the actors of this bloody deed'. Eventually, one man was hanged for it, and another suspect escaped. Contrary to the early reports, the wife of the exiled Jacobite had not been responsible at all.

Life was tolerable. One of the officers in charge of detachments sent him a young roebuck. Since it was not fit to eat, James proposed to have it tamed. When it was suitably domesticated, he would send the animal to England as a gift to his mother. If one imagines the antics of even a friendly deer in a garden at Blackheath, it may seem to be a suitable revenge for the matter of Miss Lawson. And the Macleod invited him to Dunvegan Castle on the Isle of Skye. Since James could not 'find enough work to employ me here', he accepted.

Throughout this period, one gets the impression of an amiable young man: restless, perhaps, but conscientious in his duties. His soldiers liked him, and their opinion was shared by almost everybody he met. In his relations with his parents one scents weakness, and there are traces of self-pity. In anyone else, it might have been said that he was too concerned with his health. In his case, however, such preoccupation was forgivable. Unless he watched himself carefully, he would succumb to one or another complaint.

But beneath all this there was a streak of utter ruthlessness. Once James Wolfe had made up his mind to accomplish something, nothing could stop him – even if it meant sacrificing the lives of his own men. At Fort Augustus an incident occurred which illustrated this trait dramatically. Since, at the time, few people were taken into his confidence, it went unremarked. It was not until three years later that he told the story – and then only to his friend Rickson, who had been posted to the Highlands. The account was embedded in an assortment of advice, and we must assume that he regarded his attitude as beyond reproach.

Shortly after the battle of Culloden, two French frigates landed £40,000's worth of gold coins in Scotland. The fortune passed into the hands of the Young Pretender, who was in hiding. When at last he was able to escape to France, he proposed to take the gold with him. His lieutenants, however, argued that such wealth would be better kept in store for financing another rebellion. The prince agreed, and Lord Lovat's son-in-law, Evan McPherson of Cluny, was given the custodianship. He could hand out some of it to deserving cases, but he had to keep the greater part intact.

When the Earl of Albemarle had been commander-in-chief in Scotland, several attempts had been made to round up Cluny and his agents. They had all failed, and the gold remained undiscovered. Somewhere in the hilly wilderness of the Highlands the outlaw remained at large, living off the country, but occasionally daring to make visits home to attend family gatherings. He was obviously a man with remarkable powers of endurance, and James regarded him as a worthy quarry. The fact that this singular chieftain (he was the head of his clan) had defeated much larger forces than his own did not deter him. Indeed, at the beginning, he did not even intend to deploy the whole regiment on the undertaking. But, behind his plan to get Cluny, lay something much more devious – even, some might say, villainous.

The assignment was given to Captain Alexander Trapaud, who commanded a detachment at Laggan, a few miles from Cluny Castle. Trapaud was to brief a sergeant and twenty men. Reports seem to have reached Fort Augustus that their prey was due to make one of his trips home. The patrol would raid the stronghold when he had arrived and, with a bit of luck, take him into custody. On the face of it, it sounds a straightforward operation. It would give the men something to do – even if the chances of success might seem to be small. After all, if Wolfe knew anything at all about Cluny's movements, that ingenious warrior must have known a good deal about the affairs of Captain Trapaud and his small command.

But the matter did not end there. Wolfe had little doubt that Cluny would be captured. Once Trapaud's men had taken him, the clan could be expected to set out in force to rescue their chief. By their overwhelming weight of numbers, they would kill off every member of the 20th's detachment. Once this had happened, Wolfe would put the next phase of his plan into operation. Without waiting for instructions, he intended to march the regiment into the heart of McPherson's territory, and to wipe out the entire clan of unruly Highlanders. 'Wou'd you believe I am so bloody?' he asked Rickson. ' 'Twas my real intention, and I hope such execution will be done upon the first that revolt, to teach 'em their duty and to keep the Highlands in awe. They are a people better governed by fear than favour.'

The method he advocated, and which he would have used if his plan had come off, was to dispatch a 'secret, sudden night-march into the very midst of them'. Large patrols, made up of anything from fifty to one hundred men, should be employed to terrify the presumed enemy. There should be constant 'mysterious' movements of troops, 'to keep [the Highlanders'] attention upon you, and their fears awake'. And, to intensify the atmosphere of foreboding, grim letters should be written to the chiefs. Their substance would be the promise of 'fire and sword and certain destruction if they dare to stir'. The goodwill which had been shown to the worthy burghers of Inverness did not seem to extend to their friends – and, in some cases, relatives – out in the wilds.

Part of this letter was written in rather bad French, as if James could not face an English version of his intentions. But there was no denying the gist of it: a sergeant and twenty men were to be the bait in a trap which would result in the massacre of hundreds. Fortunately for everybody, the raid came to nothing. When the soldiers arrived, Cluny was at his house – dead drunk. The moment his servants heard about the approaching troops, they wrapped up his slumbering body in a plaid, carried it out of the building, and hid it in some brushwood near a river. Although the patrol passed close to the spot, the men found no traces of their prey. They returned to Laggan empty-handed. Soon afterwards, Cluny seems to have decided that there were more congenial lives than that of an outlaw, and he escaped to France.

By a strange coincidence, his intended captor was about to make his own exit from the Highlands; for, early in June 1752, James was at last granted extended leave. There was still no mention of permission to go abroad; but at least he was able to visit Dublin, where his uncle, Major Walter Wolfe, lived. Afterwards, anything seemed to be possible.

8

THE INDUSTRIOUS TRAVELLER

James's trip to Ireland was unremarkable. He visited his uncle, who seems to have lived in a Dublin coffee house. Like a dutiful tourist, he viewed the site of the Battle of the Boyne; noticed in passing that there was room for improvement in Irish methods of agriculture; and did the sights of Dublin. He had little to say about the city, except that the women were more attractive than those in Scotland. Presently he caught the ship from Cork to Bristol. By late August he was at his parents' house in Blackheath.

During his long conversations with Lord Bury at Inverness and Fort Augustus, he must have made some telling points about the necessity for leave to go overseas. Impressed, Bury passed them on to Cumberland, and Cumberland at last gave in. The good news reached Blackheath at the end of September. Lord Bury had excelled himself. Not only had he talked the Duke out of his objections: he even enclosed a letter of introduction to his father, the Earl of Albemarle. Since the Earl was currently His Britannic Majesty's Ambassador in Paris, there could not possibly be a better way of getting into French society.

Packing up his few belongings, and after his parents had given him their customarily lavish quota of advice, James set off for Dover. At six-thirty on the morning of 4 October 1752, he embarked on the packet boat. The voyage to Calais, which took three and a half hours, was extremely rough. 'I never', he said, 'suffered so much in so short a time at sea.' However, even hell had an ending, and he eventually reached Paris in the company of two other Channel-scarred Englishmen. His first impressions of the city were that the buildings surpassed those of London, but the Tuileries were inferior to the park at Greenwich.

To a young, and presumbaly virile, man – even for one still suffering from a broken heart – the opportunities of the French capital were immense. He could polish up his knowledge of the language simply by speaking it and hearing it spoken. He could attend classes in such civilizing arts as riding, dancing, and fencing, and he would still have time for a good deal of enjoyment. He had, admittedly, not much money; but his introduction to the Ambassador should have guaranteed him plenty of invitations. To anyone else, it would, indeed, have been a pleasurable experience – but not for James. His attitude during the months he spent in Paris was prim.

While the rest of the city was entertaining itself after its fashion, James went early to bed. And, when the rest of the city was still asleep, he had already risen. He confessed in a letter home: 'My way of life that you may enquire after is very singular for a young man that appears to be in the world and in pleasure. Four or five days in the week I am up an hour before day (that is six hours sooner than any other fine gentleman in Paris), I ride, and as I told you in a former letter I fence and dance and have a master to teach me French.'

Before leaving Blackheath, he had promised his mother that he would write home at fortnightly intervals. The torrent of surviving letters shows how well he kept his word. For a period, he decided that his mastery of the French language would be improved if he neither spoke nor read nor wrote English. But, he hastened to reassure Mrs Wolfe, such a resolution would have no effect on their correspondence. 'I had rather lose this or a much greater advantage than be denied the satisfaction of expressing my regard for you in the plainest and dearest manner,' he told her.

He found that the best amusement was to be had at the opera and the playhouse, but his excitement at the performances was not nearly so great as when he caught sight of an umbrella. This very sensible invention had not yet reached England – and yet here, in Paris, the people used it 'to defend them from the sun, and something of the kind to secure them from snow and rain. I wonder a practice so useful is not introduced into England, where there are such frequent showers, and especially in the country, where they can be expanded without any inconveniency.' When, a few years later, a gentleman named Jonas Hanway was so bold as to walk through London with one of these contrivances, he received jeers and missiles from the mob. Perhaps James was wise not to bring one home as a souvenir.

The visit to the dentist, which was to be one of the highlights of his stay, was a great success. It appeared that his teeth were in much better condition than he had imagined. Two needed filling. After this modest operation, James and the surgeon had a long conversation – most of which seems to have been concerned with Mrs Wolfe's mouth. They discussed her gums, in particular, at considerable length.

His own health was seldom out of his mind. As he constantly assured his parents, 'I take great care [of it].' It was, indeed, one of the reasons why he saw so little of Parisian ladies. 'These entertainments', he wrote, 'begin at the time I go to bed, and I have not health enough to sit up all night and work all day.' He just wanted one or two hours conversation a day with 'three or four female acquaintances'. It was little enough to ask, but it seems to have been impossible. The trouble was that James Wolfe had never been, and now never would be, young at heart.

At his riding and fencing lessons, his teachers were moderately enthusiastic about his progress. Dancing was another matter. To begin with, the master doubted whether he had any natural aptitude for it. Later, he became more optimistic – though he was still uncertain whether the proposed course was long enough to achieve perfection at, say, the minuet. The standards in England were probably lower than those of the French. Whilst the Parisian expert was not prepared to say more than that James would no longer be laughed at when he took the floor, an English admirer later reported enthusiastically about his performance. 'He was generally ambitious', she wrote, 'to gain a tall, graceful woman to be his partner, as well as a good dancer; and when he was honoured with the hand of such a lady, the fierceness of the soldier was absorbed in the politeness of the gentleman.' She noticed that, on such occasions, 'such a serene joy was diffused over his whole manners, mien and deportment, that it gave a most agreeable turn to [his] features.'

When he was not studying, or at the theatre, or in bed, he was a constant guest at the Earl of Albemarle's house. The set-up there was somewhat baffling. At his town residence, His Lordship employed a staff of sixteen in the kitchen, and supplied lavish hospitality to the guests of his aides. He himself lived mostly out at Fontainebleau with his mistress. According to Horace Walpole, he received £17,000 a year from the British Government, 'which he squanders away, though he has great debts.'

Albemarle appears to have been good to James – though, heaven knows, the latter's demands were few enough. At times it must have seemed that he was trying to cut himself off from people: using them to provide the accomplishments he needed, but never really enjoying them. Even Elizabeth had now been translated into a useful experience. After brooding about her in his Parisian lodgings, he wrote to his mother: 'My amour . . . has defended me against other women.' He even went so far as to suggest that it had 'something softened the disposition to severity and rigour that I had contracted in the camp.' For those who were not thus defended, he had little but scorn. He observed that 'one terrible, frequent, and almost natural consequence of not marrying is an attachment to some woman or other that leads to a thousand inconveniences. Marshal Saxe died in the arms of a little whore that plays upon the Italian stage – an ignominious end for a conqueror.'

He sealed the letter up, blew out the candle, and climbed into bed. For James, the introspective prude, there would be no such 'inconveniences'.

Shortly after he had arrived in Paris, the young Duke of Richmond visited the city. He was, it seemed, looking for a military tutor. James was offered the job, but he turned it down. He professed that he did not consider himself 'quite equal to the task', and recommended a friend for it. When his mother wrote to him, protesting that he had refused what seemed to be a good opportunity, he flashed back a fragment of self-righteousness. 'You have known me', he told her, 'long enough to discover that I don't always prefer my own interest to that of my friends.' On the face of it, it sounds like a piece of hypocrisy. He did not wish the job, and that was that. However, he may have been irritated by his mother's constant urge to interfere.

No correspondence between the Wolfes was complete without its reference to money problems. The General was given the task of attending to this side of things. As usual, James was compelled to defend what was really a very modest style of life. The bulk of the expenditure, he explained, had gone on two suits and various accessories – a bill which 'does not exceed seventy pounds.' He pointed out that 'there are few men that live in the manner I do' and that 'the fortune of a military man seems to depend almost as much on his exteriors as upon things that are in reality more estimable and praiseworthy.' Neither remark could be denied.

The winter in Paris was almost unbelievably cold. With the spring, the French army moved into camp. Lord Albemarle decided that the Duke of Cumberland would wish a British officer to be present – and, since the Austrians and Prussians would also have troops there, James was eager to volunteer. On Albemarle's advice, he wrote to London offering his services; but he was not optimistic. He suspected that His Royal Highness would turn his application down.

When the reply came from Lord Bury, it was much more drastic than he had expected. Far from being allowed to visit the encamped foreign armies, he must come home at once. The 20th, now back in Glasgow, was, it seemed, in a fearful condition. The second-in-command was not only incompetent, but also ill (he had been seized with a fit of apoplexy). James quickly packed, and hurried home to England. By late April, after a wretchedly uncomfortable journey in one of the 'new post-chaises; machines that are purposely constructed to torture the unhappy carcases that are placed in them', he reached Glasgow. He found that the 20th was in an even worse state than Lord Bury had implied.

Shortly after James reached Glasgow, the apoplectic major died after a seizure which was violent and terrible. A few days later, an ensign was struck down with palsy, and other members of the regiment were seen to be coughing up blood. The officers were living in a state of peevish poverty, and the other ranks were in equally dire straits. But this disastrous chapter of ill health was not over. By the middle of the following month, the 20th succumbed to another complaint, which removed the skin from the soldiers' faces. James was a victim of it, too, though not so severely as the others. The one bright thing in his life at this time was the arrival of a pointer from his cousin, Edward Goldsmith. In his list of likeable creatures, dogs and horses came some way higher than humans.

There was no time for sympathy. The demoralized soldiers had to be brought back to a reasonable state of efficiency as quickly as possible. For those who were fit enough, drill parades followed one another in a seemingly endless succession. Discipline was tightened up, and James excelled himself as a martinet. Presently the regiment began to look like a body of soldiers once more. Later, the third Duke of Marlborough remarked that it was 'the best drilled and disciplined in the Kingdom'. But, or so the months when James was in Paris suggested, it could keep up this standard only if he was with them.

Just as they were perfecting their performances on the parade ground, Lord Bury suddenly made one of his few interferences. The drill movements had always been executed in quick time. While James had been on leave, His Lordship had received a commendation from the King on the regiment's behaviour in the Highlands. He was suitably gratified, and began to wonder what else they could do to distinguish themselves. The answer, he decided, was to change the tempo. Everything, Bury insisted, was now to be carried out in very slow time. Since the 20th was about to be reviewed by a visiting general, and there were not enough hours in which to practise the new routine, James was exasperated. However, thankfully, the general fell ill, and the ceremonial parade did not take place.

At last the 20th's term of duty in Scotland was coming to an end. Britain's relationship with France was deteriorating once more, and the south-east coast of England was vulnerable to a sudden invasion. In mid-September, the regiment marched away from the dreaded Glasgow on a long journey which, by way of Warwick and Reading, eventually took them to Dover. Cumberland should have reviewed them at Reading; but he, too, fell sick. It was just as well, for the men were still wearing old uniforms which, in some cases, were near to rags.

As they plodded along the road to Dover, six companies were detached to form a garrison at Maidstone. James's headquarters were in Dover Castle, which was dilapidated and cold. The kindest description he could find for it was 'this vile dungeon'. The invasion threat never materialized, and the troops had to employ such zeal as they had by looking out for smugglers. At one time, James believed that the task would be carried out better if the soldiers were deployed along the coastlines. But then he decided that it would be ineffectual. 'The villainy of the smugglers', he wrote, 'would overcome all precautions.'

In spite of the fact that he considered 'there is not in the King's dominions a more melancholy dreadful station' than Dover, his health was better at this time, and the regiment enjoyed a pleasant social life in the town. But, in James's view, nothing should be undertaken without some serious purpose in mind. His belief even extended to entertainment. 'I always encourage our young people to frequent balls and assemblies,' he wrote. 'It softens their manners, and makes 'em more civil.' To ensure that they behaved themselves, he went along to keep a fatherly eye on the subalterns. He was also concerned to make sure that the younger officers did not fall in love and marry. 'Whenever I perceive the symptoms, or anyone else makes the discovery', he told his mother, 'we fall upon the delinquent without mercy, till he grows out of his conceit and new passion.'

He was now twenty-seven. Still haunted by his overpowering ambition, he was worried that, stationed away from London, he was becoming forgotten. Whatever doubts he may have had in life, the question of his own ability never figured among them. It was high time, he decided, that he was given the colonelcy of a regiment. Unfortunately, the authorities were not of the same mind. He had been made a lieutenant-colonel at an age when many officers were still subalterns. Consequently, able though he no doubt was, he had no cause for complaint. He would have to be patient.

From Dover, the regiment moved to Exeter. They arrived there at the beginning of October 1754. If they had expected a friendly welcome from the inhabitants, they were to be disappointed. Exeter was only marginally less pro-Jacobite in its convictions that Inverness. For some time the soldiers had to suffer the sneers and, in some instances, hatred of the people. But James was as much diplomat as he was soldier. As in Inverness, he set out to win affection – and, once more, he succeeded. The arena for this battle by charm was again the dance floor. On one occasion, the regiment put on a modest ball, which must have produced a good deal of acrimony in Exeter homes. The women all turned up; the men, in a bid to snub Wolfe and his officers, stayed away. However, he was presently able to tell his mother: 'Would you believe it that no Devonshire squire dances more than I do?' He had, he informed her, 'danced the officers into the good graces of the Jacobite women hereabouts, who were prejudiced against them.' Entry into the men's good graces followed. A few weeks later, he was able to report: 'The Right Worshipful the Mayor of Exeter and myself are hand in glove.'

Although he was tolerably fit at this time, a letter written in the middle of January 1753 must have worried his mother. He had been to Bristol to serve on a court martial. When writing about the experience, he told her: 'Folks are surprised to see the meagre, consumptive figure of the son. . . . The campaigns of 1743, '4, '5, '6, and '7, stripped me of my bloom, and the winters in Scotland and at Dover have brought me also to old age and infirmity, and this without any remarkable intemperance.' Later in the letter, he again suggests his foreboding that he was not destined to live for very long. 'I am', he observed, 'perhaps somewhat nearer my end than others of my time.' Although he was obviously delicate, his maladies had not been especially serious. Gravel was a common enough ailment, and since he had taken the cure at Peterhead there had been no recurrence. The state of the medical art was not far enough advanced to make any prognosis for the future, and even the most thorough examination would have produced nothing more than superficial results. Nevertheless, the expectation of an early death was nearly always with him. Doubtless it was one of the reasons why he was impatient to achieve high rank.

In spite of the breakdown of his romance with Elizabeth, he remained on friendly terms with her uncle, General Sir John

Mordaunt. While the 20th was stationed at Exeter, James took some leave, and during the course of it discussed his future with the General. The conversation was not encouraging. Lord Bury was clearly soon to move on; indeed, he had been promised the next cavalry regiment that became available. But, if James hoped to succeed him as colonel of the 20th, he was likely to be disappointed. 'Another colonel of rank or quality or Parliamentary merit' would probably get the regiment. The majority of lieutenant-colonels had either reached the peak of their ambitions, or else they were prepared to wait for promotion without grumbling. James would be well advised to do the same. However, Sir John promised to use what influence he could on the young man's behalf.

After the War of Austrian Succession, the Marines had been disbanded once more. Nevertheless, the Navy needed soldiers to fight beside them, and for a while it seemed as if the 20th were likely to be given this role. Rumours about their probable destination varied from day to day. Virginia in North America, Minorca, or simply 'to cruise', were among them. Back at Blackheath, the old General was nothing if not articulate in his opposition to any such idea. His experiences in the West Indies had given him a considerable mistrust of any combined operation between the two services. James was less inclined to worry, and he even overcame his dread of seasickness. As he cheerfully observed, 'the sickness that we feel at first will soon be over.' There was no harm in hoping – in any case, the project died of inertia, and the 20th was left to wander round the southern counties of England. Nevertheless, in James's mind, it had been a close thing. He had even been at pains to give Mrs Wolfe instructions for the disposal of his dogs.

The period was one of profound anticlimax. Instead of travelling to battle on some distant island, they went to Winchester. In December 1754, the Earl of Albemarle died, and Lord Bury, having inherited the title, was given the 1st Regiment of Dragoons. But James, as Sir John Mordaunt had hinted, was not vouchsafed the 20th Regiment of Foot. The colonelcy was handed over to an undistinguished officer named Philip Honeywood. As might have been expected, James was outraged. If, in future, anyone were promoted over his head, he promised to resign his commission. 'I am resolved', he wrote, 'I shan't serve one moment longer than I can do it with honour, if I should starve.' However, Honeywood seems to have been a likeable enough man, and there were diversions – such as the sight of twenty-eight British men-of-war anchored in Spithead. James was invited to dine on board one of them as the guest of Lord Anson. He was impressed. He considered that this assembly of ships was 'more formidable than the fleet of England ever was [before].'

His admiration did not extend to the British infantryman. Although, in Europe there had been peace of a kind between Britain and France since 1748, the two countries were more or less constantly at each other's throats in India and North America. In the summer of 1755, General Braddock and his men received a thorough thrashing from French colonial forces in a wood near Fort Duquesne (now Pittsburg) in North America. When James heard about it, he was moderately critical of Braddock, violently so of his men. 'I have', he wrote, 'but a very mean opinion of the Infantry in general. I know their discipline to be bad, and their valour precarious. They are easily put into disorder, and hard to recover out of it. They frequently kill their officers through fear, and murder one another in their confusion.' He was echoing the views of a writer in the *Scots Magazine,* who reported: 'It is stated that the greatest slaughter among our officers [at Fort Duquesne] was not made by the enemy; but that as they ran several fugitives through to intimidate the rest, when they attempted in vain to rally them, some others, who escaped the same fate, discharged their pieces at the officers.'

The outbreak of the Seven Years War in May 1756 came as a surprise to nobody. The epidemic of invasion fever that preceded it was, in some places, little short of hysterical. When a wedding procession passed through one village, the word went round that the French had landed. The inhabitants ran to their homes in terror, and armed themselves with pitchforks. James Wolfe underwent a more restrained fit of anxiety. Assuming that both he and his father would be killed in the hostilities, he unleashed a string of letters to the General, discussing how they could best make provision for the apparently about-to-be-widowed Mrs Wolfe.

But the era of the anti-climax continued. Instead of being posted to Europe to fight the French, the 20th was sent to Devizes in Wiltshire. Their most serious engagement occurred a few months later, when they were dispatched to Stroud with some units from the Buffs. The enemy was a party of weavers who had come out on strike for better pay. The soldiers were told that they could take up arms if need be; but, since the wretched weavers were half starved, such martial action was unnecessary. Indeed, James saw the occasion as an opportunity to enlist recruits. 'The people', he wrote, 'are so oppressed, so poor and so wretched, that they will perhaps hazard a knock on the gate for bread and clothes, and turn soldiers through sheer necessity.'

Colonel Honeywood went to the earthly heaven of all good colonels – a cavalry regiment. His place was taken by an officer named William Kingsley. Once again, James had been overlooked. According to his earlier threat, this should have been his cue to resign. But the country was at war, and such a course was out of the question. He would have to suffer in silence. For one of the few times in his life, he succeeded.

The training of young officers was one of his constant concerns. A gentleman, whose younger brother was about to join the Army, asked him what subjects the youngster should study. James assumed that the lad had a good grounding in French and Latin, and that he had some knowledge of mathematics. Without it, he could not hope to master the construction of fortifications, nor could he become proficient in the science of defence and attack. He then recommended about a dozen books ranging from the *King of Prussia's Regulations for his Horse and Foot* to the *Life of Suetonius*. Several French works were included in the list, and one or two biographies. He admitted that the aspiring officer would probably 'think this catalogue long enough,' but: 'If he has the patience to read, and desire to apply (as I am persuaded he has), the knowledge contained in them, there is also wherewithal to make him a considerable person in his profession.'

To another correspondent who sought his advice on this matter, he made it clear that 'In the army, as well as in other professions, learning is absolutely necessary, and a year or two of improvement is better than one with the insignificant duty of the capital.' He might have added that the 'army' he referred to existed mostly in his imagination. Many officers got by with very little education.

On the face of it, his struggle for promotion was having disappointing results. Behind the scenes at Court, however, there were a number of people trying to advance the cause of this ambitious and unusually promising officer. One of them was an old friend of his father, the Duke of Bedford. His Grace had recently been appointed Lord-Lieutenant of Ireland. On 6 February 1757, James received a letter from the nobleman's secretary. It offered him the joint positions of Barrack-Master General and Quarter Master General in Ireland. James agreed to consider the appointments – but without very much enthusiasm. If he were to carry out the functions, he insisted that he should be given the rank of colonel. Without it he told his father, 'I shall give it up immediately and come back to the battalion.'

The King, supposedly on the advice of the Duke of Cumberland, refused to promote him. Lieutenant-Colonel Wolfe, he said, was too young. If he were made a colonel, he would receive preference over many of his seniors, and this was not to be countenanced. The fact that the monarch had given his own son the rank of major-general at the age of twenty-two seemed to be of no relevance. Shortly afterwards, James went with the Duke to a royal levée in London. During the course of it, he was permitted the doubtful pleasure of kissing the King's hand. Awed by the sovereign's proximity, he contained his fury.

But he did not have much time for recriminations. The 20th was still stationed in Gloucestershire, and there was much work to be done. Now that the country was at war, the regiment's strength was to be doubled by the formation of a second battalion. At a somewhat higher level, events were taking place which were to have a marked effect on James's career. After a period of eleven weeks, during which the nation had been virtually without a government, King George II was compelled to reinstate William Pitt (later Earl of Chatham) as Secretary of State. Pitt, unlike his sovereign, was full of ideas; and the war began to stir itself from a state of torpid inactivity. Among the projects conceived by this vigorous statesman was that of striking a blow at the French coast.

9
THE RAID THAT FAILED

On 6 April 1757, the Duke of Cumberland left London for Hanover to command the Electorate's troops against an expected French attack. The army in Britain was taken over by Field Marshal Lord Ligonier. It was, as Ligonier was compelled to admit, an ill balanced instrument of war. The junior officers and the rank and file were considered to be second to none in the world. Unfortunately, there was a fearful paucity of good generals.

Pitt believed that the proposed expedition to the French coast would create a diversion, and take the enemy pressure off Hanover and Prussia. According to his intelligence sources, the operation should not be difficult. France had an inconsiderable fleet; the country's finances were in bad shape; and the greater part of her army (150,000 men) was deployed on her eastern frontier. Only ten thousand soldiers were left to guard the entire length of the Channel and Bay of Biscay coasts. Furthermore, from Pitt's point of view, the selection of a suitable target was made easier by a report which had recently been submitted by a Captain Clarke. Clarke had returned to England from France shortly before war broke out. During the course of his travels, he had visited Rochefort, where he had diligently inspected the military installations. He discovered that the town contained a large arsenal of arms and ammunition, and yet it was comparatively lightly guarded. Indeed, the antiquated fortress was crumbling in many places and was in obvious need of repair.

From Captain Clarke's information, Pitt concluded that Rochefort would be the perfect objective for a combined operation – organized on similar lines to that of a latter day commando raid. If it was to achieve its purpose, it should be carried out at once. He ordered Lord Anson, who was at the head of the

Admiralty, to have the fleet ready by a date in July. Anson demurred; it was, he said, impossible. Pitt flew into a fury. If the Admiral did not meet his deadline, he said, he would report matters to the King – and see that he was impeached in Parliament. The threat sufficed. Anson promised to have the vessels ready.

By mid-July, plans for the expedition were almost complete. The ships were ordered to take on supplies for six months; and, to bring their crews up to strength, a large number of sailors were impressed. Two thousand were taken from the Thames alone. Scaling ladders were constructed. They were so designed that they were easy to erect and each could accommodate thirty men climbing abreast. Every transport had to be equipped with ten boats, capable of carrying thirty soldiers apiece. All told, the fighting strength of the fleet was sixteen ships of the line, plus a number of frigates, fireships and bomb-ketches. The landing party was to be made up of ten infantry regiments, fifty light horse, and a contingent of gunners – amounting to ten thousand men. It was almost exactly the number of soldiers who were strung out along the entire French coastline.

So far everything had gone without a hitch. But now the difficult part arose. Who was going to take charge of the military side of the expedition? Initially, Pitt offered the command to Lord George Sackville, but he turned it down. Next, Major-General the Honourable H. S. Conway was considered. The King rejected the idea. Conway, he said, was too young. His Majesty may also have taken into consideration the fact that the Major-General was a cold and haughty character who was cordially disliked by almost every officer and other rank with whom he came into contact. Finally, for want of anyone better, Lieutenant-General Sir John Mordaunt (Elizabeth Lawson's uncle) was approached. Sir John agreed, but the choice was disastrous. In his younger days he had been a brave and thrusting officer. Now, at sixty, he was a prematurely old man, given to spasms of nervous irritability and almost incapable of making a decision. As some contemporary wit said of the expedition, it had everything except a general. Admiral Sir Edward Hawke was to command the naval force, and there were no doubts about his ability. He had long shown himself to be an excellent seaman.

Mordaunt, then, was commander-in-chief of the land forces. Conway – and George II presumably did not object to this – was appointed second-in-command; and Edward Cornwallis (the former colonel of the 20th) was third-in-command. The post of Quarter Master General was given to James Wolfe. James was told about it by Pitt at an interview in London. He was, however, given no details of the expedition's destination – nor, indeed was anybody else outside the high command. Pitt was making sure that maximum security was observed. He even insisted that the orders should not be opened and broadcast to the officers until the fleet had been at sea for a week.

James had no doubts about his ability to carry out his new duties. As Horace Walpole observed: 'The world could not expect more from him than he thought himself capable of performing.' But, once he was down at Newport, Isle of Wight, and watching the ships assembling, he may have had misgivings about the voyage. They were to be amply justified.

By 10 August, the army was prepared to embark but the transports were not ready. While they waited, the time passed pleasantly enough. James told his mother: 'We have much company, much exercise, a theatre, and all the camp amusements, besides balls and concerts.' Eventually the troopships turned up, but then the weather became bad. One adverse wind after another roared up the Channel, and it was not until 7 September that the conditions were suitable. A week later, Sir John Mordaunt opened the sealed orders. 'You are', the text read, 'to attempt, as far as shall be found practicable, a descent with the forces under your command, on the French coast, at or near Rochefort; in order to attack, if practicable, and by a vigorous impression force that place; and to burn and destroy, to the utmost of your power, all Docks, Magazines, Arsenal and Shipping that may be found there; and exert such other efforts as you may judge proper for annoying the enemy.'

The voyage was long and tedious. At times the ships were becalmed, at others held up by fog. But even though he was able to describe the Bay of Biscay as 'smoothe as the Thames in winter', James was dreadfully ill for most of the time. 'I have not', he wrote to his mother as he suffered his nauseous ordeal in HMS *Ramillies*, 'been one hour well since we embarked, and have the mortification to find that I am the worst mariner in the whole ship. General, secretary, and aides-de-camp are all stouter, all better seamen than myself.' The troops, it seemed, were in particularly good order, and seemed to be thriving on life at sea.

On 20 September, the fleet made a landfall off the Ile de Ré. Vice-Admiral Knowles and his squadron were sent off along the channel which divides it from the Ile d'Oléron, to examine its possibilities as an anchorage. At about the same time, a large French warship, homeward bound from the Indies (nobody seems to have been sure whether they were the West or the East) was sighted. Three of the British vessels were detached to intercept her, but the Frenchman escaped. Shortly afterwards, Knowles reported back to Admiral Hawkes that conditions were entirely suitable.

At low tide, this area of the French coast looks as if the sea has rolled away into the Bay of Biscay. Channels of water, which are littered with mud banks, carve it up with a pattern of islands. Each is a small desert of soft sand capped with tough whip-like grass. The Ile de Ré and the Ile d'Oléron are like a couple of outposts. Once the lane in between clears their most easterly points, it swells out into the Rade des Basques, which resembles an enormous lagoon. La Rochelle lies on the coast at one end, facing the Ile de Ré. Rochefort, tucked away up the Charente river, is at the other. It is protected by two more islands: the Ile d'Aix and the small Ile Madame.

If the attack was not launched at once, the careful security precautions would be valueless. But these were sailing ships dependent on the wind. Just as it had delayed their departure from the Isle of Wight, so did it frustrate them now. When the leading vessels were making for the channel, it suddenly veered and increased in strength. Everything had to be postponed for another day. The date was 21 September. On the twenty-second, the ships managed to reach the anchorage, but then the wind dropped completely. By now the inhabitants of the coast were thoroughly alarmed. There was spasmodic gunfire, and one or two columns of smoke rose up. They were, presumably, signals. And the surrounding water glistened in the early autumn sunshine like glass tinted a soft brown.

By the afternoon of the twenty-third, the wind changed again. Nudged forward by a light breeze, HMS *Magnanime* penetrated into the Rade des Basques until her guns were able to bear on the small fortress that capped the Ile d'Aix. After a bombardment lasting thirty-five minutes, a detachment of infantry was landed; but the matter was already resolved. The fort's five hundred men capitulated with only small casualties. Thirty pieces of cannon and eight mortars were abandoned in perfect condition – few of them had been fired. It might have seemed to be a good omen.

With the citadel on the Ile d'Aix out of action, the road was clear for the next part of the operation. Unfortunately, the only person who seemed prepared to do anything about it was James Wolfe. Just as the *Magnanime*'s bombardment was reaching its climax, he asked Mordaunt for permission to go ashore on the island. The commander-in-chief agreed. Taking a telescope with him, James clambered into a boat. By one pm, he was climbing to the top of the fort's ramparts. He was well rewarded: the vantage point gave him an excellent view of the mainland. He noticed that another fort, perched on a thin tongue of land, guarded the entrance to the Charente. That, too, would have to be put out of action. It was, on the other hand, only a small construction. He doubted whether it contained more than six guns.

It was clearly impossible to navigate a naval task force of such a size up the narrow winding river to the town. The men would have to be put ashore on some suitable and convenient beach. Scanning the shore with his telescope, James noticed what seemed to meet the requirements about midway between La Rochelle and Rochefort. The only difficulty was that there was a short cliff with a mass of sand dunes on top of it. He estimated that a force of about one thousand foot soldiers and three or four hundred horses could hold off the invasion. But, according to intelligence reports, the French had nothing like this number. In spite of its military importance, Rochefort was garrisoned by only a few hundred troops, and their morale was poor. Most of them were Huguenots, whose Protestant faith tended to make them more sympathetic to the English than to the Catholic throne of France.

When he was back on board the flagship, James went to see Mordaunt at once. The plan he proposed was a sensible one. The first action, he suggested, should be to neutralize the fort on the headland. One man-of-war would suffice for the job. Once this had been done, the main force could move towards the beach-head. Simultaneously, the bomb-ketches should be dispatched in the direction of La Rochelle to create a diversion. Mordaunt was guardedly enthusiastic; Hawke thought the plan excellent. The operation, he said, should be put in hand at once – provided there was enough water for the ships. The pilot of the *Magnanime* assured him that there would be.

But Mordaunt now succumbed to vague misgivings. It would be a mistake, he said, to do anything in a hurry. The matter must be discussed at greater length. He called a conference for the following day. In the meanwhile, a rear-admiral and three captains were sent off to take a closer look at the mainland. They confirmed the pilot's view: the landing was possible.

The conference stretched itself out through the morning and then into the depths of the afternoon. Through the cabin windows, they watched the tide peeling the water off the sand banks close to the shore; and then, on the flood, replacing it. And the talk droned on and on. Out of it came a number of objections which became magnified in Mordaunt's mind. What would happen if the opposition turned out to be greater than they had expected, and the weather deteriorated? With a strong wind, the swell and the breakers would make it impossible to re-embark the troops. What was more, the warships would be unable to get within range of the shore. The soldiers could expect no support from their guns. To put a final blight on James's plan, Mordaunt pointed out that the element of surprise had long disappeared. Since the fleet had first been observed, there had been ample time for the French to reinforce the Rochefort garrison.

Two more days were wasted in what were described as 'mature deliberations'. Then Mordaunt suddenly changed his mind. The raid should go ahead as quickly as possible. At midnight on the twenty-eighth, the troops were put into the boats. For the next few hours they remained in the area of the anchorage, tossed about uncomfortably by the swell. At about three am, a cutter sailed into the midst of the armada of landing craft. Her captain had orders for the colonel in charge. The soldiers were to return to the ships at once. At first the officer could not believe it. 'Show me your instructions,' he demanded. The written evidence was produced, and the troops went back to the transports.

Precisely why this sudden change of heart occurred is uncertain. According to Admiral Hawke, the generals had suddenly become afraid of putting the men ashore in the dark – without being able to have (as Hawke remarked afterwards) 'a full view of the ground where they had to land.' Mordaunt's story was different. He blamed the Navy. He asserted that a strong wind had suddenly sprung up from the direction of the coast. The sailors, he said, had told him that, under these circumstances, it would be impossible to carry out the plan. The boats would take too long to reach the beach-head; and, even then, the whole force could not be landed at once.

Whichever version is true, there is no doubt about the outcome. Early on the twenty-ninth, Hawke sent Mordaunt a short and sharp letter. All this wasted time was keeping a sizeable portion of the fleet holed up in a corner of the French coast to no apparent purpose. Unless Mordaunt had something constructive to suggest, he would have no alternative but to return to England. Mordaunt's indecisiveness continued. Couldn't they meet again to discuss the matter at great length? Hawke refused. Simple seamen, he told the General, were no fit judges of what could or could not be carried out on shore. Mordaunt acquiesced. The capstans were manned by sweating tars; the anchor chains rattled on to the decks; and, one by one, the sails unfurled. The expedition which was to have wrought havoc to the French seaboard set sail for England. The sole accomplishment of an operation which had cost something like £1 million had been the destruction of an unimportant fortress.

James was furious. He told his father: 'We lost the lucky moment in war and were not able to recover it.' In another letter, he wrote that the operation had 'been conducted so ill that I am ashamed to have been of the party. The public could not do better than dismiss six or eight of us from the service. No zeal, no ardour, no care or concern for the good and honour of the country.' The authorities took a similar view. Out of the whole fiasco, only two officers, they decided, had emerged with any credit. One of them was Captain Howe, the commanding officer of the *Magnanime*. The other was James Wolfe. A court of inquiry was immediately assembled to investigate the unhappy saga of indecision and faulty judgement. The Duke of Marlborough, Lord George Sackville, and a major-general named Waldegrave, were appointed to sit on it. On 9 November they began their deliberations; on the fourteenth James gave his evidence; and on the twenty-first the findings were published. They had decided that Mordaunt was to blame and suggested that the unhappy general should be court-martialled.

But Mordaunt was now a sick man, and James doubted whether he would be able to sit through the humiliating experience. The court appears to have been merciful. They took the state of his health into consideration and – ever loyal to the service – they expressed doubt about whether he had received sufficient help from the Navy. He was acquitted and left to moulder in retirement. As it happened, he was not the only senior officer to be discredited at the time. The braggart Duke of Cumberland had been out-generalled by the French in Hanover. His forces had been cut to pieces, and the Electorate was now in the hands of the enemy. To the man in the English street, there seemed to be nobody left to lead the Army. As ever, the public wanted a hero. With the possible exception of James Wolfe, whose conduct on the Rochefort expedition had impressed everybody, there was nobody.

If James had made a name for himself at last, the fact must have escaped him. It was a miserable homecoming. Mrs Wolfe had succumbed to one of her maladies, and had gone off to Bath with her husband to take the cure. Before joing them, James rested at the house at Blackheath. He was out of condition from being confined aboard ship for so long; disgusted at the expedition; and thoroughly angry at his treatment by the Army. During his absence, he discovered, an officer some years younger than himself had been promoted to colonel. So much for the King's objections to his own advancement! He sat down and wrote a tart letter to Lord Barrington, the Secretary at War. In view of what had happened, he said, he wished to be excused duties as Quarter Master General in Ireland. All that remained, it seemed, was to return to the 20th.

At about the same time, he also wrote to his friend Rickson. Recollecting in tranquillity, he decided that the trip to the west coast of France had not been an utter waste of time. 'One may always', he observed, 'pick up something useful from amongst the most fatal errors.' In this instance, the lesson he had learned was that, in any combined operation, speed was a vital factor:

> I have found out that an admiral should endeavour to run into an enemy's port immediately after he appears before it; that he should anchor the transport ships as close as he can to the land; that he should reconnoitre and observe it as quick as possible, and lose no time in getting his troops on shore; that previous directions should be given in respect to landing the troops, and a proper disposition made for the boats of all sorts, appointing leaders and fit persons for conducting the different divisions. On the other hand, experience shows me that, in an affair depending on vigour and dispatch, the generals should settle their plan of operations, so that no time may be lost in idle debate and consultations when the sword should be drawn; that pushing on smartly is the road to success, and more particularly so in an affair of this nature.

He also remarked that 'in particular circumstances and times, the loss of a thousand men is rather an advantage to a nation than otherwise, seeing that gallant attempts raise its reputation and make it respectable.'

James was the son of a marine. His first commission had been in a marine regiment, but he had never served with it. All his career so far had been with foot regiments, and yet he now revealed an instinctive knowledge of combined naval and military operations. It was, perhaps, remarkable, especially since, after the West Indies expedition, his father had been thoroughly disenchanted with this form of warfare. But James Wolfe seldom borrowed the opinions of other people. With his enviable ability to size up a situation quickly, and to draw instant and very clear conclusions, he was perfectly capable of forming his own ideas. The time was now approaching when people would listen to them.

His career prospects were not nearly so bad as he had expected. Instead of politely acknowledging his letter of resignation, Lord Barrington asked him to delay his decision for a week. Although James was unaware of it, Admiral Hawke had been praising his conduct on the Rochefort affair to Lord Anson, and Anson had passed on the comments to the King. George II reconsidered his earlier verdict. Such a talented officer should not be neglected. The recently formed second battalion of the 20th must be turned into a new regiment. It became the 67th Foot (later, the Hampshires) and it was given to James Wolfe. On 21 October, he was promoted to the rank of brevet colonel. Later in the year, he was called before the Prince of Wales (later George III). It seemed that His Royal Highness had read the findings of the court of enquiry, and had observed that the failure of the Rochefort expedition was attributed to the fact that Wolfe's plan had not been carried out. He wanted to know more about it. During the course of the conversation, the subject of the 20th cropped up. How, the Prince wondered, had he managed to drill them into such an exceptional regiment? James described his methods, and added that 'there was in the corps a necessary degree of obedience, joined with high spirit of service and love of duty.' His Highness, James told one of the officers in his new command, was 'greatly pleased, knowing well that from good indications, joined with order and discipline, great military performances usually spring.'

At last he was content. When he heard about his promotion, he remarked that his new rank was 'at this time ... more to be prized than at any other, because it carries with it a favourable appearance as to my conduct upon this late expedition, and an acceptance of my good intentions.' In this happy frame of mind he set off for Bath, where he was to spend Christmas with his parents. It was a brief interlude in which relaxation was probably combined with the birth of a new romance. But then, in early January, he was summoned to London. The Commander-in-

Chief of the Army had another assignment for him and one which was to be far more testing than the Rochefort experience. At the age of thirty, James Wolfe had less than two years of life ahead of him. But these were to be more eventful than anything which had gone before.

Part II
THE GLORY

10

THE FIRST JOURNEY WESTWARDS

In the eighteenth century, war between Britain and France was a series of eruptions – some of which lasted for longer than either wanted. In North America, it was more or less continuous. The opponents were in marked contrast to each other. French settlers were, on the whole, an adventurous people. Many of them were trappers and hunters. They were skilled in the use of arms; experts in fieldcraft; and fiercely independent. The English, on the other hand, were more domesticated. They were farmers and traders who, when things went wrong, looked anxiously to the mother country for help. They regarded the Red Indians as savages, whilst the French made an attempt to reach terms with them. Consequently, the tribesmen were, with the exception of the Iroquois, on the French side. Most of the men had been reared as warriors; they were brutal and effective.

The British were in possession of New York and Boston on the coastline; the French held Quebec in the north and New Orleans in the south. After the defeat of Braddock at Fort Duquesne, they planned to construct a chain of forts running from Lake Ontario to Louisiana. Since they already controlled most of the country to the west of the Allegheny Mountains, there seemed to be no reason why the settlers in Canada should not link up with their compatriots on the Mississippi. The French flag would fly over the huge hinterland of the continent; the British would be pushed out of their towns and villages; those who survived would have to struggle back across the ocean to England.

When Pitt returned to power, he became absorbed by the problems in North America. Unless the French ambitions were contained, the scattering of Union Jacks on the map would rapidly be removed. The war in Europe would have to take care of itself. Pitt's ambitions lay on the other side of the North

Atlantic. Nor did they stop at halting French expansion: he proposed to launch a full scale invasion. One factor favoured the idea from the very outset. Whilst the French fleet had only sixty-three ships of the line, and whilst, of this number, only forty-five were in a seaworthy condition, the Royal Navy's score of heavyweights amounted to 130. Even if Spain threw in her fortunes with France, which seemed likely, the event would add no more than forty-six more vessels to the French score. In maritime terms, it could hardly be considered as a threat.

The key to so many things was the St Lawrence River. It was the highway to Quebec and, thence, to Lake Ontario. Whoever controlled it would be in an excellent position to attack the line of French forts which groped southwards. But, as a preliminary, the garrison at Louisburg on Cape Breton Island would have to be knocked out. For a sizable portion of the year, the St Lawrence defended itself against invading navies by becoming icebound. When the temperature rose and the waterway became navigable once more, Louisburg took over this responsibility. As a naval base, it was perfect. It provided a natural harbour, and the vessels stationed there were well placed to protect the Gulf of St Lawrence against intruders.

Apart from its strategic position, there was little to be said on behalf of Louisburg. The climate was foul: a hideous mixture of cold, high winds, and fog. The coastline of Cape Breton Island was littered with rocks; the interior was rough and, in many cases, swampy. As for the town itself, it served as a base for the cod fishing industry. According to an observer in 1758, the residential district consisted of 'narrow, stinking *Lanes* they call *Streets*. There is hardly a tolerable *House* in it, besides those of the Governor and Intendant, that are built of Stone or Brick without any elegance.' However, he was prepared to concede that the hospital, the nunnery, and the powder magazine, were better than the rest. As for the barracks, the building had been erected by the British during a brief occupation, which began in 1745, and ended with the Treaty of Aix la Chapelle, when the town was exchanged for Madras in India. It was said, quite wrongly, to be bomb-proof. All told, Louisburg had a circumference of about two miles. It was inhabited by 4,000 civilians and 3,000 troops under the governorship of a determined and patriotic administrator named the Chevalier de Drucour.

But before Pitt could embark on his master plan, he had to infuse some enthusiasm into the British colonists. His first action was to recall the commander-in-chief, an inexpert soldier named the Earl of Loudoun. Quite apart from the fact that Loudoun was no match for his French opposite number – the thoroughly professional Marquis de Montcalm – he had a singular knack of exasperating the settlers. They not only lacked confidence in him: they seldom so much as *saw* him. Had he emerged from his plush lair more often, and made some attempt to understand their points of view, he might have been more successful. But Loudoun was an inept snob, a man who, as Pitt so quickly grasped, was totally unsuitable for his role.

To replace Loudoun, Major-General James Abercrombie was dispatched across the Atlantic. As an example of military genius, Abercrombie was little better than his predecessor; but, as Pitt was rapidly discovering, talented generals were about as rare as albatrosses in Britain. However, the newcomer's duties were carefully defined in Whitehall. He was not given the task of creating policy, but simply of doing what the Government (which meant Pitt) told him. Even the details of his forces were worked out for him: he took what regular troops he was given, and, to be fair to him, his army was seriously under strength for most of the time.

Pitt now turned his attention to Louisburg. To his way of thinking, there was only one military commander fit to take charge of such an expedition – a colonel named Jeffrey Amherst, who was currently serving on the Continent. Amherst was summoned to London, and given the rank of major-general. Elderly generals who might have hoped for the position grumbled about the appointment of a relatively junior officer who was only forty-one years old. Pitt was not interested. If his search for talent could be satisfied only from the ranks of younger men, there was nothing more to say. The war, after all, was not being fought for the benefit of veterans who snoozed through the twilight of their lives in the clubs around St James's Palace. Since Pitt himself was only fifty at the time, his attitude was not surprising. What was more, he was succeeding where elder politicians had failed. England, as well as the American colonies, was at last being shaken from a fearful lethargy, which may have been full of pious hopes, but which was woefully lacking in action.

Admiral Boscawen, a seaman who had seen plenty of action and who had shown himself to be courageous, was given command of the fleet. The expedition was due to sail from Portsmouth for Halifax in early February. Once off the coast of Canada, it would link up with a force of warships commanded by Vice-Admiral Sir Charles Hardy. The object was to begin the invasion in June, after the ice had broken up.

Amherst's army was to consist of three infantry brigades supported by engineers and artillery. One of them was given to an officer named Edward Whitmore, who was probably the oldest man in the force. The second was entrusted to Charles Lawrence – currently Governor of Nova Scotia and consequently already on the spot. The third brigade, on Pitt's insistence, was put in the care of James Wolfe. Wolfe was also to act as second-in-command to Amherst during the operation. The lesson of Rochefort had evidently been absorbed – especially by Pitt, who would certainly have advocated an action similar to that outlined in James's report.

When the expedition was being planned, and Amherst was on his way back from Germany, James was with his parents in Bath. He was worried about their health, but his visit to the spa was made tolerable by a young lady who was staying in the house next door. Her name was Kathleen Lowther. She was a girl of good looks, whose father had been governor of the Barbadoes. At the beginning of January, James returned to duty in Exeter; but this, too, was for only a short period. On the eighth of the month, he was called to London and told about his new responsibilities. Two weeks later, he was given the rank of brigadier-general; and, at about the same time, he resigned his appointment as Quartermaster General in Ireland. He had held the position for ten months without ever actually carrying out any of the duties. He not unreasonably remarked to the Duke of Bedford in his letter of resignation: 'It is a mortification to have been so long in that office and so useless.'

Henrietta Wolfe, James's mother. Edward III was one of her ancestors. Her attitude to marriage and motherhood was essentially regal

James Wolfe as a young man. He was commissioned in the Army at the age of fourteen: by the time he was seventeen, he had become his regiment's adjutant

Above James fought at the Battle of Culloden as ADC to General Hawley. In his opinion, the general fought 'with wonderful spirit'. Of his own performance, he had nothing to say

The Duke of Cumberland: a recurring hazard in James Wolfe's military career

A soldier in the 20th

Glasgow in the mid-eighteenth century. While he was stationed there, James made good the gaps in his education

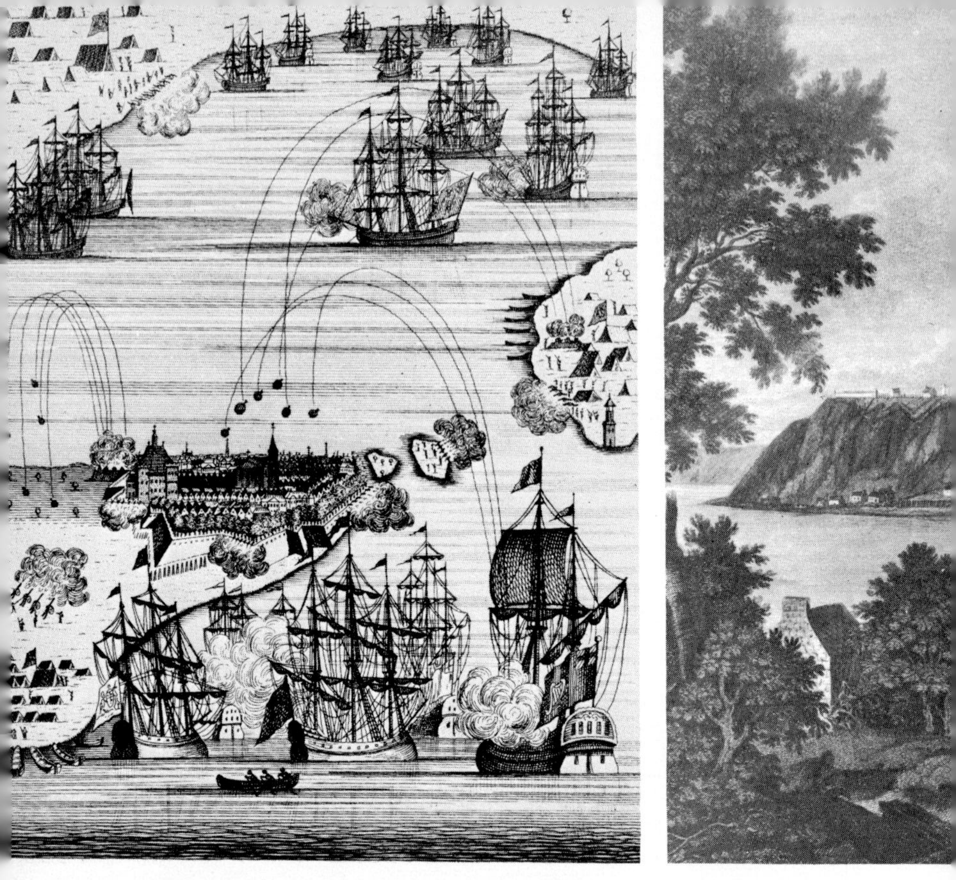

The siege of Louisburg, as seen by a contemporary artist. Most of James Wolfe's troops were encamped on the headland at the right of the picture

Boats of the Royal Navy raided Louisburg harbour: captured one ship and set fire to another

A view of Quebec from Point Levis. The capture of this promontory enabled the British guns to bombard the city

In an attempt to destroy the British fleet, the French sent an armada of fire ships down river by night

to Isaac Barré
from his friend
Geo: Townshend

Opposite Brigadier George Townshend's portrait of his general, James Wolfe

James Wolfe at the Battle on the Plains of Abraham. The black band on his arm shows that he was still in mourning for his father

Troops coming ashore at the Anse au Foulon

The most famous picture of the death of James Wolfe. In fact, it has nothing to do with reality. When James died, only two junior officers and a grenadier were present

Once again, he was about to go into action and his life was in hazard. The prospect did not daunt him in the slightest. 'All I wish for myself,' he told his mother, 'is, that I may at all times be ready and firm to meet the fate we cannot shun, and to die gracefully and properly when the hour comes, now or hereafter.' But the coming expedition had a prospect which, to James, was far more terrible than the thought of a well aimed enemy bullet. He looked forward to the fight for Louisburg, but first of all he had to get there. The voyage to Rochefort had been bad enough; the thought of spending a month or two crossing the Atlantic was almost unendurable. He poured out his misgivings in a long letter to his uncle in Ireland. To his parents, he said nothing; but there were many other things to write about.

Doubtless remembering his favourable impression of Kathleen Lowther, he hurriedly scribbled down his latest thoughts on marriage. 'I have', he told Mrs Wolfe, 'no objection to it, but differ much from the general opinion about it. The greatest consideration with me is the woman, her education and temper. Rank and fortune never come into competition with the person. Any bargain on that affair is base and mean. I could not with any satisfaction consider my children as the produce of such an unnatural union.' It was as if Mrs Wolfe's dream of the Croydon heiress as a daughter-in-law haunted the page.

His father, as James put it, seemed 'to decline apace, and narrowly escaped being carried off in the spring'. It was, he suggested, the result of being inactive, and the idea was not unreasonable. With Mrs Wolfe's talent for imagined ailments becoming sharper, and her earlier tendency to dominate transforming itself into a querulous middle age, the poor old General was liable to die of boredom at any minute. Nevertheless, it was now possible that both parents might survive him, and James had to put his affairs in order. He asked George Warde to keep an eye on his mother and father. In the case of his death, Warde and his friend Guy Carleton were to act as his executors. He gave each a letter conferring powers of attorney, but the duties were unlikely to be onerous. Once he had paid all his debts, James reckoned that he would be about £500 out of pocket if ever he returned from Canada.

On 2 February 1758, he arrived in Portsmouth. His capacity for disapproval was only just short of infinite, and it seldom had greater opportunity for exercise than it did in this port. Members of the garrison were castigated as 'vagabonds that stroll about in dirty red clothes from one gin shop to another'. As for the town itself, he dismissed it as 'this infernal den'. Nor was he much more complimentary about the force in whose hands the future of Louisburg rested. There were, he admitted, about two good battalions. The rest he described as *la canaille*. It was a word he enjoyed using – indeed seldom has an expression been more overworked without actually falling to pieces.

An average person would have found more than sufficient to occupy his time at this moment, but nothing seemed able to stem the torrent of writing which poured through his pen. There was a long letter to Lord George Sackville, now Master-General of the Ordnance, about his ideas for the invasion of Europe. He believed that the troops should be put ashore, at least 4,000 at a time, in sloops and cutters – vessels which could sail close to the beach and if necessary run aground. To support them, a fleet of round- or flat-bottomed boats armed with swivel-guns should be built.* Surprise – and therefore speed – were of the utmost importance. The dissertation was followed by another, again addressed to Lord George, criticizing the Army's new method of drilling; and then there was a testy note to Mrs Wolfe on why he would not use his influence to secure a commission for one of his cousins. The lad was, he said, a 'low dog' and an 'idle vagabond'. Portsmouth, perhaps, was beginning to colour his opinion of the rest of humanity.

He embarked in HMS *Princess Amelia* on 12 February. Three days later, the fleet sailed; but the winds were adverse. It took them a week to get to reach a point somewhere off Plymouth, and then it came on to blow really hard. They had to anchor in the Sound until the weather changed. On the way, the 74-gun *Invincible* had been driven ashore on the Isle of Wight. Otherwise, the expedition – with the exception of Brigadier-General James Wolfe – was in good shape.

* These boats were constructed along the line suggested by James. Some of them were used during his operations against Quebec.

The armada which was about to head out into the Atlantic was made up of forty-one warships. About 2,600 soldiers were crammed aboard them, and they remained on board for the next two months. Indeed, it was not until 8 May – after a voyage which had taken them by way of Madeira, the Canary Islands, and Bermuda – that they finally arrived off the coast of Nova Scotia. Three ships had sustained damage on the trip; the others were unharmed. Four days after they had sighted land, they put in to Halifax. James was wretchedly weak after such a long period, in which the nauseous antics of the ship and an enforced lack of physical activity had done everything possible to undermine his health. Even his apparently endless stream of letters had dried up. Nevertheless, once he stepped ashore, he seemed to recover immediately. The cure he advocated so earnestly for others was never more effective than it was for himself. The very promise of action seemed to sweep away the pain from his eyes, and to replace it with the gleam of energy and enthusiasm.

While Hardy's squadron had been patrolling off Cape Breton Island, contingents of troops had been converging on Halifax from other parts of the colonies. Artillery had been promised from New York and Boston, but the guns had not yet arrived. Three battalions had come from Philadelphia – though here again there were snags. With only three hundred men in each, they were severely under strength. However, there was a promise of 1,500 irregulars and five hundred rangers; and the Highland troops struck James as particularly good soldiers. He described their officers as 'the most manly corps . . . I ever saw'. Amherst, who had made a late start, was still on his way across the Atlantic in HMS *Dublin*. The medical supplies, the horses, and the oxen to haul the cannons, were also in transit.

Wolfe's own brigade was made up of twelve companies of grenadiers, Fraser's Highlanders, a company of local rangers, and, perhaps the most effective of them all, 550 light infantrymen. These were picked troops, chosen from other regiments for the high quality of their marksmanship and their physical agility. They wore green uniforms which, unlike the conspicuous red of the ordinary infantry, enabled them to blend reasonably well into the countryside. From the enemy's point of view, they seemed to materialize suddenly, strike hard and swiftly, and then to melt away into the ground. James Wolfe could not take credit for inventing them, but no other unit was so completely in accord with his philosophy of tactics. The Indians and rangers were looked upon as savages; the light infantry were regarded as 'artificial savages'.

There was still snow on the ground, and many of the local troops were in poor condition. Something like three hundred men were suffering from scurvy, and there was no excuse for it. As James pointed out, most of the contractors could buy fresh meat just as cheaply as the salted version. Fortunately, Admiral Boscawen was quick to sum up the situation and to do something about it. Soon after he first set foot on shore, he ordered six hundred head of cattle for the commissariat. But malnutrition was not the only problem. As James looked moodily at the soldiers, fretting for the campaign to begin, he noticed that: 'Too much money and too much rum necessarily affect the discipline of an army. We have glaring evidence of their ill consequences every moment. Sergeants drunk upon duty, 2 sentries upon their posts and the rest wallowing in the dirt. I believe', he concluded, 'no nation ever paid so many bad soldiers at so high a rate.'

For much of the time, he was irritable, even withdrawn. But there were moments when he became expansive and anxious to please his colleagues. On one of them, he invited forty-six guests to dinner at the local hotel. The food cost him £1 a head, and the consumption of liquor was prodigious. All told, the company drank seventy bottles of Madeira, fifty of claret, and twenty-five bottles of brandy. The bill for the evening came to £98 12*s* 6*d* (£98.62½). However, such extravagance contributed to what one officer described as 'the harmony, Spirit, and confidence, that reigns universally thro' the Army and Navy'.

While they were waiting for the latecomers to arrive, there was plenty to be done. The troops had to be trained in the use of boats, and in landing on a hostile shore. A team of carpenters and engineers was employed in building siege-works. They included a wooden fort, which could be taken to pieces for stowing aboard ship. As became apparent later in the campaign, James and Amherst had conflicting ideas on how the reduction of Louisburg should be conducted. James believed that it could be done rapidly and with economy – except in matters relating to lives and ammunition. The commander-in-chief, on the other hand, saw the operation as a drawn out and full-scale siege after the European pattern. The fact that the argument never came to a head was largely due to Amherst's tact. He gave his wilful and impatient second-in-command his head. Beyond defining his objectives, he allowed him to achieve them in whatever manner he saw fit.

By 24 May, the expedition was almost ready to sail, but Amherst had not yet arrived. Nevertheless, the prevailing mood was one of confidence, though nobody was under any illusions about the difficulty of the task ahead. In spite of Sir Charles Hardy's two-month long blockade of Louisburg, three or four men-of-war and a number of smaller vessels had slipped into the port. Others, which had been storm-bound, had been captured, but this was of small significance. Within the harbour, the enemy could rely on a punishing amount of fire power.

Work on fortifying the town had begun in 1713. Since then, it was estimated, the French had spent something like £1,250,000. Part of this large figure could be accounted for by the fact that the stone had been quarried in France. It had to be shipped across the Atlantic accompanied by labourers recruited to carry out the work of construction. It was indicative of the importance that successive French governments and two of that country's monarchs put on the place, not only as the entrance to Canada, but also as a naval base from which to police the West Indies colonies.

At last, on 28 May, the commander-in-chief made his belated arrival; but then it turned out that the warships were not ready. Two more Frenchmen reached the safety of Louisburg harbour, which brought the total up to thirteen. Estimates for the British assembly of ships vary, but it was at least 157. According to one historian,* the number was 180, with 13,000 naval ratings on board and about the same number of soldiers. An observer who travelled with the expedition put the naval strength at 23 ships of

* W. T. Waugh, *James Wolfe Man and Soldier*, (Montreal, 1928).

the line and 18 frigates; the rest were transports and supply vessels.

To his credit, Amherst wasted no time. He transferred himself from the *Dublin* to Boscawen's flag ship, the *Namur,* and requested his naval colleague to get under way as quickly as possible. The fogs which wrapped themselves around the Nova Scotia coastline had cleared. With a strong wind behind them and a bright northern sun glinting off the wavetops, the convoy headed out to sea. The voyage was uneventful and the fleet linked up with Hardy's force according to schedule. By 2 June, the main invasion force was at anchor off a bay six miles to the south-west of Louisburg, whilst Hardy's squadron was detailed to guard the entrance to the harbour. But then the wind, which had been so co-operative, suddenly veered. With the change in direction came fog, and presently gales. A frigate named the *Trent* was driven on to an outcrop of rocks, and there seemed to be a very real danger that the cumbersome transports would be blown ashore. As all the senior officers agreed, the hardest part in the reduction of Louisburg would be that of getting the soldiers ashore.

Amherst's original idea had been to make three landings, each at brigade strength, in an attempt to confuse the enemy. Shortly after their arrival, however, he and his three commanders managed to make a reconnaissance from a small boat. It was carried out under atrocious conditions – in high seas and with banks of fog suddenly obscuring the objective, clearing and then being replaced by others. Nevertheless, they saw enough to realize the impossibility of such an undertaking. The shore seemed to be heavily defended; and, as if enemy soldiers were not hazard enough, large waves were crashing on to the rocky beaches and sending up huge feathers of spray. There was, in Amherst's opinion, only one point at which they could possibly establish a beach-head. Wolfe's brigade would attempt to go in first. If it established itself, Lawrence's would follow and then Whitmore's.

Cape Breton Island is a disorderly design of land separated from the north-eastern end of Nova Scotia by a narrow stretch of water known as the Strait of Canso. At the other extremity, the

Cabot Strait lies between it and Newfoundland about seventy miles away. It is through this channel that ships sail into the Gulf of St Lawrence, and thence into the river. Louisburg lies near the eastern end of the island. The harbour, which is more in the nature of a large basin, is protected by two outcrops of land. On one of them, Battery Island, the French had erected strong fortifications.

The main fleet was anchored in Gabarouse Bay, which was one of the very few places on this unkindly coast to offer any shelter – and the nearest to the town. There were woods close to the shore and, beyond them, swamps. The reconnaissance had shown that there was a strong force of French regulars and Indians in the vicinity, and that the trunks of trees had been used to build defensive positions on the beach. There also seemed to be a battery of guns on hand. And the weather continued rough. The lightning strike, the precious element of surprise upon which Wolfe set so much importance, was missing. The enemy was having days, not hours, to consider the ominous armada off shore, and to make suitable preparations. On one occasion, the troops were disembarked into boats; but, when it became clear that only a fortunate few would reach the shore, they were stuffed back into the transports again. On 5 June, the island was blotted out by thick fog. This was followed by heavy rain. By the seventh, the mists had cleared away completely, but it was still too rough. The battery on land opened up a spasmodic fire; the frigates, closer to the coast than the larger ships, returned it.

At last – round about midnight on the eighth – the gale blew itself out. A heavy swell was now running, but the sailors judged it safe to make the attempt. At two am, Wolfe's brigade took to the landing craft, and the oarsmen bent to their task. They were heading for a kink known as Kennington Cove at the south-westerly corner of the bay. As they drew nearer, and the first glimmering of an unsatisfactory dawn stirred in the east, they could see that heavy waves were hurling themselves on to the rocks. The chances of getting a boat ashore under any circumstances seemed to be small, but small arms and cannon fire were now adding to the perils of the sea. Kennington Cove was far too heavily defended. They would have to look elsewhere.

The boats pulled away from the shore and made for the other end of the bay. At some point, the flagstaff on Wolfe's craft was shot off, but the young Brigadier was unmoved – indeed, he did not seem to notice the occurrence. He just sat there, silent, observant, and with an almost supernatural calm. His attitude affected the men: it gave them confidence. If their commanding officer was so unworried, what had they to fear? And the boats, gripped by the swell, reared up and came crashing down, shipping water for some of the time, struggling towards the menacing beach which was often obscured by clouds of spray. Even if they managed to get on to it alive, they would have to climb a fifteen-foot cliff under enemy fire.

From their positions ashore, the Frenchmen were now holding their fire. It was the lesson which James had tried to teach his men at Dettingen: don't waste ammunition – wait until you are sure of hitting somebody. Or perhaps these troops had decided there was no need for intervention. Might they not rely upon their ally, the sea? The helpless boats would be dashed to pieces on to the rocks, and the invaders would suffer an ignominious death by drowning.

But the enemy reckoned without Lieutenants Brown and Hopkins and Ensign Grant. These officers were in charge of a boat containing one hundred light infantrymen. Somehow, through the swirling spindrift, they noticed a gap in the rocks. Urging the sailors to extend themselves completely, they came as near as can be to throwing their craft at the opening. One moment, it appeared as if a wave was about to overwhelm them; the next, the prow was grating on to the beach. The light infantrymen disembarked quickly and ran for cover. The way was open: the rest of the brigade could follow.

The enemy were now firing rapidly from a range of about twenty yards, and a battery of three guns added its contribution to the inferno. A boat carrying twenty-two grenadiers was smashed on to a rock, and the men were drowned. Wolfe clambered ashore with an agility which was surprising for a man of his ungainly height. One of the first people he encountered on the beach was a Highlander. The man's bearing impressed him so much that on an impulse he gave him a sovereign. And the troops continued to come ashore. Once Wolfe's brigade was clear of the waterline, Lawrence's followed, and then Whitmore's. Amherst was, as seemed to be his habit, the last to arrive.

Miracles are welcome in any military operation, and such a manifestation was never more urgently needed than now. After scrambling ashore, often up to their waists in water, the soldiers made the not surprising discovery that their supplies of gunpowder had become a saturated mess. Their only effective weapons were bayonets. To a detached onlooker, it must have appeared improbable that they would get close enough to use them. It did, indeed, seem that little less than a master stroke of luck could save this foolhardy expedition; but that was what happened. Suddenly, unaccountably, the Frenchmen took to their heels and fled into the woods. They were obviously hurrying back to the security of Louisburg.

Had the men remained at their posts, they could have inflicted immense damage. Such invaders as survived would have been taken prisoner, and, though the fleet might have made an attempt to bombard the town, the operation would have been aborted. As it was, they became victims to the soldier's most fatal enemy: panic. It may have been that their morale had been softened by the barrage put down by the warships to cover the hazardous journey to the shore. But this, on its own, was not enough to explain it. The truth of the matter seems to be that, since the impossible had happened, there was no longer any hope for the possible. French engineers had assured the Governor of Louisburg that only madmen would attempt to land on the beaches near the town. Well, madmen had made the attempt, and they had succeeded. Astonishment had become disbelief; and, with it, the strands of courage snapped. The routed soldiers left behind them seventy prisoners, seventeen cannons, fourteen large swivel-guns, two mortars (one an eight-inch, the other a ten-inch), and the corpse of an Indian chief. The unfortunate warrior wore a medal round his neck that had been an award from the King of France. It was afterwards presented to Boscawen.

Wolfe's and Lawrence's brigades chased the fleeing enemy over the rough country towards the town. When the first rounds of artillery fire opened up from the battlements, they halted.

Unwittingly, the French gunners had served a useful purpose by revealing the range of their weapons. Beyond the line of farthest-flung shells, it would be safe to establish the main army's camp and headquarters.

During the siege of Louisburg, Wolfe went his own way, unbothered by interference from his commander-in-chief. Indeed, if one reads his dispatches, one sometimes wonders who was running the show. Often they seem more like instructions than the dutiful reports of a subordinate officer. True to military tradition, he usually signed off with the words: 'I have the honour to be, Sir, Your most obedient and most humble servant.' There may have been a rough and ready kind of obedience in the message: there was certainly nothing to suggest humility.

Amherst was prepared to take his time: Wolfe, throughout the campaign, appeared to be in a hurry. Strangely enough, he and the French Governor, Drucour, were both aware of something which seems to have escaped the other British senior officers. Louisburg, in itself, was a matter of small importance. It only assumed significance if it was regarded as the gateway to the St Lawrence – and, therefore, to Quebec. The Governor's determination to hold out for as long as possible had a single purpose: to hold the British back until winter set in, and the river was frozen once more. Wolfe, for his part, wanted to get the siege over as quickly as possible so that the army could move on before the summer ended. If his commander-in-chief acted quickly and decisively, there was no reason why they should not at least try to take Quebec that year. But Amherst was slow. He built his siege-works carefully and in large quantities, until it seemed as if a battleship had been dispatched to sink a small boat.

Nobody was more energetic than James Wolfe. In all his utterances, there was no talk of fatigue, no misgivings about his health. He drove himself at a furious pace, and his body obeyed. Once again, his philosophy that activity equals fitness, and that a poor constitution can be overcome by a strong spirit, was showing itself to be true.

The weather turned bad again. On the very day of the landing, snow storms ripped across the island. They were followed by more gales and fog, which hampered the unloading of stores. Nor were matters helped by the nature of the ground, where the swampy soil made it necessary to build roads before the siege guns could be placed in position.

Hardy's squadron was stationed at the approaches to the harbour, to make sure that the small French fleet was contained. Wolfe and his brigade were making for the far side of the basin with the idea of bombarding the enemy vessels, and later turning their guns on the town. He reached the sea wall with 1,200 men after encountering little opposition. On the eighteenth, the troops took up their positions. By the following morning, after a night of desperately hard work, the batteries for the guns had been built. His plan was that, at 10 pm, he would send up a rocket to signal that he was ready. The main army, the fleet, and his own artillery, would then open up a bombardment calculated to erase Louisburg from the North American map.

The rocket went up on schedule, but the rest of the firework display fizzled out pathetically. Two of James's 24-pounders had stuck in the mud on the way to the batteries. The touch-hole of another was so crammed with moist earth that it was impossible to ignite the charge. And, on top of all this, the range was farther than he expected. Nor was there any barrage worth talking about from the other forces. They were not, it seemed, ready. Three of James's shells did, by a happy chance, hit vessels. One of them appeared to be slightly damaged.

And there were other troubles. Before the bombardment had been due to begin, he had ordered half a gill of rum ('diluted', he insisted) to be issued to every soldier. The men were suitably grateful, but he might have conserved the spirit. The troops had, it seemed, their own supplies, which they had bought off the masters of the transports. This unfortunate fact was made clear to him when, doing his rounds, he visited a detachment that should have been watching out for a possible French attack from the rear. Every man was dead drunk.

Early on in the siege, some of the French ships were seen to unfurl their sails, and it looked as if they were about to attempt a break-out from the harbour. As things transpired, however, they were merely shifting their positions. The object was uncomfortably apparent: they meant to intensify the fire on the brigade's positions. In spite of this, and despite a substantial bombardment from the guns on Battery Island, the British casualties were relatively small. On 25 June, the island's guns fired their last rounds. Then, silence. After a fearful pounding, the Louisburg outpost had been put out of action. The way to the harbour was open, at any rate for the time being. This might have been the cue for Hardy's ships to make a quick entrance, but they left it too late. The French filled two frigates and two store ships with stones, and sank them at the mouth of the basin. Their own vessels would no longer be able to escape; but, at least, the enemy would not be able to get in.

Throughout the days of the siege, James Wolfe's activities were divided. Sometimes he was busy with the batteries: moving them, strengthening them, doing anything his fertile mind could devise to improve their accuracy and to increase the volume of fire. At others, he was concerned with keeping the French foot-soldiers confined to the town. He usually took the light infantry with him on these forays. On one occasion, he received a report that a party of four hundred enemy soldiers had reached a point about one mile from the city walls. James marched to meet them at the head of a hundred light infantrymen supported by three hundred regulars. The engagement lasted for two and a half hours. At the end of it, eight of Wolfe's men had been wounded; the surviving Frenchmen were back in town; and he had secured a piece of land which gave his guns a better field of fire on to the French ships.

Mobility was the key to the light infantry; their lightning raids became an unhappy legend within Louisburg. As a writer who was present, and who afterwards styled himself 'A Spectator' (he must have been one of the first war correspondents) put it: 'Some people of the garrison express their surprise ... [at] the suddenness of Brigadier Wolfe's motions from one Place to another, & their Sentiments of the Effect of his Operations. [They] used to say – There is no Certainty where to find him – but, wherever he goes, he carries with him a mortar in one pocket, & a 24 pounder in the other.'

Back at headquarters, the construction of siege works had

slowed down. One hundred of the carpenters had fallen ill with smallpox. However, on the credit side, two French frigates had been sunk in the harbour. Their masts could be seen sticking up out of the water. And the niceties of chivalry were still observed. Amherst sent the Governor's wife a gift of pineapples. Her husband's reply was to send the General a supply of fresh butter and some champagne.

The day was 21 July. The 64-gun French ship of the line, *Le Célèbre,* contained a day's supply of gunpowder for the garrison. At some point in the bombardment, a shot struck a piece of iron on board her. The impact caused a spark, which ignited the explosives. Suddenly a great upsurge of flame erupted. The crew valiantly tried to throw the remaining gunpowder overboard, but they were too late. *Le Célèbre* was now blazing fiercely; and, before long, the inferno spread to two more vessels. The sailors jumped into the harbour, and swam for the quays. The ships burned throughout the night. In the morning, their charred hulls drifted on to the shore.

It had been a bad day for the French. While *Le Célèbre* was on fire, a British shell blew up the magazine. Another knocked down the church steeple, which was an almost equally grave setback; for it had been invaluable as an observation post. Madame Drucour was up in the ramparts helping to keep her husband's soldiers supplied with food and ammunition. In the British camp, General Amherst reminded his officers to direct their fire on to military installations. The civilian quarters of the town were not to be harmed. And James Wolfe stalked impatiently from one post to another. Everything was progressing far too slowly for his liking. Even the siege-works that *had* been completed were unsatisfactory. He judged the parapets to be too thin, and the parallel trenches were badly made.

However, he was pleased when one of his officers likened his hit-and-run tactics to those described by Xenophon. 'You are right', he cordially agreed. 'I had it thence; but our friends are astonished at what I have shown them, because they have read nothing.' The suggestion that he was a soldier-scholar suited his image and those long hours of studying during his service in Scotland had obviously not been wasted. But he did not elaborate on the subject, for there were more urgent matters to be discussed. He quickly turned the conversation to the barbarities of American Indians. Predictably, he described them as *la canaille*.

On 23 July, the allegedly bomb-proof barracks were burned to the ground; and a party of German mercenaries, who had deserted from the garrison, reported that the people of Louisburg were going down *on their knees* to the Governor, *begging* him to capitulate. But Drucour stood firm. If he gave in now, there was plenty of time for the British to reach Quebec before the river froze.

Throughout the campaign so far, Admiral Boscawen's role had been mostly that of an interested spectator. He used to come ashore daily to confer with Amherst; otherwise there had not been a great deal for him to do. He now decided that the fleet should take a more active part. At noon on 25 July, two boats from every vessel were ordered to report to the flagship. One should be a barge or pinnace, the other a cutter. Each was to be commanded by a lieutenant, or, if one were not available, by a mate or a midshipman. The crews were to be armed with muskets and bayonets, cutlasses, pistols, and poleaxes. Once this small force had been assembled, it was put under the command of two senior captains. The craft were then dispatched in twos and threes to Hardy's squadron.

Somewhile after sunset, when the harbour was shrouded in fog, the fleet opened up its guns on to the town. Under cover of the barrage, the boats were paddled silently past the sunken ships and into the inner basin. The firing suddenly stopped; and then – moments later, it seemed – the men in the raiding party began to cheer. They had captured a ship named *Le Bienfaisant*, and they were already towing her out to sea. A second vessel, *Le Prudent*, had also been taken, but she was badly damaged, and there were several feet of water in the hold. It was impossible to move her; instead, she was set on fire. The outing had certainly been successful, but it was scarcely an epic in the Hornblower tradition. Neither vessel had many ratings on board; and, in each, there was only a young ensign in charge.

The story of Louisburg was rapidly coming to a close. There were now large breaches in the walls, and Drucour clearly could not hold out for much longer. Early on the morning of 26 July, Amherst sent the Governor a letter, setting out his terms for surrender. If they were turned down, Boscawen intended to destroy the remaining ships in harbour, and bombard the town at point-blank range. Drucour replied that he might consider hauling down his flag, but only if the French officers were permitted to return to France on parole. 'To answer Your Excellencies in as few words as possible', he wrote, 'I have the honour to repeat to you that my resolution is still the same, and that I will suffer and sustain the attack you speak of.' The note was an amazing piece of audacity, for he now had only three guns capable of being fired.

Brigadier Whitmore, who was given charge of the negotiations, sent back a brusque message. No, the French officers could not return to their native land. The surrender must be unconditional. Drucour asked whether he could have a further hour to think matters over. Whitmore replied that one hour and no more was all he would allow, and there could be *no* bargaining. The troops in the parallel trenches, the gunners in their batteries, were given the order to reload. If Drucour did not say 'Yes', they were ready to pound the smoking remains of Louisburg into dust.

The period of grace was almost up, when a French lieutenant-colonel was seen running from the garrison, waving his arms and yelling: 'We accept'. He was immediately taken to Amherst, who confirmed the terms. The main entrance to the town must be handed over at eight o'clock on the following morning. The garrison was to be paraded on the Esplanade, where they would 'lay down arms, colours, implements and ornaments of war'. The soldiers would then be taken back to Britain as prisoners of war in British ships. The civilian population would be permitted to return to France. Unhappily, some of them never got there. One of the vessels ran into a storm about one hundred miles off the English coast and foundered with three hundred people on board. There were no survivors. But, all things considered, the treatment of the French was thought to be very humane. As one observer suggested, 'it had more the appearance of transplanting an English Colony, than the behaviour of dispossessing a French Settlement.'

As for James Wolfe, he was not particularly interested in the details of surrender. Without action, he became restless, and this disagreed with him. In a way, he was sorry it was all over. The campaign seemed to have done him good. 'I would', he observed, 'much rather besiege a place than pass four weeks at sea.' For most of the time, he had been too busy to criticize, but now he had leisure in which to reflect. The affair, he concluded, had not been well done. Everything had been too slow, and it seemed unlikely that they would take Quebec that year. 'If this force had been properly managed', he wrote, 'there was an end of the French colony in North America in one campaign.'

But there was more to such a dream than the capture of Quebec. While Amherst's army had been fighting at Louisburg, another British force had been defeated inland at Fort Ticonderoga. General Abercrombie was now in desperate need of reinforcements. James was considering only part of the picture, and his next assignment was unlikely to add to his understanding. His job was the thankless, and apparently senseless, one of wiping out French fishing settlements on the shores of the Gulf of St Lawrence. It was not worthy of a young brigadier who had become a hero. Nobody realized this better than James himself.

11

THE LAST INTERLUDE

When the citizens of Halifax, Nova Scotia, heard about the victory at Louisburg, they celebrated by consuming sixty thousand gallons of rum. In Boston, the people showed their approval by lighting bonfires, and services of thanksgiving were held in the town's churches. Two officers – Captain Edgecomb and the commander-in-chief's brother, Captain William Amherst – were sent to London with the news. When Pitt was informed, he told Amherst: 'You are the most welcome messenger that has arrived in this kingdom for years.' Even the ageing monarch nodded in pleasure. At first, however, the Duke of Newcastle had to tell him where Cape Breton Island was. With some surprise, the King learned that it was not, as he had expected, somewhere off the coast of France. But, once he had absorbed the fact that it lay on the far side of the Atlantic, his enthusiasm for this distant theatre of war began to quicken. Hitherto, it had been somewhat perfunctory. He now announced: 'We must keep Cape Breton, take Canada, and drive the French out of America.' It was precisely what Pitt had been telling him for the past year or so.

The captured French colours were paraded through the streets of London from Kensington Palace, and deposited in St Paul's Cathedral. When Parliament returned to business in early November, the members put on record their thanks to Admiral Boscawen and General Amherst. Nothing was said about James Wolfe, who had been the real dynamic behind the campaign; but he was too junior to qualify for such exalted praise. Nor, in all probability, would he have wished it. Unlike everyone else, he felt that the success had been 'ill deserved', and he was in no mood for celebrating. The taking of Louisburg had not been enough. He was disgruntled that the year's score of victories had not included Quebec.

While Amherst's forces had been embattled round Louisburg, a force under General Abercrombie had been attempting to cut the French line of forts, which thrust southwards from Canada to Louisiana. At Ticonderoga on Lake Champlain, Abercrombie confronted a force of 4,000 French troops with 15,000 men. By every law of statistics, he should have amply fulfilled his purpose. But the General blundered. Putting his faith in inaccurate intelligence reports, he left his artillery behind. After launching four attacks in five hours, he was compelled to withdraw. His losses amounted to two thousand men. One Highland regiment was the poorer by five hundred officers and other ranks. At some point in the engagement, Lord Howe's unit lost its way, and ran into a French formation in a similar predicament. Howe and a good many other men died in the skirmish, which achieved nothing and should never have taken place. Since James regarded Howe as 'the noblest Englishman that has appeared in my time, and the best soldier in the army', his grief was considerable.* Furthermore, he was acid in his criticism of Abercrombie. Pitt must have shared his views, for in September of that year the incapable general was ordered back to England. Amherst took his place as commander-in-chief in North America.

Before Captain William Amherst left for London, James sent him a longish letter, which was full of advice. Still under the impression that nobody but a fool would give the vanquished Louisburg more attention than it deserved, and certain that the only sensible thing to do was to press on to Quebec, he told Amherst to 'put the General in mind of pilots; I dare say there are plenty in Louisburg; their names should be known....' Some of the men had lost their muskets in the battle; other weapons had been damaged beyond repair. But this was a matter of no importance. They could help themselves from the abundant stock of captured French ordnance. Nor should the General be too proud to issue the men with former enemy flints for their firelocks. They were, James assured the senior officer via his brother, 'very good, and may be useful in his army'. In the final

* George Augustus, third Viscount Howe, was thirty-three. He had served in Flanders during 1747 and was MP for Nottingham. At the time of his death, he was commanding the 60th Foot.

paragraph, he seems to have become unsure of himself. Did he suspect that he was being too opinionated; that he was, perhaps, laying down the law to his superior? He was quick to make amends. 'I write this by way of memorandum', he hastened to say, 'knowing how many matters the General must have on his hands in this hour of business.'

But this moment of humility, if such it was, did not last. He was fretting about the future. In early August, he was concerned that he might be sent to the mainland to join Abercrombie's force. The idea was not acceptable. If no move was made in the direction of the St Lawrence River, he wished to return to Europe. It seemed that, before he had departed for Louisburg, Field Marshal Ligonier had promised that he might go home when the work was done. 'As I am pretty much resolved not to stay in America', he told his friend Rickson, '. . . I hope the General will not put me to the necessity of insisting upon the Field Marshal's promise. . . .' Nevertheless, he found time to speculate about what reinforcement's Abercrombie's troops would need. The light infantry, he decided, would be ideal for such operations; but their establishment should be rationalized. There should be a captain in charge of every one hundred men, and each battalion should make an equal contribution (thirty men) to the units.

When Captain Rodney, RN, conveyed Captains Amherst and Edgecomb to England, he took with him gifts for General and Mrs Wolfe. There was a quantity of dried cod, but James was uncertain whether it would be worth eating. On the other hand, he felt sure his father would enjoy the supply of Madeira. The accompanying note, like so many of James's letters home, dwelt briefly on money matters. He was, as always, hard up. 'If the King had not been pleased to give me a regiment', he wrote, 'I should have ruined myself and you; for we are at a vast expense, and you know I never plunder.'

In early August, when they were preparing to dispatch the 5,637 members of the Louisburg garrison to prisoner of war camps in England, he was passing the time by picking strawberries and other wild fruit. His mind, on the other hand, was busy composing further messages to General Amherst. What, exactly, did the general propose to do next? Amherst replied that what he *wished* to do, and what he *could* do were entirely different things. Like James, he wanted to attack Quebec, but Boscawen had told him that it was not practicable. James was never patient. Ever since the fighting had stopped, he had been trying to contain his restlessness. Now it was beyond control. If the Navy was too faint-hearted to undertake the logical next step, there were many other things which could be done. Casting prudence to one side, he poured out his thoughts in a second letter to Amherst.

Four or five battalions should be sent to reinforce the soldiers on the mainland. 'With the rest of the troops', he wrote, 'we might make an offensive and destructive war in the Bay of Fundy and in the Gulf of St Lawrence. I beg pardon for this freedom, but I cannot look coolly upon the bloody inroads of those hell-hounds the Canadians; and if nothing further is done, I must desire leave to quit the army.' He might have added the words 'in Canada', for he had no intention of giving up his military career. But he was too incensed to go into such niceties of detail.

Amherst's reply was patient but firm. He reiterated that he wished to take Quebec, but this seemed to be impossible. His plans were, indeed, very similar to those which James had suggested. But, he added: 'Whatever schemes you may have, or information that you can give, to quicken our motions, your communicating them will be very acceptable, and will be of much more service than your thoughts of quitting the army, which I can by no means agree to, as all my thoughts and wishes are confined at present to pursuing our operations for the good of His Majesty's service, and I know nothing that can tend more to it than your assistance in it.'

By 15 August, the convoy carrying the French prisoners had sailed. Whitmore was appointed Governor of Louisburg. A small garrison was installed in the port; the remainder of the corps began to disperse. Amherst left for the mainland with six battalions to reinforce Abercrombie, and presently to take over from him. Robert Monckton took two battalions to the Bay of Fundy at the western side of Nova Scotia; and James was left with three battalions. He was instructed to join forces with Admiral Hardy for operations in the Gulf of St Lawrence. The object, not a very difficult one, was to distress 'the enemy's fishery and alarm them'. Brooding, he set off in his assignment. There was no point in sending any more letters to Amherst. Instead, he gave Lord George Sackville, who was now commanding the army in Europe, a taste of his feelings. The language suggests that he was carrying out what should have been an unpleasant task with a certain amount of zeal.

'I am neither inhuman nor rapacious', he wrote, 'yet I own it would give me pleasure to see the Canadian vermin sacked and pillaged and justly repaid for their unheard of cruelty.' It was clearly composed in a similar frame of mind to that in which, some years earlier, he had sent a patrol from the 20th into the heart of hostile Highland territory. Nor was his braggart ruthlessness justified. The French commander, Montcalm, was an honourable man. The villains of the piece were the Indians and, so far as James was concerned, even their depredations were a matter of hearsay. But, in his present mood, he was concerned with neither justice nor accuracy. The affair of Lake Ticonderoga and the death of Lord Howe still rankled. He was aware that nine thousand of Abercrombie's force had been provincial militia men, and this was enough to condemn all North American soldiers out of hand. He told Lord Sackville: 'The Americans are in general the dirtiest most contemptible cowardly dogs that you can conceive. There is no depending on them in action. They fall down dead in their own dirt and desert by battalions, officers and all. Such rascals as these are rather an encumberance than any real strength to an army.' Since the rangers, all of them local men, had acquitted themselves very well in the Louisburg campaign, there was nothing in his personal experience to justify such vehemence.

The letters survive; but they would be more helpful if we could watch them being written. The handwriting is neat, and gives little clue to the emotions behind it. For much of the time, James was a man who practised rigorous self-discipline. Even when he erupts on paper in an explosion of rage, the language is carefully chosen. To what extent were these emotional passages a true expression of his feelings? Were they a sign that the temperature of his mind had reached boiling point – or were they written for effect? He had an unpleasant task to perform in the

Gulf of St Lawrence. When it was completed, he observed that 'we have done a great deal of mischief – spread the terror of His Majesty's arms through the whole gulf; but have added nothing to the reputation of them.' Was this because it had all been too easy; or was it because, in his heart, he was ashamed at what he had done? And was he, when he wrote to Lord George Sackville, preparing *himself* for such inhuman conduct? Did he require the French Canadians to be villains to justify the actions he had been ordered to prosecute? Did he, it might be wondered, write that letter to inform Lord George Sackville – or to deceive himself?

It would soon be autumn. The crust of ice would presently form on the St Lawrence. The summer, a brief interlude in a calendar of snow, fog and storms, was almost over. James saw nothing more to detain him in a part of the world that he disliked. Boscawen was about to return to Britain in the *Namur*, accompanied by the *Royal William* and the captured French ship from Louisburg, the *Bienfaisant*. James decided that he would go, too. He wrote a final letter to Amherst, in which he gave the General a few pointers on the art of warfare. 'Cannonade furiously before you attack', he counselled, 'and don't let them go in lines, but rather in columns.' Then he departed. If Amherst tried to detain him, he would recall Ligonier's promise. In fact, Amherst made no such attempt, but Pitt did. When the *Namur* was leaving her anchorage and heading out to sea, a letter from the Minister was travelling in the opposite direction. It ordered James Wolfe to remain in North America, but it arrived too late.

His Majesty's ship of the line *Namur* dropped anchor off the Isle of Wight on 1 November 1758. On the following day, James set off for Salisbury, where his regiment was stationed. By the seventeenth of the month, he was with his parents at Blackheath. People remarked on how well he looked, but they were mistaken. As he observed in a letter to his uncle, 'long passages and foggy weather have left their effect upon me.' He was, to be more precise, suffering from rheumatism and his old enemy, the gravel. However, as he announced: 'I would much rather die than decline any kind of service that offers.' He intended as soon as circumstances made it possible, to repair to Bath 'to refit for another campaign'.

But for the moment there was something more pressing which required attention. When Pitt heard that the young brigadier was back in town, he was furious. He was unaware that his letter had arrived too late. Was this talented officer, whom he had picked for promotion in the face of considerable opposition, deliberately flouting his wishes? Perhaps James Wolfe had achieved too much too quickly. Some explanation, certainly, was required.

James heard about the Minister's attitude when he was in White's Club. He immediately sat down and wrote to him:

> Since my arrival in town I have been told that your intentions were to have continued me upon the service in America. The condition of my health and other circumstances, made me desire to return at the end of the campaign, and by what my Lord Ligonier did me the honour to say, I understood it was to be so. General Amherst saw it in the same light.
>
> I take freedom to acquaint you that I have no objection to serving in America, and particularly in the River St Lawrence, if any operations are carried out there. The favour I ask is only to be allowed a sufficient time to repair the injury done to my constitution by the long confinement at sea, that I may be the better able to go through the business of next summer.

The letter was a success: Pitt was mollified, and James was able to go to Bath. No doubt his enthusiasm for taking the cure was sharpened by the thought that Kathleen Lowther was down there. But, since the only surviving evidence of his sojourn is contained in letters to his mother, nobody would have suspected it. On his third day at the spa, he was writing to say that 'the women are not remarkable; nor the men neither'. Indeed, he implied that he was only too eager to finish the cure and get back to London.

Kathleen Lowther was a beautiful, if not particularly intelligent, young lady who might have been expected to appeal to any prospective mother-in-law. Her brother was to become the Earl of Lonsdale; her father had enjoyed an adequately distinguished career; and she was far from badly off. Whatever Mrs Wolfe's criticisms of Elizabeth Lawson may have been, they could not have been directed at Miss Lowther. Had she been a reasonable woman, she would thoroughly have approved her son's taste. But Mrs Wolfe was no longer reasonable. Her love for James was demanding and utterly possessive. He understood this, and he probably took pains to keep his passion a secret. Certainly no mention of her appears in his letters, though she must have discovered the truth when, after a rapid wooing, he and Kathleen became betrothed. But the only clue to her reaction lies in another direction. General Edward Wolfe's estate amounted to £15,000 (most of it invested in government securities) plus the house at Blackheath. It had been understood that, when he died, James should be his inheritor. Indeed, the gist of several replies to his son's appeals for cash had been 'wait until I'm dead'. James had felt so confident of moderate, if not great, expectations, that his own will was written as if he already had the money. But, at about this time, the old General seems to have undergone a change of mind. When he died in the following March, it became clear that he had made a new will. The entire amount was left to Mrs Wolfe. Of James, there was no mention.

Throughout their married life, Mrs Wolfe had been in command. Having heard of her son's intentions, did she persuade her husband to make this change? Such an act would have been typical – just as meek compliance would have been characteristic of the General.

James's romance with Kathleen must be one of the most poorly documented love stories in history. There is no help from within the Wolfe family, and Miss Lowther destroyed the few clues that ever existed. Six year's after James's death, she married a post captain in the Navy, who afterwards became the Duke of Bolton. With incredible foolishness, she took the occasion to burn her former fiancé's portrait, and all the letters and presents he had sent her. All that is known is that she gave him a miniature of herself and a copy of Gray's *Elegy*. The sole written survivor of the affair from James's pen is the mention of her in his will. It requests that the miniature shall be set in brilliants to the value of £500 and returned to her. Since such extravagance is totally out of character, the only measurement of his love is that expressed in a sum of money. His mother would have liked that: she expressed almost everything in such terms.

George II's instructions to Pitt about pursuing an aggressive policy in America were typical of a growing awareness of this aspect of the Seven Years War. Until the victory at Louisburg, it had been an unfashionable sphere of operations. Neither British nor French officers were anxious to serve there; to the ordinary member of the public it was all rather remote, a conflict in which uncouth colonials fought similar barbarians. In Europe, however, the war had been a good deal less than satisfactory. The French had helped themselves to the island of Minorca in 1756. Admiral Byng had been shot at Portsmouth for failing to prevent the calamity. Otherwise there was little to report after two years of desultory fighting. In America, on the other hand, things had been *happening*. Amherst's success at Louisburg more than made amends for Abercrombie's defeat at Ticonderoga, and this was not the only British victory. General Bradstreet had taken Fort Frontenac (now Kingston) with a force of American irregulars. Since the strong point controlled Lake Ontario – which, in itself, commanded the supply line to the south, it was almost as significant as the fall of the Cape Breton Island port. Nor did anyone have to wait long for the ancillary rewards. In November, the French withdrew in silence and in shame from Fort Duquesne.

North America was, indeed, appearing with greater clarity on the map. There were plenty of people only too anxious to advise Pitt on how best to conduct the campaign. A typical letter came from William Beckford, who, later on, was twice Lord Mayor of London. Mr Beckford proposed that an expedition should be sent up the St Lawrence with the dual objects of taking Quebec and Montreal. By overcoming these towns, he wrote: 'the two great heads of Canada, and of the French power in North America are destroyed; and, consequently, the limbs of that body must wither and decay without any further fighting.' It was a nice piece of rhetorical prose; but, as with the king's instructions, Pitt had already been thinking along similar lines.

The score for 1758, he might have told himself, had been reasonable. He had secured Louisburg and Fort Frontenac, but

Abercrombie had failed in the south and Quebec had not, as he had hoped, been taken. For 1759, he laid down three objectives. The American irregulars were to press westwards along Lake Ontario to eliminate the French outposts at Niagara. Amherst was to take over where Abercrombie had failed, advancing up Lake Champlain and forcing a way into Canada from the south. Finally, a force equipped for combined operations was to assemble at Louisburg, sail up the St Lawrence, and reduce Quebec.

Mordaunt's abortive expedition to Rochefort had marked James Wolfe in Pitt's mind as a man to watch. Louisburg had provided confirmation that here, indeed, was a talent far and away above the prevailing preponderance of military mediocrity. In the Minister's opinion, he was the only officer fit to take charge of the Quebec operation. When he made his decision known, there was the usual outcry from James's elders who, by reason of seniority, considered themselves to be his betters. Wolfe, they said, was not only an upstart – he was eccentric. The Duke of Newcastle was given the task of conveying this fragment of information to the King, who, as every schoolboy knows, replied: 'Oh! he is mad, is he? Then I wish he would *bite* some others of my generals.' Since the Duke had a tiresome habit of prostrating himself in front of the monarch and bursting into tears, he may not have been the best messenger for this slander.

Nevertheless, Pitt felt it necessary to make some concessions. The command he had in mind for James carried the rank of major-general. For Louisburg, he had become a brigadier-general, but this was only a local rank. The moment he returned to Britain, he automatically reverted to colonel. The minister adopted the same procedure for Quebec. While he was in Canada, James would be a major-general; but in London he would continue to be Colonel Wolfe – before, and, in theory, afterwards. In fact, the aftermath would not matter. If he succeeded, no honours would be too great for him. If he failed, his military career would be at an end. Furthermore, Pitt made it clear that, when James was in Canada, he would nominally be under Amherst's command. In fact, however, there was to be no interference from his superior officer. Whether Wolfe liked it or not, the fate of the expedition would be in his hands – and the responsibility for it.

He was down at Bath, taking the waters and dallying with the pretty Miss Lowther, when Pitt called him to his country house at Hayes in Middlesex. There is no record of the conversation, but the Minister promised him a force of 12,000 men, most of whom were already in Canada. There would be ten line battalions plus a grenadier regiment, three companies of artillery, and six companies of rangers. Strong naval support would be provided, and the expedition was due to assemble at Louisburg in early April. The choice of senior officers would be up to Wolfe. He could have whomever he liked.

Afterwards, James professed to have felt humble and inadequate at the size of his new commission. He told his uncle in Ireland: 'I am to act a greater part in this business than I wished or desired.' One suspects, however, that he was writing for effect – playing the role of a modest nephew who is amazed that anybody should so overrate his ability. Throughout his life he questioned many things about himself, but never his skill as a soldier. What was more, his criticism of other generals had been sharp to the point of cruelty. Such outspoken condemnation must, surely, have implied that he could have done better himself. Now, as he was only too well aware, he had been invited to prove it.

But, before the battle for Quebec could begin, there were skirmishes to be won in London. His first choice of officer was his old friend George Warde. Writing to him from Blackheath on 20 December 1758, he asked 'if I may mention you for distant, difficult, and disagreeable service, such as requires all your spirit and abilities. 'Tis not the Indies, which is as much as I can say directly'; but he added that it would be 'a very hazardous enterprise'. Unfortunately Warde turned out to be unavailable: he was spirited off to Germany with his regiment of Dragoons, and the offices of Adjutant General and Quarter Master General (Warde could have chosen whichever he had liked) remained unfilled.

His second choice for the post of Quarter Master General was another old friend, Guy Carleton. James had wanted to take him to Louisburg, but this had been refused. Now he tried again, but Carleton was out of favour with the King. He had made some disparaging remarks about Hanoverian troops, which had been brought to the monarch's notice. As the Elector of Hanover, George took umbrage, and Carleton was cast out into the military wilderness.

The commander-in-chief, Ligonier, had the difficult task of trying to change the monarch's mind. After two attempts had failed, Pitt chipped in with some good advice. 'Tell His Majesty', he suggested, 'that in order to render any General completely responsible for his conduct, he should be made, as far as possible, inexcusable, if he should fail; and that, consequently, whatever an officer entrusted with a service of confidence requires should be complied with.' Ligonier reproduced the speech almost word for word, and the sovereign at last gave in. Carleton was appointed Quarter Master General. For Adjutant General, James chose an unknown officer named Isaac Barré, who put the final touch to a very distinguished career when he became Secretary to the Navy in 1782. In 1758, however, Barré seemed to be very far from the great things in store for him. 'For want of friends I have lingered a subaltern eleven years,' he sadly remarked. But Wolfe, in a sense, discovered him – and, suddenly, the disappointed young officer's prospects were transformed. He was made a major and given a unique opportunity to achieve distinction.

On 21 December, James returned to Bath to complete the cure. On Christmas Eve, he sat down in his lodgings to compose a long letter to Pitt. It was mostly concerned with naval matters, but he did not allow what might have been considered an excusable ignorance to hamper his style. He was, as so frequently on paper, pragmatic. Getting off to a typical start, he remarked on 'the thorough aversion conceived by the marine of this country against navigating in the River St Lawrence.' From this, he made the point that, in his opinion, the 'second naval officer in command [Rear-Admiral Durrell] is vastly unequal to the weight of business.' Then he got down to his preliminary plans. The first thing to do, he explained, was to station eight or ten ships off the Isle of Bic at the mouth of the river. This would effectively prevent any relief from reaching the French forces up stream. Once this had been done, a 'frigate or two and sloops' were to be sent to the Isle of Orleans, which was virtually on Quebec's doorstep. They should have 'proper people on board to acquire a certain knowledge of the navigation, in readiness to pilot such men-of-war and transports as the commanders might think fit to send up.' It was a thoroughly lucid and sensible document, and Pitt must have been pleased with it.

Early in the new year, James returned to London, where there were more battles to be fought. One of them brought him face to face with Lord Barrington, the Secretary for War. It concerned that recurring flaw in his pattern of existence – pay. Had he been a commander-in-chief, he would have been entitled to £10 a day plus the sum of £1,000 for expenses. But, as Barrington pointed out, that honour belonged to General Amherst. As a major-general, his salary would be £2 a day. Nothing more. On this occasion, James seems to have been more than usually tactful. Recalling the conversation some time afterwards, Barrington observed: 'He said, however, he asked nothing; that he had no money himself, but he could borrow some off his father, so he should not be distressed.... His modesty touched me.' It did more than that: James's charm was so great that Barrington persuaded the King to sign a warrant for £500 by way of expenses. He also said that, if this were not sufficient, he would get the monarch to sign another.

As at Louisburg, there were to be three brigadiers in the corps. James had no doubt about the appointment of two of them. One brigade was to be given to the Honourable Robert Monckton, the second son of Viscount Galway. He was a quiet, straightforward, thoroughly modest gentleman, who had taken charge of the operations in the Bay of Fundy. James liked him and had complete confidence in his ability. His second choice was also a Louisburg veteran, the Honourable James Murray, son of Lord Elibank. Years previously, during his service in the Highlands, James had disagreed with Murray, but any hostility between the two men had long been forgotten. Commenting on Murray's work at Louisburg, James wrote that he 'has acted with infinite spirit. The public is indebted to him for great services in advancing by every method in his power the affairs of the siege.'

Monckton, then, was to command the first brigade, and Murray the third. The vacancy for the second remained open until a few days before departure. Indeed, when *Proposals for the Expedition of Quebec* were published, there was a blank space for this appointment. When, at last, a decision was reached, the choice was not James's but Pitt's. The officer's name was the Honourable George Townshend. He was three years older than James, the heir to a viscountcy, and the man of whom Horace Walpole wrote: 'his proud and sullen and contemptuous temper never suffered him to wait for thwarting his superiors till risen to a level with them.' He was a cavalryman who had fought at Culloden and Laufeld. After the latter, Cumberland had made him his aide-de-camp. The appointment was brief. One year later, Townshend became lieutenant-colonel of the 1st Foot Guards.

Among his less endearing characteristics (at any rate, so far as his superior officers were concerned), were his sense of the ridiculous and the fact that he was a born cartoonist. Not long after his service with Cumberland, he produced a number of brutal caricatures featuring the Duke. He was also said to have inspired a pamphlet which attacked his royal master's military methods. Such things were not to be tolerated. Townshend was compelled to retire from the service until the Duke's mismanagement at Hanover showed that the comments had not been altogether wide of the mark. He was then given the rank of colonel and appointed ADC to the King.

But Townshend wanted to get back to proper soldiering. No doubt George II mentioned the fact to Pitt, who may have considered that he had made sufficient concessions to the young major-general. He had, after all, given in to him on most questions – was it not reasonable that he should be allowed to nominate at least one of the brigadiers? After nine years in the wilderness, George Townshend, that most difficult of subordinates, was back in business. It was not long before he was exercising his abrasive artistic talents on his new commander.

The expedition was scheduled to sail from Portsmouth in the third week of February. Before this, however, there was much to be done. On 12 January, James's commission, signed by George II, was handed over to him by Pitt. James presumably sent it to his mother for safekeeping, but from that point onwards the document disappeared. Normally it would have been recorded in the minister's office and at the War Office. By some strange oversight this was never done. All James's other commissions are to be found in the Wardes' house at Westerham; but this, the most important of them all, is missing. When, after her son's death, Mrs Wolfe was engaged in a wrangle with the Army about the amount of money due to her, she was asked to produce it; but she ignored the request. Had she destroyed it in a moment of angry despair? Did it never reach her? Or was she unwilling to allow this precious fragment of paper to leave her possession – fearing, perhaps, that it would not be returned? All this is speculation; the fact remains that the official evidence of James's appointment has never been located.

James's Uncle Wat in Dublin was one of his closest confidants. Since Walter Wolfe was, himself, a military man, he was obviously very interested in his nephew's activities, and he never wanted for news. On 29 January, James wrote him a final letter. It contained his by now familiar criticisms of the North American campaign; and observed: 'The backwardness of some of the older officers has in some measure forced the Government to come down so low [in giving him the command]. I shall do my best, and leave the rest to fortune.' His farewell letter to Mrs Wolfe was, on the whole, cool. Since he was staying in London, and she was only a few miles away at Blackheath, there was no reason why he should not have said good-bye in person. But his betrothal to Kathleen Lowther may have caused him to stay away. During the course of a note which was unusually brief, he announced: 'I shall carry this business through with my best abilities. The rest, you know, is in the hands of Providence, to whose care I hope your good life and conduct will recommend your son.'

During his last days in London, he was invited to dinner by Pitt. The only other guest was the minister's brother-in-law, Lord Temple. According to Temple, who remarked on it to Thomas Grenville, who passed the account on to Earl Stanhope, who described it several years later in one of his Histories of England, the meal was not a success. At some point, James is alleged to have drawn his sword, and thumped the table top with his hilt. He then 'broke forth into a strain of gascanade and bravado'. After he had departed, Pitt is supposed to have said: 'Good God! that I should have entrusted the fate of the Country and the Administration to such hands!'

Such conduct might have been explained, if James had drunk too much. But everything suggests that his input of wine was very moderate – far less, indeed than that of his distinguished host and fellow guest. On the other hand, he was never slow to express his feelings: he was clearly extremely enthusiastic about his new command, and his conversation no doubt reflected the fact. In 1758, they had failed to take Quebec – indeed, they had not even attempted such a mission. James was determined that, this time, the town should fall. By the time the story appeared in print, it had passed through several hands. Each had doubtless added to it, until James's original remarks had been distorted into a caricature worthy of the pen of George Townshend. As for Pitt's remark, as W. T. Waugh remarked in *James Wolfe Man and Soldier* (Montreal, 1928): 'It is certain, too, that [he] did not utter the exclamation attributed to him; that great orator could never have perpetrated such a banal anticlimax.' Mr Waugh also suggests that, since James had not entirely recovered from his ailments, he was 'slightly feverish'. He may, then, have been in an excitable frame of mind, but he was certainly not delirious.

The men-of-war were assembling off Portsmouth. On 14 February 1759, a convoy of sixty transports, escorted by six ships of the line and nine frigates, under the command of Rear-Admiral Sir Charles Holmes, sailed for New York. Three days later, James embarked with Vice-Admiral Sir Charles Saunders in the 90-gun HMS *Neptune*. Their destination was supposed to be Louisburg. The last and greatest adventure of James Wolfe had begun. While they were on passage, Lieutenant-General Edward Wolfe died at Blackheath. He was in his seventieth year.

12
THE FORCES ASSEMBLE

The timing of the operations which were designed to smash the French hold on North America had been worked out by Pitt. He had promised James 12,000 men for his part in the undertaking plus a generous allocation of shipping. The total tonnage of Sir Charles Holmes's convoy added up to 20,000, and the colonies themselves were required to produce a further 6,000 tons. The vessels and the soldiers were scheduled to assemble at Louisburg at the end of April. Since most of the troops were already in America, it may have seemed to be easy. Unfortunately, Pitt did not take sufficient account of the weather.

When James embarked in HMS *Neptune*, he made the acquaintance of Vice-Admiral Sir Charles Saunders who, as commander-in-chief of the naval force, was to be his partner in the campaign. Previously, Saunders had been Comptroller of the Navy; and, before that, Senior Naval Officer in Newfoundland. Earlier in his career, he had served with Lord Anson, when Anson circumnavigated the world. He was, by all accounts, a quiet and capable officer. Horace Walpole remarked of him: 'No man said less, or deserved more.' One of Wolfe's aides agreed that he was 'a worthy gentleman and a brave man'. But, if he is to be believed, the voices which had tried to convince the King of James's insanity had also infected Saunders. He had, the ADC wrote, been 'taught to look on Mr Wolfe as a rash madman that would lead him into scrapes'.

During the voyage across the Atlantic, the two senior officers spent little time discussing the coming events. When at last they reached America, James remained uncertain about his colleague's plans for naval warfare in the St Lawrence, but this may be understandable. He was still unwell, and the Atlantic in late winter is no place for a man in poor condition who is subject to seasickness. Consequently, he spent most of the time shut away in his cabin. As for Saunders, at this juncture he may not yet have devised any strategy. Nevertheless, he had taken at least two precautions. One was that of putting Captain James Cook, who had already shown an uncommon talent for navigation, in charge of HMS *Mercury*. The other occurred on the eve of departure, when the Admiralty suddenly insisted that two vessels must be detached from the squadron for service in the Mediterranean. One of them, the instructions specified, was to be the *Stirling Castle*. In the event, Saunders ignored the small print, and sent something else. The *Stirling Castle*, he noted, was 'handy for rivers'. This may suggest that he had already determined to bring his big ships as far up the St Lawrence as possible. To have gone into greater detail with few facts to guide him would have been foolish.

The naval forces which were to be brought together under Saunders's command were now split into three. Admiral Holmes's convoy, with its cumbersome herd of transports, was struggling across the Atlantic in heavy weather. Saunders's own smaller and faster squadron was similarly engaged; and, before many days had passed, it had overtaken Holmes's slower fleet. Meanwhile, the second-in-command, Rear-Admiral Philip Durrell, was already in American waters. If he was obeying his orders, Durrell's ships should be in position across the Gulf of St Lawrence – denying it to any French units which, when the thaw came, might try to reach Quebec.

So far as James was concerned, the days passed with a wretched slowness. His fever seemed to come and go. Now and again, he suffered atrocious pains in his bladder; his joints ached with rheumatism; and, as always, he was horribly seasick. At times he wondered whether he was in a fit condition to undertake such an important task; but then the fever dropped, the nausea eased, and his self-confidence returned. Occasionally he ventured on deck in an attempt to take some exercise. Such excursions seldom lasted for long. It was bitterly cold, with a slate grey sky overhead and huge waves crashing on to *Neptune*'s decks. One day it would be spring and they would reach the shelter of the

Canadian coast, but it was hard to believe. To James, the torment seemed endless.

At last, during the final week of April, the silhouette of Cape Breton Island appeared on the horizon. But the excesses of winter were not yet done. As the squadron approached the coast, it soon became clear that Gabarouse Bay and the harbour were still covered with ice. To make matters worse, the island suddenly disappeared behind a bank of fog. Under such circumstances, it was impossible to berth. Admiral Saunders ordered the squadron to steer a course for Halifax. They arrived there on 30 April.

James found little to please him. The troops already stationed in Halifax were recovering from an epidemic of measles. Rear-Admiral Durrell, contrary to his instructions, was not on station in the Gulf of St Lawrence: his ships were still in the port. As James's aide wrote, Durrell and his captains 'began to see themselves in a devilish scrape, and that they should be called to severe account for not being in the Chops of the River early enough to prevent supplies going to Quebec. These gentlemen began to arraign Mr Wolfe's conduct in hopes to screen themselves. But all mankind joined in an opinion that nothing could be more scandalous than their proceedings, and all the bellowing of the Troops at Halifax could not persuade them to leave that harbour for fear of ice.'

So far as James was concerned, it merely confirmed his opinion that Durrell was a very second-rate commander. In a letter to Pitt, he had described him as 'vastly unequal to the weight of business'. However, in Durrell's defence, it should be said that the winter had been exceptionally harsh and that, in his opinion, he required more than the three hundred troops that had been seconded to his ships. What precisely he told James has not been recorded, but he had no cause to complain of the army commander's attitude. He was promptly given a further 250 men under the expedition's Quarter Master General, Colonel Guy Carleton. Once this had been arranged, Saunders ordered him to get out of Halifax and into the Gulf of St Lawrence immediately. But the tardy Durrell was too late. A convoy from France had just slipped through. He captured two store ships at the rear, but the others escaped. In practical terms, the net result was that the naval force was now the richer by a collection of charts relating to the St Lawrence. But these were of doubtful accuracy. James's aide forlornly wrote: 'Canada would certainly have been an easier conquest had that [Durrell's] squadron gone earlier into the River.' This, on the whole, seems doubtful; but the French ships which reached Quebec carried a valuable officer. His name was Colonel de Bougainville, and he was Montcalm's aide-de-camp. The capture of de Bougainville would have been more valuable than the sum of reinforcements and supplies on board.

The period at Halifax was one of frustration. Although Pitt had promised him 12,000 troops, it seemed very unlikely that so many would be available. In spite of the recruiting officers' efforts, it had been impossible to fill the holes in the ranks created by sickness and the previous year's campaign. Of Holmes's convoy, only an ordnance ship named *Ruby* had reached port. The remainder were said to have been scattered by a storm, and some were believed to have foundered. Five hundred men had to be taken away from the American battalions for the defence of Nova Scotia. Once they were gone, these four units had only a couple of thousand men fit to serve.

After a rest of over two months while its owner was at sea, James's pen became active again. On 1 May, he wrote to Pitt. He informed him of the late departure of Durrell's squadron; and he pointed out that, unless the units drafted to him by Amherst were up to strength, the force would contain nothing like the promised 12,000 men. Indeed, 6,000 would be nearer the figure. At the end of the letter, he observed: 'Our troops, indeed, are good and very well disposed. If valour can make amends for the want of numbers, we shall probably succeed. Any accidents on the river, or sickness among the men, might put us to some difficulties.'

Never had a General been more concerned about the welfare of his men. While he was at Halifax, he asked Amherst to send him sufficient molasses to manufacture six months' supply of spruce beer. It was, he believed, good as a preventative and as a cure for scurvy. On 9 May, he issued an order concerning life on shipboard as it affected the coming trip up the St Lawrence. 'After the troops are embarked', he wrote, 'the commanding officers will give all necessary directions for the preservation of the health of their men. Guards must mount in every ship, to keep strict order and prevent fire. When the weather permits, the men are to be as much in the open air as possible, and to eat upon deck. Cleanliness in the berths and bedding, and as much exercise as the situation permits, are the best preservatives of health.' There were also instructions about what should be done if a vessel ran aground. 'The men on shore are to make three distinct fires by night, and three distinct smokes by day, to mark their situation.' They had, he believed, little to fear from the Canadians living on the river banks. 'Fifty men with arms', he said, 'may easily defend themselves until succour arrives.'

At last the ice dispersed, and on 13 May they were able to sail for Louisburg. The voyage lasted two days. When he arrived, James found a packet of mail waiting for him. One of the letters was from Lord Barrington, the Secretary for War, instructing him to remain in Canada. It had been in transit when James was already making his way back to England, and his letter to Pitt* had repaired any damage done by his apparent disobedience. He might just as well have thrown it away, but Barrington's words seem to have rankled. Some while later, when he had many more urgent things to engage his attention, James replied at some length. He repeated his assertion that Field Marshal Ligonier (the army's commander-in-chief) had told him that it was in order to return at the end of the Louisburg campaign. Then he wrote:

> ... as General Amherst had no other commands than to send me to winter at Halifax under the orders of an officer who was, but a few months before, put over my head, I thought it was much better to get into the way of Service, and out of the way of being insulted; and as the style of your Lordship's letter is pretty strong, I must take the liberty to inform you, that though I should have been very glad to have gone with General Amherst to join the army upon the Lakes ... yet rather than receive orders in the Government of an officer younger than myself (tho' a very worthy man) I should certainly have desired leave to resign my commission; for as I neither ask nor expect any favour, so I never intend to submit to any ill usage whatsoever.

* See previous chapter.

It was strong stuff for a substantive colonel (albeit a local major-general) to send to a cabinet minister, but he was probably past caring. His future, one way or another, would be decided at Quebec. Furthermore, his sense of values may have been affected by the fact that he was, no doubt, very lonely. The tight-lipped Admiral Saunders did not encourage the exchange of personal confidences; his friend Guy Carleton was in the St Lawrence with Durrell's flotilla; and he was not on intimate terms with his three brigadiers. Back in England there was, admittedly, the fair Miss Lowther, but she was even farther away than Carleton. His mother was now an ill-tempered old woman; and his father, as the second letter in this collection of mail informed him, was dead.

The news of the old General's death saddened but did not surprise him. He wrote to his Uncle Wat in Dublin: 'I left him in so weak a condition that it was not probable we should ever meet again. The general tenor of his conduct through life has been extremely upright and benevolent, from whence one may hope that little failings and imperfections were overbalanced by his many good qualities. I am exceedingly sorry it so fell out that I had it not in my power to assist him in his illness, and to relieve my mother in her distress; the more so as her relations are not affectionate, and you are too far off to give her help. I have writ to Mr Fisher to continue the pensions which my father had assigned to his kindred; my easy circumstances enabling me to fulfil all his intentions.'

His reference to 'easy circumstances' makes it clear that James had no idea that, at the last moment, his father had changed his will. With Mrs Wolfe inheriting the entire estate, his finances were in their customary chaotic condition. According to his aide, James had 'an exceeding contempt for money'; but he had also a chronic need for it. At the moment, however, he was more concerned with the finances of his expedition. As he wrote later to Pitt: 'I writ to General Amherst for money, but he could send me none; this is one of the first sieges, perhaps, that ever was undertaken without it.'

The appeal to Amherst had been sent off on 1 May. James was unwell at the time, and observed: 'I wish you health and success

– of the former I have but a small share; of the latter as little hope unless we get into the river first. However, trust me they shall feel us.' As for the economics, he pointed out: 'There is a great siege to be undertaken and not a farthing to pay the workmen. I am not possessed of a single dollar of public money.' Poor James! One sometimes feels that, beneath the soldier's red tunic, there was an accountant struggling to get out. In transactions great and small, no matter what his ADC may have thought, everything boiled down to cash – and, throughout his life, there was never sufficient.

But the troops knew nothing of these misgivings, and their place in James's thoughts should not be exaggerated. In his letter to Uncle Wat, he was suitably concerned about his father's death, and he said all the right things. Nevertheless, the remarks only accounted for about one fifth of the length. The remainder was devoted to reflections about his plans for the investment of Quebec. Instead of the promised 12,000 men, he now expected to have only 9,000, a sum which was made up of ten battalions, three companies of Grenadiers, some marines ('if the Admiral can spare them'), six newly recruited companies of North American rangers ('not complete, and the worst soldiers in the universe'), 'a great train of artillery, plenty of provisions, tools, and implements of all sorts'. The opposition, he estimated, would amount to six battalions of infantry, 'some companies of Marines, four or five thousand Canadians, and some Indians; altogether, not much inferior to their enemy'. The town of Quebec was, he suspected, poorly defended; but the rocky ground above it would make his soldiers' task more difficult. A great deal depended upon the navy making itself masters of the river.

'If I find that the enemy is strong, audacious, and well commanded', he told his uncle, 'I shall proceed with the utmost caution and circumspection.... If they are timid, weak, and ignorant, we shall push them with more vivacity.... The army under my command is rather too small for the undertaking, but it is well composed.' As for his own conduct, 'you may be assured that I shall take all the proper care of my own person, unless in case of the last importance, where it becomes a duty to do otherwise. I never put myself unnecessarily in the way of danger.' His

ADC would not have agreed with this statement. According to his observations, 'Mr Wolfe had a very peculiar turn for war – personal bravery to excess.' In this letter, James gives the first clue that he was considering launching an attack on the city from upstream. He did not – and probably could not at this stage – go into details, but he was already talking about landing a detachment 'three, four, five miles, or more, above the town'.

Most of his information about Quebec came from his chief engineer, Major Patrick Mackellar. During the campaign of 1756, Major Mackellar had been captured by the French at Oswego. He had spent some time as a prisoner of war in the city, and had tried to put this period to good purpose by finding out all he could about the fortifications. When he was repatriated, he wrote a detailed report, which he submitted to the Office of Ordnance in London. It was considered to be 'excellent'. In fact, the information was inadequate and mostly out of date. Mackellar admitted: 'The Defences to the Land I can speak of only from the Plan and a Little imperfect Intelligence – the Plan appears to have been taken about the Year 1740, and I have not heard that there have been any Additions to the Fortifications since that Time.' There had, as it happened, been a completely new defence system put up in 1745, but he knew nothing about it. Indeed Major Mackellar's study seems to have been rather like a latter day visit to Russia under the auspices of Intourist: he saw only what his hosts wished him to see, and if his observations misled him so much the better. There is no knowing how much James was influenced by the report: not, perhaps, very much, for his opinion of the Sapper officer was not great. During the siege of Louisburg, he had described him as 'incompetent'. On the other hand, it amounted to all the information he had.

As always, James was extremely busy during those days at Louisburg. Units were coming in from stations in other parts of America. The fleet of transports under Admiral Holmes's command at last turned up after a fearful voyage. They had indeed been scattered by a storm, and one vessel had been dismasted. None, however, had been sunk. On the other hand, and to add to his difficulties, three regiments had lost all their equipment on the journey from New York. Eventually, the strength of the army settled at 8,500* men – a figure which, the pundits in London observed, would prevent him from taking Quebec that year. This view would probably have been strengthened if they had known how badly clad many of the soldiers were.

Out at sea, there were still floes of ice acting as a hazard to shipping, and the fog came and went. For much of the period, a signal gun had to be fired at fifteen-minute intervals to warn the mariners in Gabarouse Bay. But the bad weather did not hamper the men's training. Some of the commanding officers had obviously yet to get the measure of their commander-in-chief. They expected him to inspect their men in the manner of a more orthodox general. In a number of cases, they had not had time to practise the new drill, which had been laid down for the army. When one of the colonels apologized to James about this, he received a brusque reply. 'Poh! Poh!,' the young general said. 'New exercise – new fiddlesticks! If they are otherwise well disciplined and will fight, that's all I require of them.'

There were apparently endless points of detail to be resolved. One of them concerned the number of women that might accompany the force. Normally, regiments on active service were allowed to take with them six females for every hundred men. In this expedition, however, the proportion was smaller – three to every seventy-five and four to every one hundred. They were, incidentally, required to do more than simply attend to the sexual comfort of the troops. One of their duties was to act as nurses.

At last the force was ready to embark. Monckton's brigade was now made up of four regiments of foot; Townshend and Murray each had three. In addition, there were three companies of grenadiers taken from the Louisburg garrison, and six companies of American rangers commanded by Major George Scott, plus gunners and engineers. On 4 June, the main body cleared the port, and by the sixth the stragglers had left. On this day, James – now back in HMS *Neptune* – sat down to catch up with his correspondence. He also used the occasion to make his will.

He might have saved himself the trouble; for, as things turned out, the document was entirely valueless. It was based on his

* Another figure frequently quoted is 9,280.

wrong assumption about his father's estate. Nevertheless, it shows something of his state of mind at the time. The first item, not surprisingly, concerned Kathleen Lowther. Her picture was to be 'set in jewels to the amount of five hundred guineas and return'd to her'. Four colonels – among them his friends Guy Carleton and George Warde – were each to receive £1,000; and Admiral Saunders was 'to accept of my light service of plate, in remembrance of his guest'. 'My camp equipment, kitchen furniture, table linen, and wine and provisions, I leave to the Officer who succeeds me in the command [presumably Monckton].' His books and papers, 'both here and in England', were to become the property of Colonel Carleton. Major Barré – his Adjutant General, his two aides-de-camp, and four other favoured captains, were each to have one hundred guineas 'to buy rings and swords in remembrance of their friend'. There were smaller bequests to his servants; and 'everything over and above these legacies, I leave to my good mother, entirely at her disposal.' The document was witnessed by two of his beneficiaries – Captain William de Laune and Thomas Bell (who was one of his ADCs: the other was Captain Hervey Smyth).

The giant convoy plodded on through the calm waters of the Gulf of St Lawrence, gradually closing up on the river which was to decide the fate of this assembly of ships and soldiers. Some way ahead of them, its situation unknown, was Admiral Durrell and his flotilla of ten vessels. There was nobody, from Saunders and Wolfe down to the most humble private on board, who would not have given away a fortune for news of them, but no word came. It was almost as if they had vanished.

The purpose of Durrell and his force was now to carry out an armed reconnaissance. If possible, they were to penetrate into the basin of Quebec itself. On the way, the troops were to occupy various islands – including the pilot station on the Ile de Bic (170 miles from Quebec) and the Ile de Coudres, which commanded the river from a point 61 miles from the city. The captured French charts may have been helpful, but they were not enough. The flotilla needed pilots, and Durrell obtained them in the simplest possible manner. As his vessels approached the Ile de Bic, they unfurled the French flag and made the necessary signal. A small armada of boats instantly set off from the shore, each containing a talkative French pilot who badly wanted the money for a trip up to Quebec. When, however, they discovered the deception, most of them became silent – and those who spoke were angry. They were obviously not going to be co-operative, but as things turned out this did not matter much. Even when they were doing their best, they were unreliable; and the French had not made any great attempts to survey the river. Indeed, their knowledge was apt to be as misleading as the charts. On the other hand, Durrell had an officer who was worth a dozen of them. For the purpose of this expedition, Captain James Cook had been transferred to the command of HMS *Pembroke*. Captain Cook seemed to be able to feel his way through unknown and potentially hazardous waters simply by sniffing the air.

The main force sailed cautiously on. James was no doubt planning and re-planning the operations ahead of him; and the troops were in good order. Their spirit is best summed up by Sergeant Edward Botwood of the 47th (Lascelles') Foot, who, until his death in action, seems to have been the unofficial bard of the force. Wrote Sergeant Botwood:

Come, each death-doing dog who dares to venture his neck,
Come, follow the hero that goes to Quebec;
Jump aboard of the transports, and loose every sail,
Pay your debts at the tavern by giving leg-bail;*
And ye that love fighting shall soon have enough:
Wolfe commands you, my boys; we shall give them Hot Stuff.

Up the River St Lawrence our troops shall advance,
To the Grenadiers' March we will teach them to dance.
Cape Breton we have taken, and next we will try
At their capital to give them another black eye.
Vaudreuil,† 'tis in vain you pretend to look gruff,
Those are coming who know how to give you Hot Stuff....

... and so on. There were two more verses in similar rollicking style.

* An expression meaning to run away – in other words, the debts would never be repaid.

† The Governor-General of Quebec.

13
THE IDENTITY OF AN ENEMY

The destination was Quebec, the capital of New France and the key to the colony's conquest. If Quebec fell, the theory suggested, the rest of the territory would automatically pass into British hands. The city was built on a rocky headland on the north bank of the St Lawrence, about 350 miles from the sea.

Thirty-two miles down stream, the river was twelve miles wide. By the time it reached the town, however, it had narrowed to about one thousand yards. The Isle of Orleans, a strip of land about twenty miles long, was in a natural position to guard the eastern approaches; and, near the western tip of the island, a tributary named the St Charles River wriggled its way northwards into the hills. The only navigable channel was a stretch of water known as the Traverse, which separated the Isle of Orleans from a smaller island known as the Ile Madame.

Quebec had been founded by Samuel Champlain in 1608. For the first sixty-five years of its existence, it had been governed by adventurers with no interference from France. In that year, the King had taken it under his control by appointing an official known as the *Intendant de Justice, Police et Finance*. The post was unpopular with the colonists just as, over the years, all visitors and residents from the mother country were viewed with suspicion. Nevertheless, the settlers believed that it had a duty to protect them in an emergency. The French view was that the government would do what it could, provided it did not interfere with the more serious business of Europe.

In 1759, the population of New France amounted to about 65,000 people. Seven thousand of them inhabited Quebec; four thousand lived in Montreal, 140 miles up the river; and the remainder were scattered over the colony in villages and isolated farms. Most of these settlements were situated in clearings amid massive forests. The river itself was still something of an unknown quantity, insufficiently explored and badly charted. Indeed the Governor-General of Quebec was under a similar impression to that of his former colleague at Louisburg, who had put all his faith on the unkind coast of Breton Island. So long as Quebec had the St Lawrence as an ally, he seemed to say, who needed more elaborate defences? No fleet of any size would ever be able to come up it. His opinion was confirmed by the pilots on the Ile de Bic, who had a vested interest in making the river appear to be difficult to negotiate.

Had James Wolfe been able to receive an accurate intelligence report from the city, the contents would have pleased him. Conditions within Quebec and in the surrounding countryside were appalling. The people were short of food, and they had little confidence in their defenders. Part of the reason for the prevailing famine lay in the previous year's campaigning, when too many men had been taken from the fields and put into the army. As a result, the harvest had never been properly reaped.

But this was not the whole reason. The current holder of the Intendant's office was a man named François Bigot, who had been given the job at the end of the War of Austrian Succession. During the eleven years which had elapsed, Bigot had become a most accomplished crook. His house, which was conveniently situated next door to the Quebec granary and warehouse, has been described as a 'palace'. It was the centre of the city's social life, and the scene of its most expensive debaucheries.

While the rest of New France went hungry, Bigot flourished. One of his rackets was based on the commercial adage of buying cheap and selling dear. He would purchase the colony's entire harvest for a pittance, and sell it at an enormous profit to France. Having sent it across the Atlantic in his own ships, he would then appeal to the French authorities for help. The colony, as he not unreasonably pointed out, was short of food. The officials sold the corn back to him at a price far less than they had paid; and, on the return of this by now much travelled cargo to Quebec, Bigot retailed it to the colonists at an even greater profit. If it failed to come back, they went hungry.

This was by no means his only method of increasing his

personal fortune. From time to time, he consulted with the Governor and, as an outcome of these conversations, he decided that the city's fortifications should be improved. Montcalm, for one, would have agreed with him. As that officer had noticed, Quebec's 'situation should have inspired any engineer other than M. de Léry* with the means of making an exceedingly strong place of it; but it seems that he has, although spending immense sums of money, devoted himself to destroying the advantages with which nature had, with such prodigality, supplied it.' Bigot's contribution to what were obviously much needed improvements was minimal. A selected builder was invited to purchase a contract from him; and, once the man had paid his money, he could do whatever he liked. Indeed, slipshod work was smiled upon by the Intendant. It meant that, before very long, it would require attention – and, once again, he would profit.

It was hardly surprising that the Governor preferred to put his faith in the steep cliffs which guarded two sides, and the river which flowed past it. Nevertheless, this senior official had confidence in Bigot. He once wrote: 'Nobody is a better citizen than he is, or has the King's interests more at heart.' It seems surprising that anybody could be so gullible; but, in a society which was rotten with corruption, the Governor-General had doubtless enjoyed more than his fair share of the pleasures to be found at the Intendant's 'palace'.

For the past four years, the Governor of Quebec had been a gentleman named the Marquis de Vaudreuil. His father had been in charge of the colony's troops, and for twenty-two years had served as Governor. With such influence behind him, it was not surprising that his son, Pierre, had been commissioned as an ensign at the age of six, nor that he had become a captain at seventeen. But, despite this rapid and suspiciously youthful promotion, his military knowledge amounted to hardly anything. He was far more adept at playing the game of politics, and his skill had availed him well. In 1742, at the age of forty-eight, he began

* Gaspard Chaussegros de Léry, an engineer who had begun an attempt to rebuild the fortifications of Quebec in 1720. After a stop-start project which went on for over twenty years, de Léry was compelled to admit that, in the event of an attack, the defenders' only hope was to prevent the enemy from landing near the city.

an eleven-year stint as Governor of Louisiana. King Louis XV rewarded him with the title of Grand Marquis, and in 1755 his successor, Louis XVI, had elevated him to the governorship of New France.

Vaudreuil had been successful; there was no gainsaying the fact. His character, however, was not equal to his rank. Stripped of the frills of office, he was a vain and rather pompous individual, who was intensely jealous of his position. In particular, he had a considerable dislike for the commander-in-chief of the colony's regular forces, a general imported from France named Louis-Joseph, Marquis de Montcalm. He resented Montcalm's more sophisticated ideas and graces, just as the soldier deplored the fact that Vaudreuil was in effective command of the entire army. It was, after all, ridiculous that a dedicated professional should be compelled to take orders from an official who was, at best, an amateur. Montcalm had put this point to the King, but the monarch was adamant. 'M. de Montcalm', he wrote, 'shall have only to execute and see that the troops under his command execute all the Governor's orders.' An attempt by the French Minister of War to change the decision was unsuccessful.

Montcalm had been born near Nîmes on 29 February 1712. His ancestors were all soldiers, and it was almost a matter of course that, at the age of fourteen, he himself joined the army. As in James's case, being commissioned at a precociously early age had cut short his education; and, again like James, he had tried to rectify the omission by reading. Most of his studies had concentrated on Greek and German. He fought in his first action at the age of twenty-one.

During the War of Austrian Succession, he served in Bohemia and Italy, where he took over the colonelcy of a regiment. In 1746, he was involved in a disastrous battle at Piacenza. The battalion was annihilated; he received five sabre cuts and was taken prisoner. On his return to France after an exchange of captives, he was given the rank of brigadier. On 25 January 1756, having spent five years of idleness at his château, he received a letter offering him the post of commander-in-chief of the French forces in North America. His wife advised him to turn it down; his mother counselled him to accept. Montcalm accepted –

though with no very great enthusiasm. He was given the rank of major-general, and set off from Brest with a flotilla of six ships and 1,139 men during the early part of 1756.

Montcalm had a just reputation for being a brave and efficient officer. He was also impatient, impulsive, talkative, and ambitious. His second-in-command, the Chevalier de Lévis, made an attempt to come to terms with Vaudreuil, which was not very difficult. All that was needed was a sufficient supply of flattery. Montcalm made no such effort. On one occasion, he wrote in a letter: 'I am on good terms with him [Vaudreuil], but not in his confidence, which he never gives to anybody from France. His intentions are good, but he is slow and irresolute.' In his diary that night, however, he noted: 'This evening at 10 o'clock the M. de Vaudreuil sent me his ridiculous, obscure and misleading orders.'

On another occasion, he wrote: 'M. le Marquis de Vaudreuil, Governor-General and in this capacity general of the army, made his first tour [of new defences]; after all, youth must be instructed. As he had never seen either a camp or a work of defence, everything seemed to him as new as it was amusing. He asked singular questions. He was like a man born blind who has been given sight.'

Vaudreuil's newly acquired 'sight' did not, however, permit him to see weaknesses which were all too apparent to the professional eye of Montcalm. For example, the General was anxious to build batteries at Cap Tourmente, a headland which controlled the approaches to the Isle of Orleans and consequently Quebec. The Governor-General refused. There was, he considered, no need for such an outpost: the river, with its reefs and shoals and difficult currents, was worth a hundred guns. Similarly, Montcalm proposed that Point Lévis, a promontory which overlooked the city on the south bank, should be heavily fortified. Again Vaudreuil turned the idea down. He remarked that, if the enemy occupied it, they could do small damage to Quebec – whilst guns placed in the Upper Town could wreck havoc with the invaders. Montcalm argued with his stubborn colleague, but it was in vain. The Governor considered that Quebec was impregnable, and that was enough.

All told, there were about 16,000 men at arms ready to defend the city and its surroundings. Of these, however, only six thousand came under Montcalm's command. These were regulars sent from France, and they could be relied upon to give a good account of themselves. The remainder were local militia recruited from the townspeople and the outlying settlements. Some of them, with a countryman's instinctive knowledge of field craft, were proficient at scouting and raiding. As soldiers, however, they had neither discipline nor morale. Nor were the Indians who, in theory, were under Vaudreuil to be relied upon. They came and went according to their mood of the moment. In so far as they had any preferences, they preferred Montcalm's command to that of the Governor.

Just as the two men at the top were divided in their opinions, so were the troops. The French regulars had a considerable regard for Montcalm and little time for Vaudreuil. The local irregulars, on the other hand, put such trust as they had in the Governor. They had no time for interlopers from France.

Once Louisburg had fallen, it seemed to be only a matter of time before the British launched an attack on Quebec. Food supplies became scarcer until the daily ration of bread for soldiers and civilians alike was a mere two ounces. Morale in the colony became lower and lower. Vaudreuil might think that the city could never be taken. Nobody else, with the possible exception of Bigot, shared his opinion. There might, indeed, have been civil strife, but there was no way of arousing popular opinion. Among the things which were denied the colony was a printing press. Consequently, the only medium was word of mouth, and the leading broadcasters were the Governor and the Bishop. The former let it be known that, if the British overcame New France, they intended to slaughter all Canadians, regardless of age, sex, or whether or not they bore arms. The Bishop, for his part, grossly exaggerated the British strength. If fear was a good comrade in arms, these two men were doing an excellent job. Unfortunately, it was not sufficient to rouse minds which had already accepted the idea of defeat, and it could not remedy an empty stomach.

During the autumn of 1758, the point came when even Vaudreuil admitted that the colony needed help from France. A small convoy was assembled, and Montcalm's aide-de-camp, an extremely intelligent twenty-nine-year-old officer named Colonel Louis-Antoine de Bougainville, was put in charge of it. On 20 December, Colonel de Bougainville presented himself at Versailles. His proposals contained four main points.

The first was a plea that France should create a diversion by sending an expeditionary force to invade either Virginia or the Carolinas. These targets were selected on the grounds that the bulk of British naval power was concentrated in the north. Consequently, it would be easier for the armada to avoid interception. Nor were these two colonies heavily defended: if the British wished to hold them, they would have to deploy troops from the northern theatre.

Point number two was an appeal for aid in the shape of small arms, cannons, and troop reinforcements; and point number three, inserted by Montcalm, was that the structure of the colony's militia should be completely overhauled. Vaudreuil was opposed to it: he suspected (rightly) that the General was making another attempt to bring the entire collection of troops under his command. Finally, the manifesto suggested that, if the worst came to the worst and the colony was compelled to capitulate, the regular soldiers should be withdrawn before the event. It should still be possible to evacuate them to the Mississippi and thence to Louisiana, where they would live to fight another day.

Some of the report was turned down. Madame de Pompadour favoured the idea of a diversionary expedition, but it was too expensive and there were not sufficient ships available. As for the rest, four vessels were filled with ammunition and reinforcements; Montcalm was to be promoted to the rank of lieutenant-general and was not, as Vaudreuil had once suggested, to be recalled to France. Far from it. The Governor was now ordered to defer to him on military matters. Finally, the King promised that the whole question of the colony would be reviewed in 1760.

Colonel de Bougainville returned to Canada. It was, in fact, his convoy that, with the exception of two store ships, had evaded Durrell's squadron. Those that reached Quebec had spotted the British sails on the horizon, and de Bougainville was in no doubt about their significance. The promise of a reconsideration of the colony's affairs in 1760 had been a waste of words. It would be too late: the moment of truth would come in the summer of the present year.

The Colonel's report on his mission brought little for anyone's comfort. The supplies and reinforcements did not amount to very much, for the King was more immediately preoccupied with affairs in Europe. Vaudreuil read in a dispatch addressed jointly to himself and to Bigot: 'His Majesty's intention is that M. le Marquis de Montcalm shall not only be consulted on all operations but also on all areas of administration relating to the defence and preservation of the colony; you will ask his advice, communicating to him the letters I write to you on all these subjects.' The effect of the instructions should have been to make Montcalm supreme commander. In practice, however, it is doubtful whether either Vaudreuil or Bigot ever told him about the matter. It certainly did nothing to change their methods of working, and Montcalm was to note: 'I have to allow him [Vaudreuil] to play the role of general. I act as secretary and major for him.'

Vaudreuil's reaction to the emergency was to call a daily council of war. The meetings were attended by the officers, Indian chiefs, and the civil authorities. As might be expected, they achieved little; but they may have served to distract the Governor from the fact that, quietly and with consummate professionalism, Montcalm was going about the business of preparing the city's defences. There was obviously no time in which to improve its inadequate fortifications, nor to instal guns on the much debated headlands of Cape Tourmente and Point Lévis. Consequently, the General decided to leave Quebec in the hands of 2,000 Canadian militia men supported by artillery, with floating batteries and fireships moored in the river. The main force, which now included five battalions of seasoned French regulars, was to be entrenched along a seven-mile stretch of the St Lawrence's north bank, between the rivers St Charles and Montmorency, and with a headquarters in the village of Beauport. There were steep cliffs which would make a British landing difficult if not impossible, and they would be able to frustrate any attempt to invest Quebec overland from a north-westerly direction. If, on the other hand, the enemy decided to move its troops by river for an attack upstream, the transports would have to pass the batteries and fireships. This, Montcalm devoutly hoped, would be impossible. Two fords and a bridge over the St Charles linked the newly dug positions with the city. All that Montcalm, Vaudreuil, and the unhappy population of Quebec could do now was to wait.

14
THE APPARENT FAILURE

James Wolfe's assessment of the military strength of Quebec had been surprisingly accurate. He had not, however, managed to surmise the intentions of Montcalm. He had assumed that the 'Old Wolf', as he called him, would concentrate his forces in the immediate vicinity of the city. The French general, on the other hand, had shown a far better anticipation of the British intentions. By entrenching his men in strong positions downstream, he had ensured that any assault from this direction would be virtually impossible. Up to a point, he had been right. James had, in fact, proposed to land his soldiers on a beach which was now covered by enemy guns. Once they were assembled, his plan was to march them round Quebec to the far side. He would then take the offensive at a point where the enemy depended upon man-made fortifications and not upon nature – and where, consequently, they were weakest.

Such a plan did not, however, absolve the navy from clearing the river opposite the city; for, without a great deal of assistance from Admiral Saunders, he would have to contend with impossibly difficult lines of communication. Furthermore, he needed to be sure of covering fire from the warships' guns. In considering this aspect of the operation, he must have drawn confidence from the sailors' performances so far. The St Lawrence was a long and treacherous enigma. Vaudreuil had believed that it was the ultimate guardian of Quebec. He was soon to be disillusioned. A succession of signal fires, lit by the settlers on the banks, marked the British progress. The unhappy Governor soon realized that, far from littering the river with wrecks, the invaders were feeling their way relentlessly towards him.

On 10 June, the leading vessels cleared Bird Rocks at the entrance to the Gulf of St Lawrence; on the thirteenth the flagship *Neptune* entered the estuary. The winds were variable, the fog came suddenly and departed just as unexpectedly, but neither proved to be a substantial hindrance. On the fifteenth, when seventeen sloops-of-war, five frigates, and a number of transports and supply ships were already two hundred miles upstream, there was a sudden storm. According to Vaudreuil's calculations, it should have been sufficient to drive the vessels ashore, where they would have broken up on the rocks. In fact, it did nothing of the kind. Seldom in its history had the Royal Navy shown such magnificent seamanship.

At last, on 18 June, the leading vessels of the main force reached the Ile de Bic. As the pilot station came into view, they noticed the reassuring sight of two British warships lying at anchor. One was the *Prince of Orange,* the other a frigate named HMS *Richmond.* Both had been sent back by Durrell, who had now reached the Ile aux Coudres. Among those on board was the master of the *Princess Amelia,* who brought with him Durrell's report. It was from this document that James and Admiral Saunders learned that de Bougainville's convoy had got through. The French pilots, Durrell explained, were useless, but this did not matter much. With the help of such officers as James Cook, the flotilla had found its way through the badly charted waters without very much difficulty. They had even been able to mark the channel by a succession of small boats with flags on them. Later, when Vaudreuil heard about the achievement, he received the news with a mixture of wonder and despair. 'The British,' he sadly announced 'passed sixty ships-of-war where we had hardly dared to risk a vessel of 100 tons.'

One story in particular indicates the apparently sixth sense which guided the sailors through these waters. When, on 20 June, the main force weighed anchor and set sail from the Ile de Bic the island's complement of French pilots was impressed into the fleet's service. They were, as might have been expected, unhelpful, and none more so than the man allocated to a transport named the *Goodwill.* He had much to say about his dislike of the English, and he echoed Vaudreuil's beliefs that the river would be the graveyard of the invaders. Eventually, when the ship was entering the Traverse between the Isle of Orleans and the Ile

Madame, the *Goodwill*'s master – a seasoned tarpaulin named Killick, who was normally employed by Trinity House – lost patience. According to Captain John Knox of the 43rd Foot, who was on board the transport, Mr Killick 'fixed his Mate at the helm, charged him not to take orders from any person except himself, and, going forward with his trumpet to the forecastle, gave the necessary instructions.' The pilot, according to Knox,

> declared we should be lost, for that no French ship ever presumed to pass there without a Pilot; 'aye, aye, my dear (Killick replied), but dam me, I'll convince you that an Englishman shall go where a Frenchman dare not show his nose'. The *Richmond* being close astern of us, the Commanding Officer called out to the Captain and told him our case; he inquired who the Master was? – and was answered from the forecastle by the man himself, who told him 'he was old Killick, and that was enough'. I went forward with this experienced mariner, who pointed out the channel to me as we passed, showing me by the ripple and colour of the water, where there was any danger; and distinguishing the places where there were ledges of rock (to me invisible) from banks of sand, mud or gravel. He gave his orders with great unconcern, joked with the sounding boats who lay off on each side, with coloured flags for our guidance; and, when any of them called to him, and pointed to the deepest water, he answered 'aye, aye, my dear, chalk it down, a damned dangerous navigation – eh, if you don't make a sputter about it, you'll get no credit for it in England.'

Later on, Mr Killick observed: 'Damn me, if there are not a thousand places in the Thames fifty times more hazardous than this; I am ashamed that Englishmen should make such a rout about it.'

While the fleet was spending two days at anchor off the Ile de Bic, James took the opportunity to transfer himself and his baggage into the *Richmond* for the last part of the voyage up river. Previously, the banks had been remarkable for the unbroken edge of an apparently impenetrable forest. Now, the line of trees became punctuated by small farms. Each had the smouldering remains of a bonfire, which had passed on the news that the invaders were moving towards Quebec. At last, on 26 June, the long journey was over. The *Richmond* dropped anchor off Saint

Laurent on the most southerly tip of the Isle of Orleans. By this time, the procession of vessels was spread out over a distance of fifty miles. One by one, the bulky transports and the more agile frigates and sloops turned into the wind, furled their sails and came to rest. Before many days had passed, the Traverse was packed with an assembly of sea power such as had never been seen in French Canada before.

James had been busy. When the first troops disembarked on the twenty-seventh, they took with them one of his compositions which was immediately nailed to the church door. It was a message addressed to the colonists:

The King, justly exasperated against France, has set foot a considerable armament by land and sea, to bring down the haughtiness of that Crown. His aim is to destroy the most considerable Settlement of the French in North America. It is not against the Industrious peasants, their Wives & Children, nor against the Ministers of Religion that he designs making War. He laments the misfortunes to which this quarrel exposes them and promises them his protection, offers to maintain them in their professions, and permits them to follow the worship of their religion, provided that they do not take any part in the difference between the two Crowns, directly or indirectly.

The Canadians cannot be ignorant of their Situation: the English are Masters of the River, and are blocking up the passage to all succour from Europe. They have besides a powerful Army on the [American] Continent under the Command of General Amherst.

The resolution the Canadians ought to take is by no means doubtful. The utmost exertion of their valour will be entirely useless, and will only serve to deprive them of the advantages that they might enjoy by their neutrality. The cruelties of the French against the subjects of Great Britain in America, would excuse the most severe reprisals; but Englishmen are too generous to follow barbarous examples. They offer to the Canadians the sweets of peace amidst the horrors of war. It is left to them to determine their fate by their conduct. If their presumption and a wrong placed, as well as fruitless courage, should make them take the most dangerous part, they will have their own selves to blame, when they shall groan under the weight of that misery to which they expose themselves.

General Wolfe flatters himself that the whole world will do him justice, if the inhabitants of Canada force him, by their refusal, to have recourse to violent methods. He concludes by laying before them the

Strength & Power of England, which generously stretches out her hand to them. I stand ready to assist them on all occasions, and even at a time when France, by its weaknesses, is incapable of assisting them, and abandoning them in the most critical moment.

It was, James must have told himself, an impressive document. Unfortunately, there were no settlers to read it. They had all fled from the island to take sanctuary in Quebec. Before departing, the parish priest had left a letter behind, imploring the invaders to treat his church with suitable reverence, and to inflict no damage upon it. Nevertheless, he had taken the precaution of removing the altar cloth and the plate.

Although he was still far from well, James was as active as ever. While the transports were arriving at the anchorage, and a river of redcoats was pouring on to the shore, he took Major Mackellar and a light escort to the most westerly edge of the island. He was anxious to catch his first glimpse of the city which had occupied his thoughts for so long; and, which was of more practical importance, to see what he could of Montcalm's defences. The trip was not encouraging. Over at Quebec, the imposing, slate-grey headland of Cape Diamond was crowned by the citadel from which the French flag fluttered in defiance. As he had rightly assumed, no attack could possibly be made from that quarter. Furthermore, and as he had not expected, the line of the river-bank reaching from the St Charles river to the Montmorency showed ample evidence of the hastily prepared redoubts and entrenchments. Nature, here too, was on the defenders' side. Before his men grappled with the enemy soldiers, they would have to scale precipitous cliffs. His original plan was out of the question, and he would have to think again.

Admiral Saunders was also given cause for uneasy reflections. As James's party made its way back across the island to Saint Laurent, a sudden storm broke out. Rain lashed horizontally across the land; the trees were shaken until it seemed as if they would be torn from their roots; and the ships strained uneasily at their anchors. On several occasions, it seemed as if a number of transports must be driven ashore. The damage to the smaller vessels was considerable: all the whaleboats and most of the cutters were demolished, and a number of flat-bottomed landing craft were destroyed. As a haven, the place was much too exposed. If he was to safeguard his fleet, Saunders decided, the ships would have to be moved into the basin opposite the city. The operation could be carried out if the floating batteries were shot to pieces, and provided Point Lévis on the south bank was in British hands. If the French had batteries of guns up there, they could destroy one vessel after another with very little opposition. The first priority, he and James decided, was to capture this headland. Brigadier Monckton was given the assignment.

Meanwhile, Vaudreuil, from his stronghold in Quebec, had determined on his initial course of action. Saunders feared for the safety of his ships: the Governor-General proposed to demonstrate how well founded these misgivings were. Having purchased seven hulks from Bigot at a considerable profit to this official, he ordered them to be loaded with gunpowder and almost anything else which would burn. At some time on the night of the twenty-eighth they were set loose and drifted down river towards the fleet. They might have caused considerable loss and havoc, if the officer in charge of the scheme, a Captain Delouche, had kept his head. As things were, Delouche gave the order to ignite the fireships too soon. One of them became trapped by the others. The commanding officer and the seven-men crew were unable to escape and were burned alive. The others were surrounded by small boats from the Navy. The seamen threw grappling irons on board, and towed them on to the shore, where they burned for the rest of the night. 'They were certainly', that constant writer Captain Knox confided to his journal, 'the greatest fireworks (if I may be allowed to call them so) that can possibly be conceived, every circumstance having contributed to their awful, yet beautiful appearance, and afforded a scene infinitely superior to any adequate description.'

The British losses were nil, though an outpost at the western end of the island fled in panic when the men saw the ships erupt, and four warships had to be moved. The soldiers do not seem to have been punished for their conduct, though James was quick to censure them. 'Next to valour', he pointed out, 'the best qualities in a military man are vigilance and caution.' The officer in charge of the detachments was put under arrest; but, when Monckton had pointed out that he was a man of an excellent character, James pardoned him.

Point Lévis, as Montcalm had rightly judged, was a vital factor in the capture of Quebec. A strong force of artillery on the headland could have inflicted untold damage on the fleet. Conversely, in British hands, guns could wreck havoc and destruction upon the city. But Vaudreuil had discounted its value, and the General had been compelled to yield. Consequently, when Monckton landed with his four battalions on the twenty-ninth, he encountered only small opposition from a handful of militiamen and some Indians. When Vaudreuil heard about the affair from Montcalm, he seems to have reconsidered his opinion. He might even have agreed to the General's idea for a counter attack. At the last moment, however, he changed his mind again. The evidence suggests that, during the brief encounter between Monckton's men and the militia, the latter had captured a prisoner whom they managed to take back to Quebec. When he was interrogated, this man said that the British intended to launch an attack that night against the main French positions. Nothing of the kind had been contemplated, and he must have been an accomplished deceiver.* Even when the assault failed to take place, he stuck to his story. Perhaps, for some reason, the operation had been delayed; but this, he assured his captors, was the ultimate intention, and it would take place soon. The French were convinced. Monckton and his brigade were left unmolested. The British troops were now able to occupy a line extending up river, and to build batteries overlooking Quebec itself. By 3 July, 5,000 men and a strong force of artillery were established on the south bank.

James was feeling no better. On 2 July, he noted 'bladder painful. A good deal racked'. Nevertheless, his energy was at its usual feverish intensity. According to Captain Knox: 'No man can display greater activity than he does between the different camps of the army.' Nor was he ever neglectful of the welfare of his men. For example, he decreed that the hospitals were to receive supplies of beef and mutton before anyone else. His treat-

* Or else he had the dates mixed up in his mind. By 27 June, James had determined to attempt a landing on the left flank of the French positions.

ment of prisoners was humane, so long as they observed his rules. The Canadians had a second opportunity to study his terms, when a proclamation, similar to that displayed at Saint Laurent, was attached to the church door at Beaumont shortly after the taking of Point Lévis. Those who were honest enough had to admit that he was as good as his word. To make sure that his men fulfilled their share of the bargain, he issued an order to the following effect: 'The Peasants that remain in their habitations, their Women & Children are to be treated with humanity; if any violance is offered to a woman, the offender shall be punished with death.' The death penalty was also promised to anyone found guilty of looting; and he insisted that no churches, houses, or buildings of any kind were to be burned or destroyed without orders. Only men capable of bearing arms were held captive in the transports; on the few occasions when women and elderly civilian men were taken, they were usually entertained to a meal by the officers before being escorted into Quebec under cover of the white flag. Predictably, perhaps, the soldiers detailed for the task received an unpleasant reception. Their charges were unwanted: they served merely to increase a population which the civil authorities were already finding it difficult enough to feed. But these visits to the enemy capital were not to continue for much longer. The settlers were less impressed by James's manifesto than he had expected. Instead of meekly complying with its terms, they embarked on a campaign of terrorism. Just as he had promised mercy in return for capitulation, so, now, did he fulfil his pledge of violence.

Some habitations were razed to the ground, and their inhabitants killed. A settlement which had dared to fire on the sounding boats off the Ile aux Coudres was wiped out. Closer to hand, Captain Alexander Montgomery of the 43rd Foot was sent on a mission to a small village west of the Montmorency River. He had been ordered to take no prisoners, and the captain was faithful to his instructions. Every member of the eighty inhabitants, including the priest, was either shot or cut down by the sword. On this occasion, the troops seem to have gone too far, for shortly afterwards James issued an order condemning scalping. 'The General strictly forbids the inhuman practice . . .' he announced, 'except when the enemy are Indians, or Canadians dressed like Indians'. There was, it seemed, one code of treatment for regular soldiers, and another for the rag-tag *canaille* in which James included most of the colonials. But if the French settlers considered that his attitude towards them was harsh, they might have taken comfort from the fact that the English general was, when the occasion called for it, no less ruthless with his own men. Robbing tents and the commissariat became a capital offence; any soldier who strayed outside the camp was liable to a court martial; and: 'If any sutler has the presumption to bring Rum on shore, in contempt to the General's Regulations, such sutler shall be sent to their provost in irons & his goods confiscated.' On the other hand, when the men showed merit, James was quick to reward them. On one occasion a company of grenadiers was presented with '2 sheep and some rum . . . for the spirit they showed in rushing those scoundrels of Indians'. And: 'The General has ordered 5 guineas to be given to the Centinels of Otway's (later 1st Bn the Royal Sussex Regiment) for taking an Indian alive, whose business 'twas to surprise some negligent centinels and assassinate them.'

That was the beauty of soldiering with James Wolfe: a man knew where he stood. Nor were his appeals for effort and courage simply outpourings of rhetoric. Unlike most generals, he treated the common soldier as a creature with a mind, and he supplied facts to keep it busy. One of his best compositions was an order of the day, which he issued on 5 July. He wrote:

> The object of the Campaign is to compleat the conquest of Canada & to finish the War in America. The Army, under the Commander in Chief [Amherst], will enter into the Colony on the side of Montreal, while the Fleet and Army attack the Governor General & his forces.
>
> Great sufficiency of Provisions & a numerous Artillery is provided, and from the known Valour of the troops, the Nation expects success. These Battalions have acquired reputations in the last campaign [Louisburg] & it is not doubted but they will be careful to preserve it; from this confidence the General has assured the Secretary-of-State in his letters that whatever may be the event of this Campaign, His Majesty & the Country will have reason to be satisfied with the Army under his Command.

The General means to carry the Business thro' with as little loss as possible & with the highest regard to the safety and preservation of the Troops; to that end he expects that the men work chearfully and diligently, without the least unsoldierly murmers of complaints, & that his few but necessary orders will be strictly obeyed.

The rest of the document contained homilies on the importance of vigilance and a reminder about the sterner aspects of camp discipline. If any offender hoped for leniency he was likely to be disappointed. Those who were condemned, he stated, would 'certainly [be] executed'.

On 18 July, an important event took place, when two frigates, the *Sutherland* and the *Squirrel*, accompanied by a number of sloops and two transports with troops on board, sailed past the city to the waters up stream. The floating batteries did little to hinder them. Three days later, James made the trip in a barge, and embarked for a short spell in the *Sutherland*. He also took the opportunity to visit the troops on the south bank.

Within the city, a priest was writing: 'The English are too many for us; and who could have suspected it? Part of their fleet passed all our batteries, and are riding in safety above the capital. They have made this town so hot, that there is but one place left where we can with safety pay adoration to our most gracious, but now wrathful and displeased God, who, we fear, has forsaken us.' The trouble was that the English – or, to be more precise, James Wolfe – were not sure what to do. It was getting on for one month since the army had arrived. During this period, they had occupied the south bank; destroyed a small fleet of fire ships; and penetrated up the river. Given time, they might have starved Quebec into submission, but this was not James's way. He had fretted that the siege of Louisburg had been too slow. He had no intention of laying himself open to similar criticism over the conduct of Quebec. The accomplishments may have seemed to be considerable; but, as he was only too well aware, they had been easy to carry out. The main French army had not yet been brought to battle; indeed, very little had been done against it. To James's way of thinking, there could only be one successful outcome to the siege of the capital, and that would be when Montcalm's army had been routed.

The French had clearly dug excellent positions, and Montcalm's confidence is shown in a note he wrote to his second-in-command. By this time, James had crossed over from the Isle of Orleans, and was encamped on the north bank of the St Lawrence, overlooking the Montmorency River. This officer, the Marquis de Lévis, had suggested a sudden attack in an attempt to dislodge the intruders. 'Drive them thence', Montcalm said, 'and they will give us more trouble; while they are there, they cannot hurt us. Let them amuse themselves'. He was right. Every attempt to winkle the French soldiers out of their trenches had failed. Even when Monckton had marched and counter-marched his men along the cliff tops of the south bank in an effort to draw their fire, they had refused to be provoked. The inhabitants of Quebec itself would have done well to have heeded their example.

The gun fire from Point Lévis was creating a good deal of suffering and damage in the Upper Town. When, presently, the cathedral was set on fire, the population decided that the time had come to hit back. Led by the town major, a force consisting of five hundred leading citizens, three hundred students, seven hundred militiamen, and a number of Indians, was assembled. They crossed the river at night and inspected Monckton's positions. Having assessed their strength, they decided to withhold their attack until they were reinforced by three hundred colonial troops. The judgement was sound; the execution, when it took place, was appalling. Moving at night, one part of the force mistook the other for the enemy. The two fired upon each other. When seventy men had been killed, they retreated in confusion. Later, in case James had drawn any wrong conclusions from the affair, Montcalm sent him a letter. 'We do not doubt but you will demolish the town,' he wrote; 'yet we are determined that your army shall never get footing within its walls.' James's reply was suitably brusque: 'I will be master of Quebec', he said, 'if I stay here until the end of November.'

It was all very well to make such a bold statement, but he was still a long way from giving substance to it. His first plan had been frustrated by the presence of the enemy soldiers on what should have been the landing points. His second idea had been to land troops above the town, where they would dig in and wait for reinforcements. It became possible after the successful passage of the *Sutherland* and *Squirrel*, and it would no doubt have been a useful accomplishment. Looked at in isolation, however, it would have been far from decisive. He worked on other projects, which were variants of plans one and two, until, towards the end of July, he began to reconsider the situation across the Montmorency. Were the French really so securely dug in that nothing could dislodge them? Perhaps, if he brought troops across the river in landing craft, Montcalm's men would come out and fight? The possibility was worth considering.

While he was working on the idea, Vaudreuil made another attempt to burn the fleet with his fireships. The date was 28 July. A considerable number of smallish vessels were chained together, until they formed a gigantic raft about six hundred feet long. They were then loaded with the customary collection of gunpowder, shells, and combustible materials. Escorted by gunboats, the deadly contraption was taken by the outgoing tide towards the British fleet. The ignition was better timed on this occasion, but the escorting ships withdrew too soon. Once again, the English sailors were able to get their grappling irons on to the inferno and to tow it safely away. According to an observer, a seaman was heard to ask his mate: 'Damn me, Jack, dids't thou ever take hell in tow before?' Afterwards, according to the log of HMS *Stirling Castle*, an officer was instructed to 'serve the boatmen for above service ½ pint of brandy each'. For his part, James felt that the time had come to put a stop to these pyrotechnical displays for once and for all. Under a flag of truce, he sent the following warning to Vaudreuil: 'If you presume to send down any more fire-rafts, they shall be made fast to the two transports in which Canadian prisoners are confined, in order that they may perish by your own base inventions.' The Governor made no more attempts to burn the fleet.

James Wolfe had finally made up his mind: the time had come to bring the main French force to battle. So far as his telescope could tell him, Montcalm's men appeared to be in a state of confusion. If he could get his soldiers across the river and into the forward French redoubts, the enemy general might be lured into making a counter attack. This could be the beginning of a bigger battle and one which might well be decisive. HMS *Centurion** was moved into the channel between the Isle of Orleans and the mainland to bombard the French flank. Part of Monckton's brigade (two hundred men from the Royal American Regiment) was ferried across the St Lawrence from Point Lévis. These men and thirteen companies of grenadiers were to spearhead the operation. Murray's and Townshend's brigades were to be ready to ford the river at a point above the beachhead in case their services were needed. The assault was scheduled for 31 July.

The boats used for conveying the troops from the transports to the shore were flat-bottomed craft that had been built in the previous year for raids on the French coast. Each had twenty sailors to man the oars, and could carry sixty-three soldiers. A seaman sat up front with a swivel gun; an ensign seated in the stern proudly held aloft the great Union flag; and a drummer situated amidships could tap out orders or a martial beat, according to the needs of the moment. The boats were no doubt excellent for the purpose for which the Navy Board (on Admiralty order) had purchased them. For manœuvring intricately in very shallow water, they were, however, somewhat less than suitable.

According to James, who wrote a long letter to Pitt afterwards: 'The place where the attack was intended has these advantages over all others hereabout. Our artillery may be brought into use. The greatest part, or even the whole, of the troops might act at once; and the retreat, in case of a repulse, was secure, at least for a certain state of the tide. Neither one or other of these advantages can anywhere else be found.' No doubt, he was right: the three brigadiers appear to have been less sure, but they had nothing better to suggest. Montcalm himself may have doubted the wisdom of such an undertaking; for, among his convictions at this time, was a feeling of certainty that the British would never threaten his left flank. He no doubt knew the state of the river better than James.

* Lord Anson's flagship during his voyage round the world.

It was a clear, hot, morning. The water shone in the sunlight like polished steel with no ripples ruffling its bland surface. The lack of wind made the work of the oarsmen easier, but it also meant that the men-of-war could not move, and were therefore powerless to assist the operation. It was left to HMS *Centurion*, some lesser warships, and the artillery on the other side, to batter the French lines. To the accompaniment of the barrage, the boats headed for the far bank of the river. They left the Isle of Orleans at about 12.30 on what should have been a short trip. As things turned out, they were still in mid-stream several hours later. Meanwhile, Townshend's brigade, which was marching to the ford, had been halted. The trouble was that, some yards offshore, a ledge of rock jutted out. At this state of the tide it was covered with water, and a number of the landing craft grounded on it. Once they had come to a stop, the French soldiers up on the cliff tops opened fire.

So far, everything had been against the attack. In their efforts to dislodge the stranded boats, the sailors suffered heavy casualties. Nor had James, who was in the leading wave, been unmarked. He had been struck by splinters three times, and a cannon ball had knocked his stick out of his hand. Under such unkind auspices it might have been wiser to call off the operation. But this was not in his nature. As the tide came in and the depth of water increased, he set off with a naval officer to search for a more suitable beachhead. Meanwhile, paralysed by indecision, the grenadiers and Monckton's foot soldiers sat and sweltered aboard the landing craft in the river.

By the time James returned, it was getting on for five o'clock. He had, he announced, discovered a suitable stretch of shore. Once it had landed, the assault force would form up in readiness for an attack. Townshend's and Murray's brigades would resume their march; and, as soon as the two formations linked up, the offensive would begin. Overhead, the sun had disappeared, and a mass of black clouds was darkening the scene. At five-thirty the soldiers climbed out of the landing craft, only to discover that they were waist-deep in water. They struggled ashore in surprisingly good spirits, which were by no means justified. By now their supplies of gunpowder were wet through. However, as somebody observed, the French appeared to be running out of ammunition.

According to his ADC, James, 'the Friend of the Brave, an Enemy to the Base ... work'd up courage to such a pitch in his little army that it became necessary often to desire the soldiers not to expose themselves without necessity for it.' It may sound an enviable gift for a commander, but on this occasion he had cause to regret it. Instead of forming up obediently on the sand, the grenadiers went beserk. Without waiting for orders, they ran towards the French positions the moment they had reached dry land. Monckton's men had not yet completely disembarked; there was still no sign of Townshend's brigade; and yet there they were, charging towards the enemy in a formation which can only be described as chaotic. The enemy's fire increased, and this senseless progress had to stop. Eventually they were forced to take cover in an abandoned redoubt. At last the Royal Americans arrived, but now the worsening weather took charge of the situation. To the rattle of French musket fire from the heights above was added the growl of thunder. Presently the storm unleashed its charge of rain in, according to Captain Knox, 'the dreadfullest [manner] that can be conceived'. Even James was compelled to admit that the difficulties of landing, the French positions – which were more strongly held than he had imagined – and now the deluge, all added up to impossibility. The survivors re-embarked in the landing craft, and headed back to the island. The retreat was covered by Fraser's Highlanders, who had turned up belatedly with Townshend's brigade. The battle, such as it was, had ended; but they were able to vent their martial fury on the Indians, who were killing off the British wounded with relish and efficiency. When at last it was all over, James reckoned that this unhappy affair had cost him 210 killed and 230 wounded. In fact he may have exaggerated the casualties, for he had a poor head for figures of this kind. Later, on 2 September, a return listed 182 officers and other ranks as killed, 651 wounded, and 17 missing – and these applied to the campaign as a whole.

On the following day, James had some harsh things to say about the foolhardy conduct of the grenadiers. In his orders, he complained: 'The check which the Grenadiers met with yesterday will, it is hoped, be a lesson to them for the time to come. Such impetuous, irregular, and unsoldierlike proceedings destroy all order, make it impossible for the commanders to form any disposition for an attack, and put it out of the General's power to execute his plans.... The very first fire of the enemy was sufficient to repulse men who had lost all sense of order and military discipline....' He was not, however, entirely pessimistic about the outcome. 'The loss, however, is inconsiderable', he noted, 'and may be easily repaired when a favourable opportunity offers, if the men will show a proper attention to their officers.'

Who was to blame? One officer noted afterwards that James appeared to be 'much out of humour with Colonel Burton [the CO of the 48th Foot who was in charge of the grenadiers] for advancing the attack without positive orders.' His wrath, however, did not seem to extend to the others. When they were back in camp, he visited all the wounded before taking any rest himself. Furthermore, as if to show that he was not critical of their conduct, he invited those officers who were uninjured to dine with him that night. Perhaps one of the captains was less deserving of sympathy; for, on the evening before, he had fought a duel with a colleague. As a result, his right arm was injured, and he was urged to remain in camp. But this intrepid warrior was determined to receive his share of whatever glory there was to be had, and he insisted on taking part. During the battle, he was hit in a lung. Eventually he was taken back to Quebec by a French soldier, where he died in a hospital run by the garrison commander's wife, Madame de Ramezay. James was impressed by this example of chivalry. He sent the soldier a gift of £20, and told his messenger to assure Madame de Ramezay that, if he captured the city, he would protect her and her community of surgeons and nurses.

According to one of Colonel Fraser's subordinates, the real culprits of Montmorency were the sailors. They had taunted the grenadiers about their lack of action until one of the captains lost patience. In a moment of anger, and forgetting all other instructions, he ordered his drummer to beat the advance. The soldiers, who were equally exasperated by an overlong period in the boats, and who were now disgusted at the seamen's gibes, needed no more bidding. The stampede began.

Each of the leading players in this drama drew his own conclusions from the affair. Vaudreuil noted: 'I have no more anxiety about Quebec.' Montcalm felt more secure, for he believed that the British would be unwilling to attack the city of Quebec from upstream, and his moderate success had shown the strength of his present positions. Nevertheless, he did not believe that too much importance should be placed on the victory. In an effort to diminish what he considered to be the Governor's excessive optimism, he told him: 'You see, monsieur, that our affair is undoubtedly a small prelude to something more important, which we are waiting for.' The question was: what? Only James could answer that; and, with his plans once again thrown into disarray, he had not, at that moment, the slightest idea. But perhaps the most unkind cut of all was the death of the 47th's indefatigable bard, Sergeant Edward Botwood. Before the battle, he had foretold a British victory in his usual exuberant style. Wrote the sergeant:

> Tho' our clothing is changed, yet we scorn a powder-puff;
> So at you, ye bitches, here's give you Hot Stuff.

There would be no more 'hot stuff' from Botwood. As one of the valiant if misguided grenadiers, he now lay dead on the beach at Montmorency. It was sad that the only music at the passing of a man who had created so much doggerel was the snap of the French sharpshooters and the roar of a nearby waterfall.

15
THE CHOICE OF DIFFICULTIES

With much depression and small comfort, James returned to the house he was occupying outside the main army's camp. His strategic inspiration seemed to have run dry. The brigadiers had opposed the attack at Montmorency, and they had been right. They had not, on the other hand, suggested an acceptable substitute. Now James had to admit that he, too, could think of nothing else. Within a few days of the battle, he dispatched Brigadier Murray and 1,200 men to assist Rear-Admiral Holmes in operations above the town. One of the objects was to destroy the French ships, which were now sequestered some distance upstream. They had been sent there on Vaudreuil's insistence, partly for safety, and partly to block any attempt by the English to reach Montreal.

Murray was also instructed to 'open a communication with General Amherst'. Otherwise, he was given a fairly free hand. He was told to engage any French outposts he might come across ('provided he could do it upon tolerable terms'), which would obviously have little effect upon the campaign as a whole. Nevertheless, such actions would necessitate landing on the north bank of the river. This, as time was to show, would be of the most profound significance.

Murray and his men departed on 5 August. Four days later, they made two attempts to land at Pointe-aux-Trembles, about twenty miles up river from Quebec. The brigadier's intention was to destroy three floating batteries moored offshore. On the first occasion, which took place at low tide, a reef of rocks made it impossible to bring the boats in close enough. On the second, he was repulsed by a strong garrison commanded by de Bougainville. After that, the force seemed to vanish. By the twenty-fourth of the month, James was becoming anxious. 'Murray, by his long stay above, and by detaining all our boats', he said, 'is actually master of the operations, or rather puts a stop to them.' He ordered rockets to be sent up, which was the only method anyone could think of to order the truant brigadier's return. On the following day, Murray reported at James's headquarters. He seemed pleased with himself – and not without reason.

It appeared that a French deserter had informed him that there was a considerable amount of the French army's clothing, arms, and baggage, stored in a magazine at a place named Deschambault. On the eighteenth, he had managed to land there with surprisingly small opposition. His men set fire to the magazine; and a party of prisoners told him that, over in the west, the fort at Niagara had fallen to the British. From a packet of intercepted mail, he also discovered that General Amherst was making good progress up Lake Champlain, and was about to join battle with a force of three thousand French regulars and Canadians.

After Murray had departed on this mission, James began to consider the contents of a long letter to Pitt. When, at last, he started to write it, he described the fiasco at Montmorency in the lucid and objective style he always used when reporting battles. He made no excuses; nor did he attempt to show the situation as being anything other than disappointing. His opening paragraph set the tone:

I wish I could, upon this occasion, have the honour of transmitting to you a more favourable account of the progress of his majesty's arms; but the obstacles we have met with, in the operations of the campaign, are much greater than we had reason to expect, or could foresee; not so much from the number of the enemy (though superior to us), as from the natural strength of the country, which the Marquis de Montcalm seems wisely to depend upon.

A commendably succinct account of the campaign so far followed, reaching a climax with the Montmorency affair. He suggested that the grenadiers' conduct might have been due to 'the noise and hurry at landing, or from some other cause'. Concluding this section, he observed: 'The Enemy have been fortifying ever since with Care, so as to make a second Attempt still more dangerous.'

Later on, he referred to his health, which was giving him more than common cause for anxiety. He would, he said, have sent the dispatch sooner (it was not finally completed until 2 September) 'if I had not been prevented from writing by a fever. I found myself so ill, and am still so weak, that I begged the general officers to consult together for the public utility.' Indeed, by the time Pitt received the letter, the matter of Quebec had been resolved. The text was, in fact, printed in an issue of *The London Chronicle* dated 16–18 October, the same edition that carried news of the victory.

The rest of the document continued the story of frustration. He explained that he had offered the Canadians humane terms, if they laid down their arms. But: 'I found that good Treatment had not the desired Effect, so that of late, I have changed my Measures & laid waste the Country, partly to engage the Marquis de Montcalm to try the Event of a Battle to prevent the Ravage . . .' He and the chief engineer (Major Mackellar) had, it seemed, examined Quebec with a view to making a direct assault on the town, but the idea was out of the question. He had even considered fortifying the Ile aux Coudres, and leaving behind three thousand men to defend it 'in case of a Disappointment'. 'But', he sadly explained, 'it was too late in the Season, to collect Materials sufficient for covering so large a body.'

He ended by writing: 'In this situation, there is such a choice of difficulties, that I own myself at a loss how to determine. The affairs of Great Britain, I know, require the most vigorous measures; but then the courage of a handful of brave men, should be exerted only, where there is some hope of a favourable event. However, you may be assured, Sir, that the small part of the campaign which remains shall be employed (as far as I am able) for the honour of his majesty, and the interest of the nation, in which I am sure of being well seconded by the admiral, and by the generals.'

Some of the delay in sending the letter was because he submitted a draft of it to Admiral Saunders. The admiral complained that he had been too critical of the fleet's part in the Montmorency action. Consequently James cut out the offending paragraphs. As he made clear to Saunders, 'I am sensible of my own errors in the course of the campaign; see clearly wherein I have been deficient; and think a little more or less blame, to a man that must necessarily be ruined, of little or no consequence.' The rest of the note was a detailed reappraisal of the battle. A postscript, added on 30 August, is much more interesting. It informed the Admiral: 'It will be necessary to run as many small craft as possible by the town, with provisions and rum for six weeks for about 5,000, which is all I intend to take.'

Meanwhile the days had been dragging on. The batteries stationed on the south bank up river from Point Lévis kept up an almost continuous bombardment on Quebec. The church in the Lower Town caught fire and the blaze spread to a neighbouring magazine, which exploded. Out in the countryside, contingents of rangers toured the villages. Each man carried a copy of James's manifesto in one hand, and a rifle in the other. Farm buildings were relentlessly burned down; hostages were taken; any settlers who showed the smallest defiance were shot. The regions adjacent to the St Lawrence were in the grips of a reign of terror which foresaw some of the worst excesses of World War II. It might be tempting to imagine that the villainous operations of these troops were conducted without the consent of James, that, indeed, he was unaware of them. But there is not the slightest evidence to suggest any such thing. Indeed, his letter to Pitt suggests that the work was carried out under his instructions. The best one can say of his behaviour at this time is that he was true to his word. Had the colonists accepted his terms, he would have stood by them – just as he was ready to make good his threats. James, in the final analysis, was an efficient instrument of war. He might question orders from superiors on the grounds that they were not the best solution to a particular problem. He never queried their ethics.

Round about the twentieth of August, his health compelled him to retire to bed in an upstairs room of the house. Two days later, Captain Knox was noting in his journal: 'It is with the greatest concern to the whole army, that we are now informed of our amiable General being very ill of a slow fever. The soldiers lamented him exceedingly, and seemed apprehensive of this event, before we were ascertained of it, by his not visiting the camp for several days.' The officers missed his company at dinner, for it had been his practice to entertain a number of them every evening. On one occasion, the story goes, a Scottish captain was invited to a meal by some friends. 'You must excuse me', he said, 'as I am already engaged to Wolfe.' A subaltern suggested that he should have spoken with greater respect. *General* Wolfe, he said, would have been more appropriate. 'Sir', the Scotsman replied, 'we never say General Alexander or General Caesar.' James is supposed to have overheard the remark, and to have been pleased by it.

But for the time being there was to be no more entertainment. He was lying on his bed with a high fever, and telling his medical attendant (according to an issue of *European Magazine* published that year): 'I know perfectly well you cannot cure my complaint; but pray make me up so that I may be without pain for a few days, and able to do my duty; that is all I want.'

There are many theories about the ill health of James Wolfe. The most common is that he was suffering from consumption. His brother Ned had, admittedly, died from it; but there is nothing to suggest that James experienced any of the symptoms. Another idea is that he was the victim of a serious illness affecting the bladder – cancer, possibly. Again, there is nothing to support the supposition. From time to time, he complained of pains in this area, and we know he took cures for the gravel on at least two occasions. But the malady was far from lethal, and the general opinion is that, by now, he had only a comparatively short period to live – no matter what happened to him in the campaign. Indeed, James himself was dogged by presentiments of an early death. Scurvy was among the other afflictions that had contributed to his misery, and this might seem to have been an appropriate moment for it to recur. Food was in short supply – for most of its sojourn outside Quebec, the army was on half-rations. But James knew enough about the disease to take suitable precautions. In any case, his energetic conduct in the battle of Montmorency does not indicate the state of lethargy, which is one of the symptoms. On the whole, then, the most convincing suggestion seems to be that he was now suffering from rheumatic fever. The high temperature, the aching joints, the abdominal pain: they all meet the case. Without the proper treatment, the sickness would have produced a heart condition that, in a matter of months, would probably have been fatal.

Perhaps the strongest indication of the severity of the present illness was the fact that he was compelled to abdicate authority to the three brigadiers. Monckton and Murray had been appointed to the expedition on his own insistence. Nevertheless, his aide – whose views were doubtless coloured by James's opinions – had some harsh things to write about the two officers. He described Monckton as being 'of a dull capacity and may properly be called Fat Headed – timid and utterly unqualified. A month of his command would be sufficient to ruin that excellent army.' His opinion of Murray was even worse. He condemned him as 'the deadly nightshade – the poison of a camp. Envy and Ambition are the only springs that work him. The more brilliant and excellent any character is, the more his Envy is excited and the more he detracts. . . . Mr Wolfe was the means of his being Brigadier General, in return he was the very bellows of Sedition and Discord and would have been the first Partisan to arraign Mr Wolfe's conduct had the campaign miscarried, in hopes to succeed the Command.'

Finally, there was Townshend – an appointment that had not been of James's own choosing. The ADC dismissed him as being of 'a feeble inconstant mind, his line of life not directed by any first principles, and he is exceedingly subject to very high and very low spirits'. He had, the young officer wrote, 'a great deal of humour, well stain'd with bawdy'. The best he could find to say of him was that he 'may be esteemed an excellent Tavern acquaintance'.

Townshend was three years older than James. He was bitter at what he considered to have been unjust treatment in the past, and extremely sensitive. Doubtless, James did not treat him with sufficient tact, and this provoked trouble – especially since, in his vanity, Townshend considered himself to be the better general. He confided the resentment to his journal. When he had built some elaborate breastworks overlooking the Montmorency, for example:

The next morning the General having gone early to rest in the evening, I reported to him what I had done, and in the evening he went round and disapproved of it, saying I had indeed made myself secure, for I had made a fortress; that small redoubts were better than lines; that the men could not man these lines, nor sally out as they pleased....

The next day I perceived with my glass an officer with an escort very much answering the description of M. Montcalm, examining our camp from the same spot. I acquainted the General with this, who rather laughed at it and at my expectation of any annoyance from that part....

Whilst I was directing the work, I heard the General had set out for the Point of Orleans, thence to pass over to the Point of Lévis, leaving me, the first officer in the camp, not only without orders but also even ignorant of his departure or time of return.

As a talented cartoonist, he found his pale and gangling commander-in-chief a splendid subject for his pen. It would have been unreasonable to expect him to keep these drawings to himself: at least once he exhibited an example to his fellow officers. This particular sketch depicted the General searching a privet for spies. By a stroke of ill fortune, James happened to see it. He crumpled the sheet of paper into his pocket, and with a bleak smile observed: 'If I live, this shall be inquired into; but we must beat the enemy first.' Nevertheless, the talented Townshend could also produce more serious work. Indeed, one of the better portraits of James is a head-and-shoulder study painted in water colours by the normally biting brigadier. The gentle humour about the mouth, and the observant and worried eyes, suggest a sympathy with his subject – even, perhaps, an affection.

From his sickbed, James struggled to direct his feverish mind towards a new appreciation of the situation. When he had dictated his thoughts, the document confirmed his belief that 'the army should be attacked in preference to the place'. There was nothing new about this: nor did one of the three plans outlined suggest anything original. He appeared to be obsessed by the fact that, since the French army was established to the east of the city, this was where the ultimate battle must be fought. Each idea was a variation on this theme, and there was no mention of any operations upstream.

Why? The letter was a poor performance, and suggested a lack of flexibility remarkable in a man of James's undoubted talent and originality. His initial idea had been to march the army overland in readiness for an attack from the west. The disposition of Montcalm's troops had made this impossible, but there was an alternative method, and one which experience had already shown to be feasible. The frigates *Sutherland* and *Squirrel* and two transports carrying the 3rd Royal Americans had sailed past and beyond Quebec with minimal opposition. Murray, on his excursion to Deschambault, had shown that it was possible to land soldiers on the north bank upstream of the city. And yet, despite these two pieces of evidence, and in spite of the disastrous attack across the Monmorency, he still insisted that the French lines in the Beauport area had to be the scene of the battle. Had the rigours of his illness affected his judgement? Had they clamped his mind in one direction, and made him unaware of any less obvious solution? His uneasy relationship with the three brigadiers begins to intrude into the picture. He never gave them his confidences, nor accepted theirs. Was he now, in his dangerously ill condition, suspicious of them? Did he see some need, which was illogical and eccentric to a fault, to mislead them – just as he had sometimes tried to deceive the French? Had they, in his mind, become the enemy within? This is one of the mysteries of Quebec which will never be solved.

The brigadiers, on the other hand, were neither sick nor suffering from warped judgement. They replied to James's letter on 29 August with a crisp and well reasoned note. Accompanied by Admiral Saunders, they had made a thorough reconnaissance of the city's surroundings from all points of view, and they spoke with authority. So far as they were concerned, James could forget about his ideas. 'The natural strength of the enemy's situation between the rivers St Charles and Montmorency,' they wrote, 'now improved by the art of their engineers, makes the defeat of their army, if attacked there, very doubtful.' After elaborating on this theory, they came to the crunch of the matter. 'We are therefore of opinion that the most probable method of striking an effectual blow is to bring the troops to the south shore, and to carry the operations above the town. If we can establish ourselves on the north shore, the Marquis de Montcalm must fight us on our own terms; we are between him and his provisions, and between him and the army opposing General Amherst. If he gives us battle and we defeat him, Quebec, and probably all Canada, will be our own, which is beyond any advantage we can expect by the Beauport side. . . .'

As the postscript on James's letter to Admiral Saunders shows, he was quick to acknowledge their proposals – and equally anxious to put them into practice. He was only too well aware that there was not a great deal of time left. When Vaudreuil wished to encourage the settlers to oppose the occupying army, he used to tell them that the British fleet had only sufficient provisions to last a month. This was an exaggeration, but, like all good propaganda, it contained an element of truth. Nor were shortages of food and the French and colonial soldiers the only enemies. September was almost upon them, and it would not be long before the brief summer was over. When the river froze over, and the ships were locked in position by the ice, the situation would become impossible. Whatever had to be done must be accomplished quickly. If it were not, the bulk of the army would be buried beneath the Canadian snow.

Nevertheless, his ready acceptance of the brigadiers' plan does not carry complete conviction. He had already begun to put it into effect by the time he completed his report to Pitt. There is, however, no mention of it in a document which is remarkable for its pessimism. He appears to have drawn no significant conclusions from Murray's outing to Deschambault – indeed, he put more weight on an earlier plan to land troops at a village three miles above the city. 'But', he wrote, 'perceiving that the enemy were jealous of the design, were preparing against it, and had actually brought artillery and a mortar . . . to play upon the shipping: and as it must have been many hours before we could attack them (even supposing a favourable night for the boats to pass by the town unhurt) it seemed so hazardous that I thought it best to desist.' As for the proposals he had dictated from his sickbed, he told Admiral Saunders: 'My ill state of health hinders me from executing [them].' They were, he said, 'of too desperate a nature to order others to execute'. In view of all this, he may have assented to the new scheme out of despair rather than faith. It was, after all, the only suggestion he had.

But now James seemed to be getting better. On 31 August, he appeared in the camp once more. The troops noticed that he looked frail and haggard, but something of his old magic had returned. That evening, he sat down to write what, as things transpired, was to be his last letter to his mother. Characteristically, it contained no mention of his illness – indeed, it was designed to reassure her. 'My writing to you', he said, 'will convince you that no personal evils, worse than defeats and disappointments, have fallen upon me. The enemy puts nothing to risk, and I can't, in conscience, put the whole army to risk. My antagonist has wisely shut himself up in inaccessible entrenchments, so that I can't get at him without spilling a torrent of blood, and that perhaps to little purpose. The Marquis de Montcalm is at the head of a great number of bad soldiers, and I am at the head of a small number of good ones, that wish for nothing so much as to fight him; but the wary old fellow avoids an action, doubtful of the behaviour of his army.'

He had evidently heard about his father's new will, and his comments were dutiful and moderate. 'I approve', he wrote, 'entirely of my father's disposition of his affairs, though perhaps it may interfere a little matter with my plan of quitting the service, which I am determined to do the first opportunity, – I mean so as not to be absolutely distressed in circumstances, nor burdensome to you or anyone else.' Strangely enough, the knowledge did not make him aware of the effect that the old general's sudden change of heart would have on his own legacies. Far from destroying the by now worthless scrap of paper he had completed during the voyage to the St Lawrence, he added to its content. On 30 July he had inserted two codicils. Both were additional bequests of £1,000: one for his Uncle Wat in Dublin, the other to his Irish cousin, Edward Goldsmith.

But this is another sector of his affairs which is fogged by mystery. In a letter written to Pitt on 30 November of the following year, Mrs Wolfe stated: 'My dear son, not knowing the disposition his father had made of his fortune – which was wholly settled on me for life, and magnified by fame greatly beyond what it really is – has left to his friends more than a third part of it; and though I should have the greatest pleasure imaginable in discharging these legacies in my lifetime, I cannot do it without distressing myself to the highest degree.' Had James misread the letter about his father's affairs? Did Mrs Wolfe not receive his note from Canada? Or, since her letter to Pitt was an appeal for a pension, did she tamper with the truth? Such conduct would not have been beyond the old lady; but, by making additions when he should have been busy with subtractions, James's own actions remain unexplained. In death, as in life, his finances were chaotic.

On 1 September, preparations began to bring the army over to the south bank of the St Lawrence. When Montcalm saw what was happening, he hurriedly marched two battalions to the ford across the Montmorency, with the idea of attacking the British rear. Monckton reacted with commendable promptness by making a feint in the direction of Beauport, and the Frenchmen were withdrawn. Thereafter, the evacuation of the camps overlooking the Montmorency and on the Isle of Orleans went ahead without any interference. By 4 September, the greater part of the British force was established in the Point Lévis area, and was ready to march in an upstream direction. On the same day, a dispatch arrived from General Amherst. The rub of it was that no reinforcements could be expected from this source. James was disappointed; and, that night, the fever returned. His condition seemed to be worse than ever. The pessimists wondered whether he would survive until morning, and even the more optimistic troops doubted whether he would be sufficiently recovered to lead them into action. But neither school of thought took sufficient account of his amazing determination. On the following day, almost as if he had willed himself into making a recovery, he was back on duty. It had, he said, been nothing more than a brief relapse. Nevertheless, anybody who studied him closely could see that he was a good deal weaker.

16
THE HANDS OF PROVIDENCE

The dark tunnel of James's life, which should have been emerging into the daylight of achievement, was thrusting into an even deeper gloom. At some point during the latter days of the siege of Quebec, he destroyed his journal. Consequently, the only surviving pieces of evidence from his own hand are his order book and his letters. The former is objective and practical, as an order book should be. The latter, mostly written to members of the Government, are almost unrelieved outpourings of depression, as if he were preparing Pitt and his colleagues for the news that he had been unsuccessful. Montcalm, evidently, believed that this had already happened – and with some justification. When the units began their journey across to the south bank of the St Lawrence, Major George Scott and a thousand rangers were detached from the force. Their assignment was to burn and destroy as many French settlements as possible. Was this, Montcalm asked himself, the action of a general who was about to fight a victorious battle? Is it customary to lay waste to lands that are soon to be conquered? To deny oneself the fruits of success by the apparently insane act of reducing them to ashes?

Montcalm doubted it. He saw the depredations of Scott and his men as the final, desperate, action of a leader who had failed. Having been unable to bring the French forces to battle, and now certain that such an action could not take place before winter set in, it seemed as if James were determined to inflict as much damage upon the colony as he could. Montcalm and Vaudreuil felt a cautious sense of relief. Some of the Canadian militia were even encouraged to return to their burnt-out homes and begin the work of rebuilding them.

The French general assessed the man correctly, but not the situation. If James was compelled to quit Canada with his work undone, he certainly intended to inflict the utmost suffering upon the colony. The evidence appears in one of the few documents he wrote during the Transatlantic crossing. It was a letter to General Amherst. Much of it was devoted to misgivings about the size of his force. But he concluded by saying:

> If, by accident in the River, by the Enemy's resistance, by sickness, or slaughter in the Army, or, from any other cause, we find, that Quebec is not likely to fall into our hands . . . I propose to set the Town on fire with Shells, to destroy the Harvest, Houses, & Cattle both above & below, to send off as many Canadians as possible to Europe, & to leave famine and desolation behind me; *belle resolution, & trés crêtienne!* but we must teach these Scoundrels to make war in a more gentlemanlike manner.

But the moment of destructive despair had not yet arrived. The purpose of dispatching Major Scott and his rangers on their mission was to safeguard British troops from the guerilla activities of the colonists. We know from further testimony by James that 'a wood country, so well known to the enemy, and an enemy so vigilant and hardy as the Indians and Canadians are, making entrenchments everywhere necessary, and by this precaution we have saved a number of lives; for scarce a night passes that they are not close upon our posts, watching an opportunity to surprise and murder.'* The fact that Montcalm may have drawn the wrong conclusion from these operations was an unexpected bonus.

By 3 September, the greater part of the British force had been withdrawn from the Isle of Orleans, leaving behind a battalion under Guy Carleton to act as garrison. Two days later, the Navy's sloops, each with a month's supply of provisions on board, were ordered up river. By now, a sizable collection of ships under the command of Admiral Holmes was anchored above Quebec. On the sixth, the main body of soldiers marched to the mouth of a tributary named the Etchemin, where they were rowed out to the tranports. Burton and the 48th Grenadiers remained at Point Lévis. If all had gone according to plan, 1,500 men under

* Letter to the Earl of Holderness.

Monckton and Murray would have landed on the north bank on the eighth. The object was to mislead; but it rained continuously on the eighth and ninth, and the raid was abandoned. It did not matter. Saunders's men-of-war mounted a bombardment on the French positions around Beauport, and the presence of a substantial portion of the fleet above the town was adding to the enemy's confusion. It had, indeed, already caused Montcalm to split his force by sending de Bougainville and one thousand crack troops to the Pointe-aux-Trembles, about twenty miles upstream. They were soldiers he could ill afford to lose.

James suffered no further recurrence of his illness, but he was withdrawn and irritable. He told the brigadiers no more than he considered absolutely essential, and even the trusty Guy Carleton, his friend for many years, had done something to displease him and was in disgrace. His behaviour is understandable. The sickness had severely weakened him: he must have been afraid that, when it came to the final confrontation with the French, he would be too ill to take part. And, as if this were not enough, he had an even more fundamental worry on his mind. He had accepted the brigadiers' idea that the landing should take place upstream. The question was, *where?*

The brigadiers had been unanimous in their choice of objective. Anywhere close to Quebec, they had decided would be difficult, if not impossible. Montcalm would have to march only a short distance to bring them to battle, and the conditions were against any conception of a full-scale landing. The craggy headland of Cape Diamond was the ultimate physical custodian of Quebec, but the line of cliffs which reached a climax at this point extended for several miles above the city. Not only were the beaches small for the disembarkation of a large force, the climb to the heights above the river would be exhausting and potentially hazardous.

As a result of this, Monckton, Townshend and Murray had suggested that the Pointe-au-Trembles might be best. According to their calculations, the troops would be able to get ashore without too much interference; and, once on the beach, the topography was more moderate. The men would be able to march rather than scramble to the high ground.

Murray's excursion up river should have convinced them that a landing here might not be so easy as they had imagined. When James went upstream to study the headland on 7 September, his observations convinced him that it was impossible. The knowledge did not disappoint him, for he was already beginning to conceive another plan. Unlike the brigadiers, he did not believe that a landing near Quebec was impossible – indeed, it suggested a number of advantages which his senior officers had either discounted or had not perceived.

If the attack were made too far up river, one battalion would have to remain behind guarding the Isle of Orleans, another at Point Lévis. His force was already short of one thousand men, for Major Scott and his rangers were still busy laying waste to the countryside, and he did not encourage them to return. If he had to deny himself a further two thousand or so, he would be in no position to meet the enemy on anything approaching equal terms. The difficulty of climbing the cliffs did not daunt him. He credited his men with an ability to accomplish the difficult, and he was not beyond ordering the impossible. Finally, the road linking Quebec with its supply depots was close to the clifftop. If he could place his army astride it, Montcalm would have to come out and fight. The alternative would be starvation.

One place seemed to answer all James's requirements. It was a small cove, two and a half miles from the city, named the Anse de Foulon. Two eminences protected it; a path, on which two men could walk abreast, led to the top of the cliff. The climb was the better part of 250 feet but, once up, there was a natural battlefield. It was known as the Plains of Abraham, a tableland hemmed in on the west and north sides by forest. To the east lay the smouldering ruins of the city; and, as if to complete its list of merits, Montcalm's supply road ran slap across the centre.

Precisely when James decided that the Anse de Foulon deserved serious consideration is uncertain. The expedition's assistant engineer, an officer of Dutch extraction named Captain Samuel Jan Holland, thought that it probably dated back to July. One day that month, James went on a reconnaissance along the south bank with Captain Joseph Gorham of the Rangers, Holland, and a party of Gorham's men. They walked as far as the

Etchemin River, which flows into the St Lawrence at a point a mile or two upstream of the cove. Looking across the river through his telescope, James noticed a number of Indians. Some of them were in canoes, others were bathing. Before they returned to camp, Gorham was ordered to establish a post at this point. While he was supervising the earthworks, Holland had (as he recalled) to note 'the number of people that came to the water's edge, the time of their coming down, the length of their stay', and so on. Possibly being wise after the event, he remembered them as 'remarks which in my mind all tended to show his design of landing at the Foulon to be pre-determined.' That night at dinner, according to Holland, James told him that the Anse de Foulon would be his last resort – but the matter must be kept secret. As reported by the engineer, the conversation was conducted in such bad French that it virtually defies translation. One wonders why. Was the use of a foreign language a piece of theatre designed to emphasize how confidential the information was? Or was it a figment of Holland's imagination?

He was, admittedly, recalling it after an interval of thirty-three years (his own journal of the campaign vanished when his baggage was stolen from a post chaise near London). Nevertheless, there is little in the document to suggest that his memory was at fault, though he may have exaggerated the closeness of his association with Wolfe. For example, his account of James's death gives him a prominent place in the drama, whilst other reports ignored him.

If James had seriously considered the merits of the Anse de Foulon in July, it shows the battle of Montmorency in a different light. Instead of a blunder, it becomes a brilliant piece of deception, for it turned Montcalm's attention away from the area up river, and made him expect the main attack to fall on his positions around Beauport. However, the web of deception – inside and outside the army – was so complex, that it is difficult to come to any firm conclusions. Indeed, as if to confuse still more, there was James's subsequent letter to the brigadiers, written from his sick-bed, in which he made absolutely no reference to the possibility of operations upstream.

On 9 September, James sat down in his cabin aboard HMS

Sutherland and wrote his last dispatch to the Government. Addressed to one of the Secretaries of State, Lord Holderness, it was a doleful document. Everything would have been easier, he wrote, 'if the Marquis de Montcalm had shut himself up in the town of Quebec'. Unfortunately, he had done nothing of the kind. As things were, he had 'a numberous body of armed men (I cannot call it an army), and the strongest country, perhaps, in the world, to rest the defence of the town and colony upon'. The British had emerged with some credit however: 'The town is totally demolished, and the country is in a great measure ruined, particularly the Lower Canada. Our fleet blocks up the river, both above and below the town, but can give no manner of assistance in an attack upon the Canadian army. We have continual skirmishes; old people seventy years of age, and boys of fifteen fire on our detachments, and kill or wound our men from the edges of the woods.'

But the natives were not the only enemy: the river, itself, was a peril. 'The stream is so strong, particularly here, that the ships often drag their anchors by the mere force of the current.' As for his future plans, he mentioned his illness; and explained that he had been compelled to ask 'the Generals to consider amongst themselves what was fittest to be done. Their sentiments were unanimous, that, as the easterly winds begin to blow, and the ships can pass the town in the night with provisions, artillery, etc, we should endeavour, by conveying a considerable corps into the upper river, to draw them from their inaccessible situation, and bring them to an action. I agreed to the proposal, and we are now here, with about 3,600 men, waiting an opportunity to attack them when and wherever they can best be got at.' The letter ended on a despondent note. 'I am so far recovered as to do business, but my constitution is entirely ruined, without the consolation of having done any considerable service to the State, or without any prospect of it.'

When James was writing to Holderness, a considerable part of his army was confined aboard the transports in abominably overcrowded conditions. In spite of the rain, the weather was still warm, and he began to worry about the men's health. If they spent much longer cooped up in the floating versions of Hades, they would be in poor shape for any fighting that lay ahead. Consequently, after he had concluded his letter, he ordered 1,500 of them to be put ashore.

His dispatch to Lord Holderness had given no clue to any intention he may have had to land at the Anse de Foulon. At no time was the name of the place ever mentioned in his orders, but this was not surprising. Men were still deserting, and, unlike the prisoner taken at Point Lévis, they could not be relied upon to mislead the French. On the contrary, most of them would have been only too pleased to pass on information to the enemy.

Within his high command, on the other hand, James might have been expected to be more informative. But it was not until the tenth that mention of the cove appeared in a letter. It was addressed to Lieutenant-Colonel Ralph Burton, commanding officer of the 48th Grenadiers. After giving a reasonably detailed account of his ideas (Colonel Burton must have won his way back into James's favour after the affair at Montmorency), he wrote: 'The fleet sails up the river a little higher, as if intending to land above on the north shore, keeping a convenient distance for the boats and armed vessels to fall down to the *Foulon;* and we count (if no accident of weather or other prevents) to make a powerful effort at that spot about *four* in the morning of the 13th.'

Burton now knew both the date and location of the landing. Isaac Barré, the expedition's adjutant-general, was probably also told, but the three brigadiers were still in a state of melancholy ignorance. On the evening of the seventh, James had called them to a conference on board the *Sutherland*, but the talk had mostly centred around the order of battle. He probably also disabused them of any ideas about a landing at the Pointe-aux-Trembles; for, afterwards, Townshend wrote that 'by some intelligence, the General has had, he changed his mind as to the place he intended to land.' When they asked him to be more precise, however, he parried the request with the vague remark: 'When the coast has been examined, and the best landing place pitched upon, the troops will be ordered to disembark, perhaps this night's tide.' Perhaps – and then, again, possibly not. Fifteen hundred soldiers did, indeed, go ashore, but merely to have a breath of fresh air. No operations were planned for the next twenty-four hours, so why did he take the trouble to be misleading? Was it further evidence of his mistrust of the brigadiers, which had been inflamed by his illness? It was almost as if he were suffering from paranoia, for his attitude was passing the bounds of reason. Who, if not these senior officers, could be regarded as a good security risk?

On the following day, if they had been quick-witted enough to grasp it, Monckton and Townshend might have begun to guess their commander-in-chief's intention; for, with Major Mackellar, they went with him to study the Anse de Foulon through telescopes. In an attempt to mislead the small French force on the far bank, they disguised themselves by wearing grenadiers' coats. In fact, they deceived nobody. The enemy merely wondered what eccentricity had prompted the British high command to put on fancy dress. It was noticeable that, during this survey, James told Monckton and Townshend nothing, and never, at any time, asked for their opinions.

Afterwards, Mackellar wrote that 'the bank which runs along the shore is very steep and woody, and was thought so impracticable by the French themselves, that they had then only a single picket to defend it. This picket, which we supposed might be about 100 men, was encamped upon the bank near the top of a narrow path.' For James, who found it easy to translate the impossible into the difficult, this seemed to be a good sign. The brigadiers, on the other hand, would have been less sanguine. They would probably have shared the French view, and they would no doubt have made their opinions known to James. This, perhaps, is why he refused to confide in them. He knew how hazardous his plan was; he had the courage to put it into operation – but not, possibly, to argue its merits. His own belief in it was too fragile to withstand the attack of men he felt to be hostile. He knew that Townshend lampooned him. He suspected that Murray was devious. Even Monckton would be unable to give him the sympathetic understanding he so desperately needed.

A great deal depended on the Navy – not least the timing, for everything was governed by the tide. Admiral Holmes had to be briefed, and he afterwards described the operation as 'the most hazardous and difficult task I was ever engaged in'. As for

Admiral Saunders, he considered the achievement of reaching the cliff top as 'scarce credible'. But James had made up his mind. True to his letter to Burton, the date was fixed for the thirteenth. On the twelfth, he composed his final order to the troops. It began by stating: 'The Enemy's Forces are now divided, great scarcity of Provisions in their Camp, & universal discontent among the Canadians.'* Then he explained:

> A vigorous blow struck by the Army at this juncture may determine the fate of Canada; our troops below [on the Isle of Orleans and at Point Lévis] are ready to join us, all the light artillery and tools are embarked . . . & the Troops will land where the Enemy seems least to expect it.
>
> The first Body that gets ashore is to march directly to the Enemy, & drive them from any little post they may occupy.
>
> The officer must be careful that the succeeding bodies do not by any mistake fire upon those who go before them.
>
> The Battalions must form upon the upper ground with expedition, & be ready to charge whatever presents itself.
>
> When the Artillery & Troops are landed, a Corps to be left to secure the landing place, while the rest march on & endeavour to bring the French & Canadians to battle.
>
> The Officers & Men will remember what their Country expects from them, & what a determined body of Soldiers are capable of doing against five weak Battalions mingled with a disorderly Peasantry.
>
> The Soldiers must be attentive to their Officers & Resolute in the Execution of their Duty.

Characteristically, the end of the document showed his continuing concern for the men's welfare. It concluded with the comforting words: 'The ships with the Blanketts, Tents, and Necessaries &c will soon be up.'

Everybody now knew what had to be done, and how it was to be done. But the three brigadiers still did not know *where* it was to take place. At last, they could stand it no longer. Meeting in a cabin on board HMS *Lowestoft,* they conferred among themselves and composed the following letter:

* This was not entirely wishful thinking: information along these lines had been brought in by a French deserter.

Sir, – As we do not think ourselves sufficiently informed of the several facts which may fall to our share in the execution of the descent you intend tomorrow, we must beg leave to request from you as distinct orders as the nature of the thing will admit of, particularly to the place or places we are to attack. This circumstance (perhaps very decisive) we cannot learn from the public orders, neither may it be in the power of the naval officer who leads the Troops to instruct us. As we should be very sorry, no less for the public than our own sakes, to commit any mistakes, we are persuaded you will see the necessity of this application.

It was signed by all three of them.

James treated each according to his status. Monckton, as second-in-command, was given a reasonably full explanation, which included the name of the landing place. Nevertheless, he was chided by the reminder: 'It is not a usual thing to point out in the public orders the direct spot of our attack, nor for any inferior Officers not charged with a particular duty to ask instructions upon that point.'

As Monckton must have complained to himself, it was unjust and very nearly insulting. The second-in-command of any army might expect to be told more than was considered fit to be published in 'public orders'. As for the remark about 'inferior officers', James, surely, was treating him as if he were a subaltern. But Townshend received even shorter shrift, with a brusque: 'General Monckton is charged with the first landing and attack at the Foulon, if he succeeds you will be pleased to give directions that the troops afloat be set on shore with the utmost expedition, as they are under your Command, and when 3,600 men now in the Fleet are landed I have no manner of doubt but that we are able to fight and beat the French Army, in which I know you will give your best assistance.'

Murray received no reply at all.

James had one more duty to discharge from his headquarters in HMS *Sutherland*. That evening, a young naval lieutenant who was in command of HMS *Porcupine* was summoned to his cabin. The officer's name was John Jervis (later the first Lord St Vincent). He had been at school with James at the Reverend Samuel Swinden's academy in Greenwich. More recently, James had been carrying out a reconnaissance in *Porcupine,* when the wind dropped and the tide began to carry the small ship within range of the French guns. Jervis lowered his boats. Amid a storm of French shells, the oarsmen towed the vessel to safety. If it had not been for this prompt action, James would at best have been taken prisoner, at worst killed.

But now he had an important personal request to make to Jervis. After the two men had chatted for a while, he shyly took a small picture of Kathleen Lowther from his pocket. He had, he told Jervis, a presentiment that he was going to die on the following day. Would he take the miniature back to England, and return it to Miss Lowther? Jervis agreed, though at some point his mission went astray. Instead of being delivered to Miss Lowther, the portrait fell into the rapacious hands of Mrs Wolfe. It was given to her at the same time as his will.

Late that evening, the 1,800 troops of the first division were ordered into the flat-bottomed landing craft. At 1.35 am on the thirteenth, the tide – which was the army's industrious if unwitting ally – began to ebb. A signal light appeared on the mainmast of HMS *Sutherland.* Quietly, carefully, the boats were lowered into the water. The sailors gently dipped their oars into the river; the soldiers sat erect and silent; and, with the precision of a parade ground movement, the fleet of invaders formed into line. The night was dark. The moon, which had risen at ten o'clock, was in its final quarter. According to an entry in Sutherland's log book, there was 'fine weather, the night calm, and silence over all'.

Propelled by the current, assisted by the oarsmen, the line of boats made its way towards the Anse de Foulon. The French – surprisingly, it seemed – did nothing. It was only when the leading craft had come within yards of the shore, that a sentry uttered a challenge. 'Qui vive?' he demanded. A Captain Fraser in the 78th Highlanders happened to speak French. 'La France' and 'vive le Roi,' he called back. The soldier was satisfied. The convoy could proceed.

It seemed to be almost too easy. As it happened, a happy accident had virtually guaranteed the army a safe passage, for the

French were expecting ships to pass by on that night. A convoy of supplies for the beleaguered garrison should have been on its way from its depot up river. At the last moment, however, Vaudreuil had decided to cancel it. By some oversight, nobody had taken the trouble to inform the soldiery; and nor had anybody bothered to arrange that most elementary of security precautions, a password. The result was that the sentry made a fatal misjudgement. It never occurred to him that the boats were carrying enemy soldiers. Responding to the subject which was, no doubt, uppermost in his mind at that moment, he believed they were transporting food.

James may have intended to mislead Montcalm with his apparently ill judged attack at Montmorency. The French general, certainly, had drawn the wrong conclusions from it. Indeed, during the past month, his flair for divining his opponent's intentions had deserted him. He now believed that the main attack would be made on his positions in the Beauport area. Even de Bougainville, who had witnessed a great deal of British naval activity from his outpost up the river, misread the signs. He believed that the fleet intended to strike a blow at the ships, and possibly launch a small diversionary assault. Like his general, the notion that this might be the main target had not occurred to him. Least of all, he and Montcalm imagined, was there any danger of a landing at the Anse de Foulon. The conditions were impossible; the picket on the cliff top was allowed to doze through the dark hours of the night, when no senior officer ever took the trouble to visit it.

Silent, almost invisible, the tribe of landing craft edged towards the small beach. At some point on the journey, James is said to have whispered his recitation of Gray's *Elegy*, and then to have remarked: 'I would rather have been the author of that piece than beat the French tomorrow.' The anecdote was reported by a future Professor of Natural Philosophy at Edinburgh University named John Robinson. At the time, Robinson was acting as tutor to a young naval officer, for which he had been given the rank of midshipman. He was no doubt near James during the trip downstream; but, since he never wrote the story down, and since it was passed on (doubtless inaccurately) from one mouth to another, the timing is probably wrong. It is, after all, a nice literary fancy to imagine the general preoccupied with a poem as he moves towards his moment of destiny. But if this were so, why did he use the word *tomorrow*? On the early morning of 13 September, tomorrow was now. Nor, when he had issued such imperative instructions that every man should be silent, was he likely to break his own order by mumbling aloud the lines of Thomas Gray.

He probably thought about it, about the copy of the *Elegy* which had been given to him by Kathleen Lowther, and about Miss Lowther herself, but this can only have been a brief moment of distraction. The greater part of his attention was devoted to watching the neighbouring boats, to peering at the indistinct river bank, and trying to compare it with the map which was printed on his mind. It seems much more probable that the celebrated recitation took place on the previous day. 'I would rather have been the author of that piece ...' a quick smile, and then back to business. Nobody, one cannot help feeling, would have been more surprised than James to find it recurring in one dictionary of quotations after another.

The first troops ashore were the men of the Light Infantry commanded by Colonel Howe. When James stepped out on to the beach and glanced upwards, he experienced an instant of doubt. A Captain McDonald of Fraser's was standing beside him. With a chilly smile, James remarked: 'There seems scarcely a possibility of getting up, but you must do your endeavours.' To the young major-general with his ailing heart, the prospect must indeed have appeared formidable. The tough, wiry Light Infantry men in their dark green uniforms were less impressed by the size of the obstacles. Led by Captain William Delaune, they swarmed up the path, and quickly overpowered the post at the top. The officer in charge was taken prisoner; but not before he had sent an orderly off to inform Montcalm. A second or so before he was grabbed, he fired at an officer. He missed, but his captors decided to teach him a lesson. He was wearing the Cross of St Louis, which had been an award from his monarch for some deed of valour. Muttering an obscenity, a soldier cut it off and pocketed the decoration.

About three-quarters of an hour after the first division had departed, the second wave set off from Cape Rouge. Among the warships were *Lowestoft*, *Squirrel*, and *Seahorse*. As the light improved, they would be able to provide covering fire. Meanwhile, the third division, made up of Carleton's men from the Isle of Orleans, and Burton's battalion at Point Lévis, were assembling on the south shore opposite the cove. They were due to be ferried across as soon as sufficient boats became available.

It began to rain. Once the outpost at the top of the path had been overpowered, and a battery at Point Samos – a few hundred yards to the left – has been silenced by some of Murray's men, there was no more opposition. Clawing, cursing, and sweating, the men struggled up to the Heights. Each had been issued with twenty rounds of ammunition, and by some miracle of manpower they had actually succeeded in getting two cannons up the path. By six o'clock, the Plains of Abraham were covered by a scarlet-jacketed mass of men. Estimates of the numbers vary. According to that industrious diarist Captain Knox, there were 4,828; Townshend put the figure at 4,441; and James himself estimated his army's strength at a more modest 3,600. But there they were, fighting-fit after a landing operation few people would have believed possible. Almost to a man, their attention was directed towards Quebec. When would the French arrive? Would they *ever* come? James knew that they must, and that it would not be long. Montcalm simply could not allow his precious supply line to be cut.

The army was now formed up in line, waiting for orders. In spite of his exhausting struggle up the cliff path, James appeared to be in tolerably good condition. For the moment, however, he was abstracted. His long figure walked impatiently from one point to another, and all the while his brow was furrowed in a thoughtful frown. What would he do, if he were Montcalm? Where would the French attack, and how could he best place his men to cut off a retreat? The battleground, if such it was to become, was a large field speckled with bushes and shrubs. At this moment, however, it was more like a chess board, and James was a player arranging his pieces. Now and then he murmured something to an aide, and the ADC went running. Seconds later, somebody barked an order and a battalion moved into place.

So much ground, and so few men: that was his overwhelming impression. The line was eight hundred yards long, which was an unreasonable distance. Consequently, he was compelled to deploy the forward troops in two ranks instead of the usual three. At the front there were the Grenadiers and six battalions of infantry. Monckton was stationed in the centre, and Murray on the left. James proposed to put himself on the right Three infantry battalions commanded by Townshend made up the second line, Burton and the 48th were in reserve, and the Light Infantry were detailed to cover the rear.

It was still raining, and a light breeze had sprung up.

Over at Beauport, Montcalm had at first refused to believe the messenger. The man was exaggerating, he said. It was just a small raiding party, which would burn a few houses and retire. However, he was persuaded to walk to the top of a hill and take a look through his telescope. The sight amazed him. The impossible had happened. He told another officer: 'Yes – I see them, where they ought not to be.' De Bougainville must be told at once, but de Bougainville was more than twenty miles away at Pointe-aux-Trembles – too far distant to be of any use.

Once he had sent off the runner, he ordered a detachment of Indian sharpshooters to move round to the woods on the British left flank. They were to begin sniping at once, and inflict the greatest possible number of casualties before the main army arrived.

Meanwhile his troops had been leaving their defensive positions and forming up in three columns. They marched to the Plains of Abraham by way of Quebec, where some cannons on the west wall were brought into action. The guns began firing at eight o'clock. For the moment there was little the British could do, and James ordered his men to lie down. Standing up in their red tunics, they made painfully easy targets.

By half-past nine the pieces were all in position. Montcalm, with his regular battalions – each clad in smart white uniforms, and with a party of less elegant militia attached to it – and his assortment of local troops, could count on about 7,000 men of very varying efficiency. He himself was riding a conspicuous black charger. The elongated James was wearing a new red uniform jacket, with a black band in mourning for his father on one arm. Both men were easy to see – too easy, for neither survived that day.

At ten o'clock, Montcalm gave the order to attack. A roll of drums signalled the advance, the colours were unfurled, and the Frenchmen began to cheer. They advanced at the double, expecting the British line to open fire at any minute. But the British infantrymen did nothing. The French came on – shouting, whooping – until they were 130 yards away. Then they fired the first volley, but the British infantry still did nothing. It was uncanny, frightening, to watch these men: immobile, apparently unafraid, a great force of destruction which seemed unwilling to unleash its fury. The French moved forwards again. The distance was one hundred yards, eighty yards, sixty yards, and then forty. . . . The British line exploded like a thunder clap. Suddenly the French halted. It was as if an invisible wall of concrete had been placed between the two armies. One moment, Montcalm's men were an integrated, efficient fighting force; the next, they wavered, holes torn in their ranks by the British musket-fire, a collection of dazed men who might soon become a rabble.

In his first action, all those years ago at Dettingen, James had told his men to hold their fire until they could be sure of hitting the enemy. Now, for the umpteenth time, he had repeated his doctrine. According to a quartermaster-sergeant in the British lines, 'General Wolfe had given positive orders, not to fire a shot until the Enemy should be within Forty Yards of the point of our Bayonets.' The men had obeyed; they had stood firm, and then unleased what one historian has described as the 'most perfect volley ever fired on battlefield'.*

Within fifteen minutes of the battle's beginning, the French were in a disorderly retreat. Not long afterwards, the breeze dropped, and the sun came out.

James could switch his mind from the large things to the small, from the strategy of a battle to the plight of one man. During the skirmishing which acted as a brief prologue to the main clash of

* Sir John Fortescue, *History of the British Army*.

arms, one of his captains was shot through the lung. James, who was standing nearby, bent down and pressed his hand. The officer, he said, had done well. He must not give up hope of survival. When he had recovered, he would be given leave and an early promotion. He then instructed one of his ADCs to pass these instructions on to Monckton should he himself be killed. Shortly afterwards, he took up his position on a hillock from which he could see the entire field.

He received his first wound within seconds of the battle beginning. The bullet struck his right wrist and tore the tendons. He turned to his ADC, Captain Hervey Smyth, who was standing beside him, and asked him to bandage it with his handkerchief. Then he sent Hervey Smyth off with a message to one of the brigadiers. The injury did not seem to hurt him much. As soon as his aide had departed, he walked briskly along the front line. When he was in front of the 43rd Foot, which was in the centre, he seems to have been hit again. The location is uncertain: some accounts say that a piece of metal tore into his belly just below the navel; others mention the groin. He staggered, and almost fell. But this, too, cannot have been serious; for he was able to return to the right of the line, and to take up a position between the 28th Regiment and the Louisburg Grenadiers.

The French attack was broken, and the redcoats were just about to charge forward, when he received his third wound. There are two theories about who actually fired it. One suggests that a former British sergeant pressed the trigger. This man had deserted after being reduced to the ranks for striking a private soldier. Some time later, he was captured by one of Amherst's units and condemned to die. Shortly before he was hanged, he confessed to shooting Wolfe as an act of personal vengeance.

Without doubt, the man existed, and was hanged. He may even have made the confession; but was it true? Did he, in his final moments, look for some notoriety, which would set him apart from other criminals? It seems possible – although another theory attributes the shot to a lad of fifteen who was serving with the militia. But, no matter who was responsible, there was no doubt about the result. James Wolfe had been hit in the breast, and this time it was fatal. As he began to fall, he called out to Lieutenant Henry Browne of the Grenadiers. 'Support me, support me', he managed to say, 'lest my gallant fellows see me fall.' But it was too late. Before Browne could catch him, he had slumped to the ground. Afterwards, Browne recalled that 'as they carried him off, he wav'd his hat to Otway's Regiment to move up and flank the enemy; soon after he desired to know how the field went, being told that the enemy was beaten, he smiled and said 'Twas as he expected, soon after he died.'

Only two other men were present. One was a volunteer officer in the 22nd named Henderson; the other was a private soldier whose name is unknown.

There are other versions of the story. 'All is over with me' and 'I die in peace' are attributed to him. Captain Knox, who was not on the spot, but who was a diligent reporter, suggested: 'Now, God be praised, I die in peace.' But Henry Browne was actually there, which was more than could be said of many people who tried to achieve a small glory from proximity to the dying general. Indeed, the biggest travesty of truth is a picture painted by Banjamin West in 1770. It shows the mortally wounded James surrounded by eleven people – including, improbably enough, a Red Indian. The one thing nearly all of them had in common is that they were nowhere near him at the time.

Indeed, James died as he had lived for most of his life: alone in an ocean of people. Everybody else was too busy chasing the French to pay much attention to an expiring general, even if he was the commander-in-chief. The waves of infantry ran past him, unheeding, and the journey down the path of glory came to an end.

The British losses that day amounted to 58 officers and men killed – 600 wounded. Estimates of the French casualties vary. Vaudreuil put the figure at 644, whilst Townshend estimated as many as 1,500. Among those who were certainly fatally wounded was Montcalm. He was carried back to Quebec, where he died early on the following morning. Monckton was hit in the lung; and Townshend ended up in what he had always considered to be his rightful place – at the head of the army. A few days later, after Vaudreuil had escaped to join de Bougainville's force (which did not reach the field in time), Quebec surrendered. Murray was appointed its Governor-General, but the better part of a year went by before the rest of the French forces eventually surrendered, and Canada passed into British hands.

James's body was brought back to England by Admiral Saunders in HMS *Royal William*. The ship sailed from Quebec on 18 October and arrived at Spithead on 16 November. On the twentieth of that month, he was buried beside his father at St Alphege Church, Greenwich. In the following year, Mrs Wolfe moved to Bath, where she began a long battle with the Army authorities. Appropriately, it was about her son's pension, and whether or not he had really been a commander-in-chief. The old lady died in 1764. She, too, was buried at Greenwich.

The story of the Wolfe family was done; the work of building a hero began. . . .

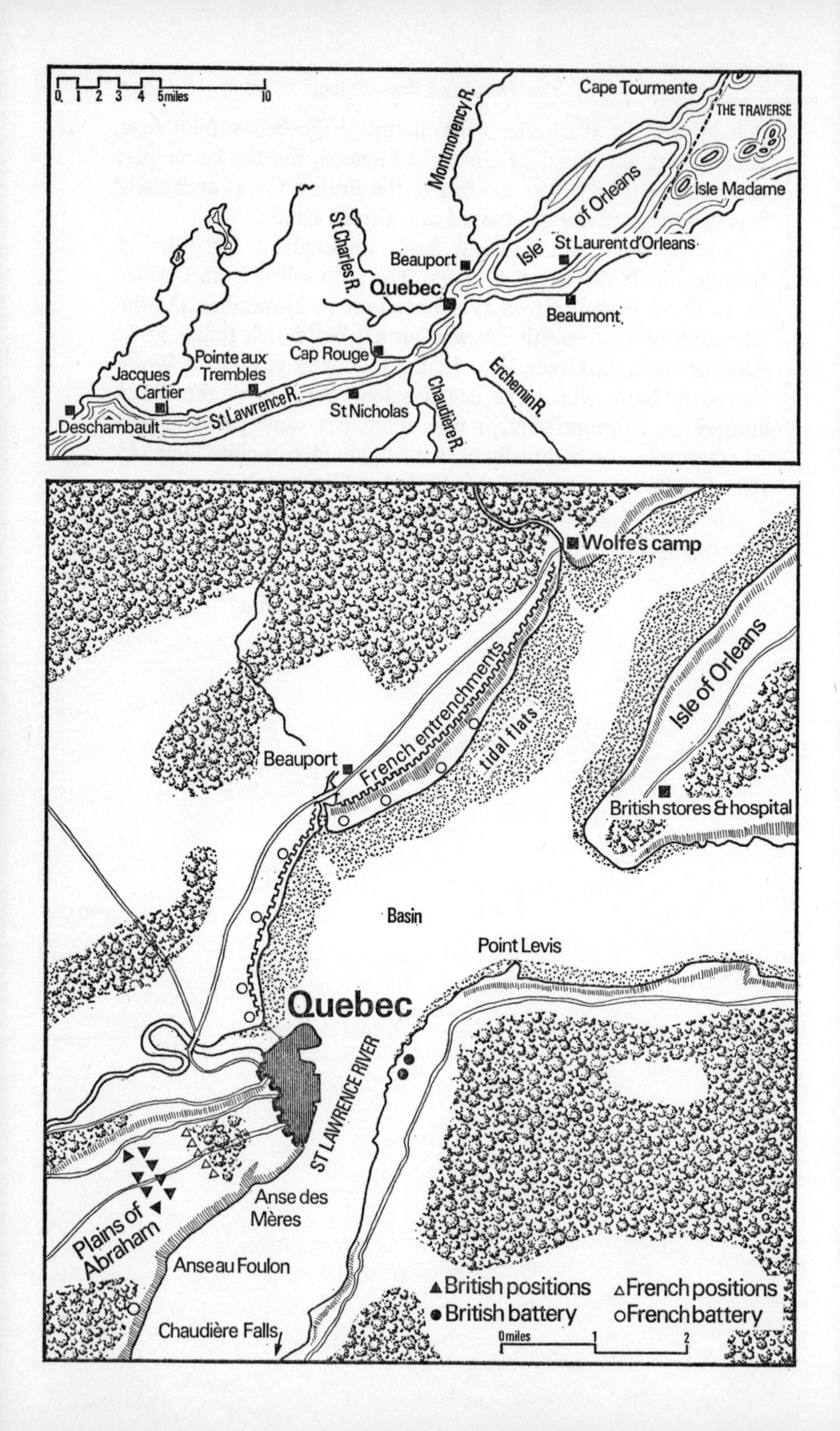

0 1 2 3 4 5 miles 10
Cape Tourmente
THE TRAVERSE
Montmorency R.
Isle of Orleans
Isle Madame
St Laurent d'Orleans
St Charles R.
Beauport
Quebec
Beaumont
Cap Rouge
Pointe aux Trembles
Jacques Cartier
Deschambault
St Lawrence R.
St Nicholas
Chaudière R.
Etchemin R.
Wolfe's camp
Isle of Orleans
French entrenchments
tidal flats
Beauport
British stores & hospital
Basin
Point Levis
Quebec
ST LAWRENCE RIVER
Anse des Mères
Plains of Abraham
Anse au Foulon
Chaudière Falls
▲British positions
△French positions
●British battery
○French battery
0 miles 1 2

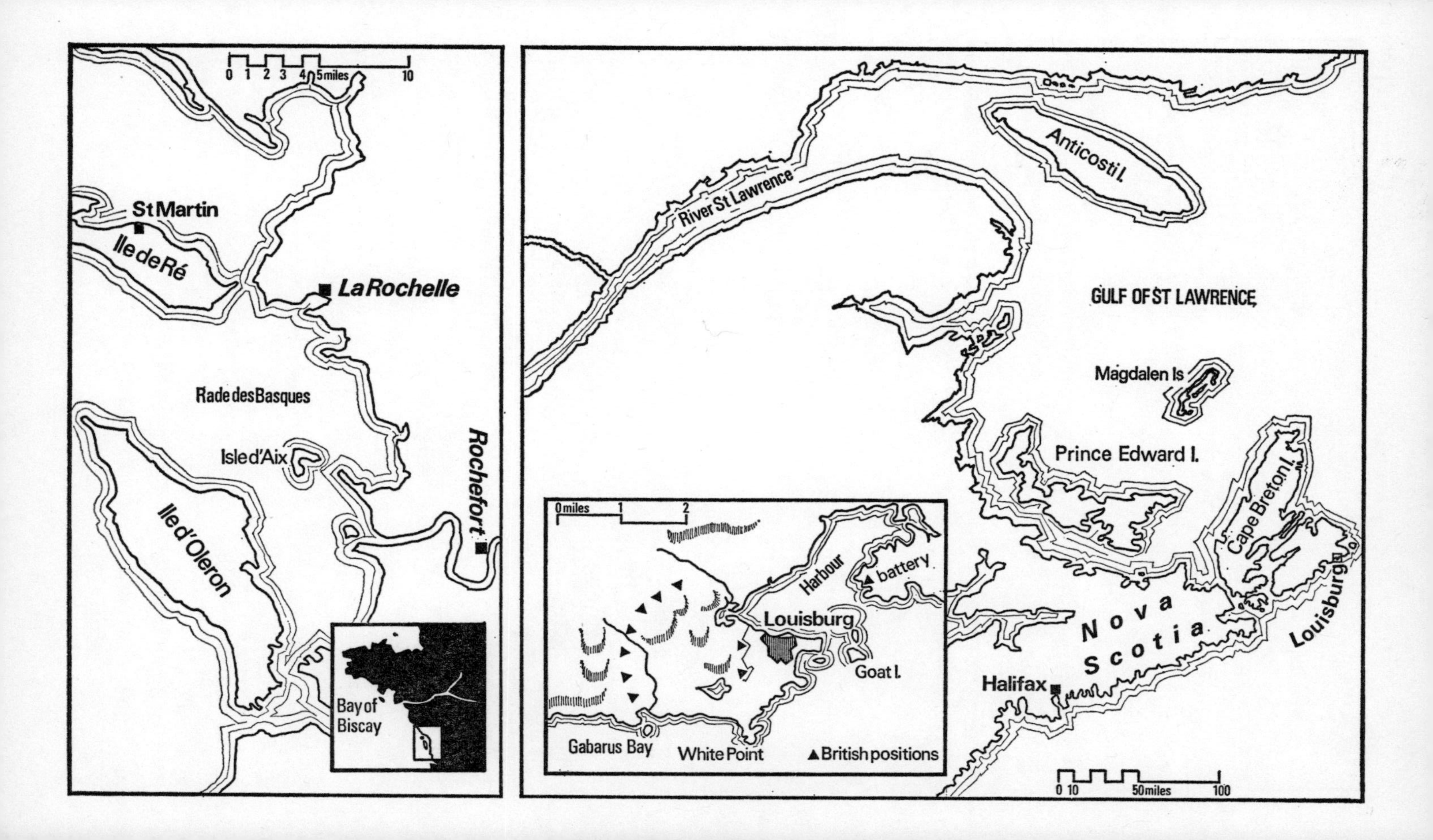

0 1 2 3 4 5 miles 10
St Martin
Ile de Ré
La Rochelle
Rade des Basques
Isle d'Aix
Ile d'Oleron
Rochefort
Bay of Biscay
River St Lawrence
Anticosti I.
GULF OF ST LAWRENCE
Magdalen Is
Prince Edward I.
Cape Breton I.
Louisburg
Nova Scotia
Halifax
0 10 50 miles 100
0 miles 1 2
Harbour
battery
Louisburg
Goat I.
Gabarus Bay
White Point
▲ British positions

BIBLIOGRAPHY

Alison, Gen. Sir A., *Wolfe* (in *From Cromwell to Wellington: Twelve Soldiers*), 1899.

Aylward, A. E., *Wolfe – General Wolfe and his Kentish Home*, 1919.

Aylward, A. E., *Wolfe – The Pictorial Life of Wolfe*, 1924.

Bradley, A. G., *Wolfe* (English Men of Action), 1895.

Carver, P. L., *Wolfe to the Duke of Richmond: unpublished letters* (extract from *The University of Toronto Quarterly*), 1938.

Casgrain, H. R., *Wolfe and Montcalm*, 1964.

Clair, C., *General James Wolfe: hero of Quebec*, 1963.

Durtnell, Lt-Col. C. B., *Notes on the Death of General James Wolfe* (typescript), 1959.

Findlay, J. T., *Wolfe in Scotland in the '45 and from 1749 to 1753*, 1928.

Gleig, G. R., *Maj-Gen. James Wolfe* (in *Lives of the Most Eminent British Commanders*), 1832.

Hart, Capt. B. H. L., *General Wolfe* (*Great Captains Unveiled*), 1927.

Hibbert, C., *Wolfe at Quebec*, 1959.

Hollandt, Capt. S. J., *The Death of Major-General James Wolfe: letter from Captain Samuel Jan Hollandt* (extract from *Journal of the Society for Army Historical Research*), 1928.

Jones, Capt. H. Oakes, *Wolfe and his Portraits: a critical study of the uniforms depicted* (extract from *Journal of the Society for Army Historical Research*), 1936.

Milne, D. W. Grinnell, *Mad is He? The character and achievement of James Wolfe*, 1963.

National Portrait Gallery, *Some Portraits of General Wolfe, 1727–1759*, 1959.

Parkman, F., *Montcalm and Wolfe*, new edition 1964.

Quebec House, Permanent Advisory Committee, *Wolfe: Portraiture and Genealogy*, 1959.

Reilly, R., *The Rest to Fortune: the life of Major-General James Wolfe*, 1960.

Salmon, E., *General Wolfe*, 1909.

Schull, J., *Battle for the Rock: the story of Wolfe and Montcalm*, 1960.

Stacey, C. P., *Quebec 1759*, 1959.

Thornton, Lt-Col. T. H., *Maj-Gen. James Wolfe* (in *Campaigners Grave and Gay*), 1925.

Waugh, W. T,. *James Wolfe, Man and Soldier*, 1928.

Webster, J. C., *Wolfe and the Artists: a study of his portraiture*, 1930.

Webster, J. C., *Wolfiana: a potpourri of facts and fancies culled from literature relating to the life of James Wolfe*, 1927.

Whitton, Lt-Col. F. E., *Wolfe in North America*, 1929.

Willson, B., *The Life and Letters of James Wolfe*, 1909.

Wolfe, Maj-Gen. James, *Instructions to Young Officers*, 2nd edition 1967.

Wood, W., *The Winning of Canada: a chronicle of Wolfe*, 1920.

Wright, R., *The Life of Major-General James Wolfe*, 1864.

INDEX

(E) 332023
General Wolfe